JESUS WALKED ALONG WITH THEM

A Devotional Reading of the Gospel of Luke

Pastor Rea Grant

Copyright © 2013 by Pastor Rea Grant

JESUS WALKED ALONG WITH THEM
A Devotional Reading of the Gospel of Luke
by Pastor Rea Grant

Printed in the United States of America

ISBN 9781628712698

All rights reserved solely by the author. The author guarantees all contents are original and do not infringe upon the legal rights of any other person or work. No part of this book may be reproduced in any form without the permission of the author. The views expressed in this book are not necessarily those of the publisher.

Scripture quotations [marked NIV] taken from the Holy Bible, New International Version Anglicised. Copyright © 1979, 1984, 2011 Biblica, formerly International Bible Society. Used by permission of Hodder & Stoughton Publishers, an Hachette UK company. All rights reserved 'NIV' is a registered trademark of Biblica UK trademark number 1448790.

Zondervan Title: New International Version "Scripture taken from the Holy Bible, New International Version ®, NIV®. Copyright © 1973, 1978, 1984, 2011 by Biblicia, Inc, ™ . Used by permission of Zondervan. All rights reserved worldwide. WWW.ZONDERVAN.COM" "The "NIV" and "NEW INTERNATIONAL VERSION" are trademarks registered in the United States Patent and Trademark Offices by Biblicia, Inc., ™ "

www.xulonpress.com

Soli Deo Gloria

'Thank You, Heavenly Father
for my wife Ruth,
our six children and their spouses,
and our sixteen grandchildren.'

TABLE OF CONTENTS

1.	Luke 1:1 - 4	Introduction	17
2.	Luke 1:5 - 7	Meet Zechariah and Elizabeth:two of God's Senior Citizens.	20
3.	Luke 1:8 - 17	An Angel of the Lord appears to Zechariah	22
4.	Luke 1:18 - 25	The Angel of the Lord has a message for Zechariah	25
5.	Luke 1:26 - 33	The Angel Gabriel visits the virgin Mary	28
6.	Luke 1:34 - 38	Mary's Acceptance of Gabriel's Message	31
7.	Luke 1:39 - 45	Mary visits Elizabeth	33
8.	Luke 1:46 - 56	Mary's Song	36
9.	Luke 1:57 - 66	The Birth of John the Baptist	39
10.	Luke 1:67 - 80	Zechariah's Song	42
11.	Luke 2:1 - 7	The Birth of Jesus	45
12.	Luke 2:8 - 20	The Shepherds and the Angels	48
13.	Luke 2:21 - 39	The Presentation of Jesus in the Temple	51
14.	Luke 2:41- 52	The Boy Jesus at the Temple	55
15.	Luke 3:1 - 20	John the Baptist Prepares the Way	58
16.	Luke 3:21 - 23	The Baptism of Jesus	61
17.	Luke 3:23 - 38	The Genealogy of Jesus	64
18.	Luke 4:1 - 13	The Temptation of Jesus	67
19.	Luke 4:14 - 30	Jesus Rejected at Nazareth	70
20.	Luke 4:31 - 37	Jesus Drives Out An Evil Spirit	74

21.	Luke 4:38 - 44	Jesus Heals Many	77
22.	Luke 5:1 - 11	Jesus Calling Disciples	80
23.	Luke 5:12 - 16	The Man with Leprosy	83
24.	Luke 5:17 - 26	Jesus Heals a Paralytic	86
25.	Luke 5:27 - 32	The Calling of Levi	90
26.	Luke 5:33 - 39	Jesus Questioned about Fasting	93
27.	Luke 6:1 - 11	Lord of the Sabbath	96
28.	Luke 6:12 - 16	The Twelve Apostles	100
29.	Luke 6:17 - 26	Blessings and Woes	103
30.	Luke 6:27 - 36	Love for Enemies	106
31.	Luke 6:37 - 42	Judging Others	109
32a.	Luke 6:43 - 45	A Tree and its Fruit	112
32b.	Luke 6:46 - 49	The Wise and Foolish Builders	112
33.	Luke 7:1 - 10	The Faith of the Centurion	114
34.	Luke 7:11 - 17	Jesus Raises a Widow's Son	117
35.	Luke 7:18 - 35	Jesus and John the Baptist	120
36.	Luke 7:36 - 50	Jesus Anointed by a Sinful Woman	123
37.	Luke 8:1 - 15	The Parable of the Sower	126
38a.	Luke 8:16 - 18	A Lamp on a Stand	129
38b.	Luke 8:19 - 21	Jesus' Mother and Brothers	130
39.	Luke 8:22 - 25	Jesus Calms the Storm	132
40.	Luke 8:26 - 39	The Healing of a Demon-possessed Man	135
41.	Luke 8:40 - 56	A Dead Girl and a Sick Woman	138
42.	Luke 9:1 - 9	Jesus Sends Out the Twelve	141
43.	Luke 9:10 - 17	Jesus Feeds the Five Thousand	144
44.	Luke 9:18 - 27	Peter's Confession of Christ	147
45.	Luke 9:28 - 36	The Transfiguration of Christ	150
46.	Luke 9:37 - 45	Healing a Boy with an Evil Spirit	153
47.	Luke 9:46 - 50	The Disciples Argue over Position	156
48.	Luke 9:51 - 56	Samaritan Opposition	159
49.	Luke 9:57 - 62	The Cost of Following Jesus	162
50.	Luke 10:1 - 16	Jesus Sends Out the Seventy-two	165
51.	Luke 10:17 - 24	The Seventy-two Return with Joy	168
52.	Luke 10:25 - 37	The Parable of the Good Samaritan	171
53.	Luke 10:38 - 42	At the Home of Martha and Mary	174
54.	Luke 11:1 - 13	Jesus' Teaching on Prayer	177

Table Of Contents

55.	Luke 11:14 - 28	Jesus and Beelzebub	180
56.	Luke 11:29 - 32	The Sign of Jonah	183
57.	Luke 11:33 - 36	The Lamp of the Body	186
58.	Luke 11:37 - 53	Six Woes	189
59.	Luke 12:1- 12	Warnings and Encouragements	193
60.	Luke 12:13- 21	The Parable of the Rich Fool	196
61.	Luke 12:22 - 34	Do Not Worry	199
62.	Luke 12:35 - 48	Watchful Servants	202
63.	Luke 12:49 - 53	Not Peace but Division	205
64.	Luke 12:54 - 59	Interpreting the Times	208
65.	Luke 13:1 - 9	Repent or Perish	211
66.	Luke 13:10 - 17	A Crippled Woman healed on the Sabbath day.	214
67.	Luke 13:18 - 21	The Parables of the Mustard Seed and the Yeast	217
68.	Luke 13:22 - 30	The Narrow Door	220
69.	Luke 13:31 - 35	Jesus' Sorrow for Jerusalem	223
70.	Luke 14:1 - 14	Jesus at a Pharisee's House	226
71.	Luke 14:15 - 24	The Parable of the Great Banquet	229
72.	Luke 14:25 - 35	The Cost of Being a Disciple	232
73.	Luke 15:1 - 33	The Parables of the Lost Sheep, the Lost Coin, and the Gracious Father	235
74.	Luke 16:1 - 15	The Parable of the Shrewd Manager	240
75.	Luke 16:16 - 18	Additional Teachings	244
76.	Luke 16:19 - 31	The Rich Man and Lazarus	246
77.	Luke 17:1 - 10	Sin, Faith, Duty	250
78.	Luke 17:11 - 19	Ten Healed of Leprosy	253
79.	Luke 17:20 - 37	The Coming of the Kingdom of God	255
80.	Luke 18:1 - 8	The Parable of the Persistent Widow	258
81.	Luke 18:9 - 14	The Parable of the Pharisee and the Tax Collector	261
82.	Luke 18:15 - 17	The Little Children and Jesus	264
83.	Luke 18:18 - 30	The Rich Ruler	267
84.	Luke 18:31 - 34	Jesus Predicts His Death	270
85.	Luke 18:35 - 43	A Blind Beggar receives his Sight	273
86.	Luke 19:1- 10	Zacchaeus the Tax Collector	275
87.	Luke 19:11- 27	The Parable of the Ten Minas	278

88.	Luke 19:28 - 44	The Triumphal Entry	282
89.	Luke 19:45 - 48	Jesus at The Temple	285
90.	Luke 20:1 - 8	The Authority of Jesus Questioned	287
91.	Luke 20:9 - 19	The Parable of the Tenants	289
92.	Luke 20:20 - 26	Paying Taxes to Caesar	292
93.	Luke 20:27 - 39	The Resurrection and Marriage	294
94a.	Luke 20:40 - 47	Whose Son is Christ?	296
94b.	Luke 21:1 - 4	The Widow's Offering	296
95.	Luke 21:5 - 38	Signs of the End of the Age	299
96.	Luke 22:1 - 6	Judas Agrees to Betray Jesus	303
97.	Luke 22:7 - 18	The Last Passover	305
98.	Luke 22:19 - 23	The First Lord's Supper	308
99.	Luke 22:24 - 38	Jesus' Pastoral Ministry After the Supper	311
100.	Luke 22:39- 46	Jesus Prays on the Mount of Olives	315
101.	Luke 22:47 - 54	Jesus is Arrested	317
102.	Luke 22:54 - 62	Peter Disowns Jesus	320
103.	Luke 22:63 - 65	The Guards Mock Jesus	322
104.	Luke 22:66 - 71	Jesus Before The Jewish Council	324
105.	Luke 23:1 - 7	Jesus Before Pilate	326
106.	Luke 23:6 - 12	Jesus Before Herod	328
107.	Luke 23:13 - 25	Jesus is Sentenced by Pilate	330
108.	Luke 23:26 - 43	The Crucifixion	333
109.	Luke 23:44 - 49	Jesus' Death	337
110.	Luke 23:50 - 56	The Burial of Jesus	340
111.	Luke 24:1 - 12	The Empty Tomb	343
112.	Luke 24:13 - 35	On the Road to Emmaus	346
113.	Luke 24:36 - 43	Jesus Appears to the Disciples	350
114.	Luke 24:50 - 53	The Ascension of Jesus (& Acts 1:1 - 11)	353

INTRODUCTION

I am a retired Baptist Minister. After having served nine Baptist Churches in Ireland between 1962 and 2006 I thank God for his goodness and mercy.

I married Ruth in May 1963 and together we thank God for each other and the six children he gave us in our marriage. Five of them are married, one is single, and we have sixteen grandchildren. We celebrated our 50th Wedding Anniversary on 28th May this year.

One of our sons followed his dad into the Baptist ministry and is currently Pastor of Armagh Baptist Church in Northern Ireland.

I look back over my years in the ministry and thank God for the discipline of the ministry in keeping my soul fresh. For almost nineteen of those years I was Secretary of the Baptist Union of Ireland from 1976 until 1995. Alongside the administrative position, I held three consecutive part time pastorates in the churches at Ballykeel (Dromara), Millisle and Donaghadee. I enjoyed every minute of those busy years. My final pastorate was in Tobermore Baptist Church, County Londonderry from 2000 until 2006.

Being retired is the worst occupation I've ever had! I miss the routine of regular pastoral life. I miss the stimulation of being with people in their everyday lives, in their homes and workplaces, in sickness and in health, in joy and in sorrow, in thanksgiving for the birth of children, in weddings and in funerals. So from time to time I have to take a firm grip of myself and take stock of my spiritual life.

In mid 2013 I came to such a point where I felt that my relationship with the Lord was below par. One day I sat down in my study and opened my Bible at the gospel of Luke. Sitting there quietly, knowing I was in the Lord's presence, I began reading a verse at a time or a longer section as necessary. Very soon I realised that my spiritual hunger was being satisfied. Thereafter I just kept reading Luke in this way for about three months, making notes each day, until I finished the book.

This book represents my study and is structured on the **Section Headings** of the **Anglicised New International Version**. The text is considered **sentence by sentence**, followed by a **Reflection** with a set of points for **Thanksgiving** at the end of each section. In my devotions, Thanksgiving was soon followed by **Supplication** and **Intercession**.

I imagine that those who read the book will find that the suggested *'Thank You, Heavenly Father'* pointers will also promote private supplication and intercession in their hearts and minds.

I thank God for the refreshing experience He was pleased to give me.

In retirement I am grateful for preaching engagements in Ireland and also in the USA. Groups of churches in Virginia and Texas invite me every year to conduct what Southern Baptist Convention Churches are pleased to call the 'Winter' or 'January Bible Study'. Preparation for these visits is stimulating and reviving. Ruth has travelled with me for the past 18 years. Being there is beyond description because the fellowship factor goes *'through the roof.'* We have many dear friends in the USA.

I also gratefully acknowledged the fellowship I have enjoyed with evangelical ministers in other denominations in Ireland down the years. These friendships are very precious to me. If I meet another believer, I put out my hand immediately and expect to see a hand coming the other way. I have rarely been disappointed.

If this book proves heart-warming
and helpful please send an email to

jamesgrant754@btinternet.com

and let me have your comments or criticisms as the case may be.

Introduction

My first name is James, but my given name is Rea, by which most people know me. Since medical records were computerised in hospitals and doctors' surgeries, only my first name is used. I've become used to answering to both names.

Your friend in the Lord,
REA GRANT
September 2013

DEVOTIONAL READINGS IN THE GOSPEL OF LUKE

1. Luke 1:1-4
Introduction

Luke 1:1-2
Many have undertaken to draw up an account of the things that have been fulfilled among us, ² just as they were handed down to us by those who from the first were eye-witnesses and servants of the word.

Luke believed that he was the custodian of a story worth telling: *'an account of the things that have been fulfilled among us.'*

The subject of the story is Jesus Christ the Son of God. It has a lengthy preface, having been chronicled by many writers over many centuries. At this stage of history it *'has been handed down to us.'*

It is a God-given stewardship to own a copy of *'The Gospel according to Luke'*. It wasn't given to us to be kept in a drawer or a bookcase or to be deposited in a museum, but to be circulated to our generation.

The story was transmitted to us *by those who from the first were eye-witnesses and servants of the word*. Luke believed that their mantle had fallen on him and he was resolved to discharge his task with integrity and thoroughness. Luke had a well-trained mind that he placed at the service of Jesus Christ.

Next to the divine inspiration of the Holy Scriptures, *eye-witness testimony* was an important factor in the reliability and compilation of both the Old and New Testaments.

The eye-witnesses were prophets and apostles, not secular journalists writing for a popular press. They believed they had been entrusted by God with a sacred task which they discharged as *'servants of the word.'*

Luke 1:3-4
Therefore, since I myself have carefully investigated everything from the beginning, it seemed good also to me to write an orderly account for you, most excellent Theophilus, ⁴ so that you may know the certainty of the things you have been taught.

The ministry of personal correspondence has been used by God in more ways than we can imagine. In past centuries a large amount of personal evangelism was carried on through letter writing.

Before IT (Information Technology)' came along the major method of communication was by handwriting and/or typewriting. In the business world the golden rule was *'get it in writing'*. *'Word of mouth'* was not enough.

However much we may miss personal correspondence (the postman doesn't deliver as many letters as he used to) we can thank God for the invention of printing. It is a boon in the production and circulation of many millions of Bibles in numerous languages around the world.

Luke decided to write a letter to a respected friend of his, *'most Excellent Theophilus.'* This man was a Roman civil servant, holding a position of prominence in local government.

He explained to his friend *'since I myself have carefully investigated everything from the beginning, it seemed good also to me to write an orderly account for you, most excellent Theophilus,'*

He was frank about the purpose of his letter: *so that you may know the certainty of the things you have been taught.*

Whether Theophilus was a convinced believer by this time we are not sure. He was at some stage on a journey of spiritual discovery. Luke was God's penman to Theophilus so that his friend could come to assurance about Jesus.

THANK YOU, HEAVENLY FATHER

For *'The Gospel according to Luke'*;
For the divine inspiration of the Holy Scriptures, and for the vital
    role of eye-witnesses in transmitting the story of salvation;
For the ministry of prophets and apostles in Biblical times, and for
    Bible translators and publishers today;
For all your *'servants of the word'* who were influential in teaching
    us the Scriptures and pointing us to Jesus Christ your Son;
For the stewardship you have given us to discharge in our generation;

For all ministers and evangelists around the world who are faithful witnesses to Jesus in their personal lifestyles, and in preaching and writing, so that by all means they may save some;
For all who are on a journey of spiritual discovery about who Jesus is and for believing friends who are showing them the way of salvation;
For all who will come to know Jesus today through reading the Scriptures and the witness of Christian friends;
For *'friendship evangelism'*.

IN JESUS' NAME, AMEN

2. Luke 1:5-7
Meet Zechariah and Elizabeth: two of God's Senior Citizens.

Luke 1:5
In the time of Herod king of Judea there was a priest named Zechariah, who belonged to the priestly division of Abijah; his wife Elizabeth was also a descendant of Aaron.

We are grateful to Luke who alone among the Gospel writers includes Zechariah and Elizabeth in the nativity narratives of John the Baptist and Jesus.

These two people were servants of God who had been nurtured in the priestly culture of their tribe. They brought these spiritual values to their marriage. It was a case of *'each for the other and both for the Lord'* from the first day of their marriage.

They served the Lord *'in the time of Herod the king of Judea.'* This infamous man was given the title *'King of Judea'* by the Roman Senate. He was a puppet *ruler* and his entire reign was marked by bloodshed. He died, unwanted by his family and hated by his people. Such was the political era in which Zechariah and Elizabeth were placed.

Luke 1:6
Both of them were upright in the sight of God, observing all the Lord's commandments and regulations blamelessly.

They had not allowed increasing age to dull their spiritual sensitivity or lessen their service to the Lord. Their daily lives were moulded by obedience to God's commandments. They were alert to God's guidance and their lifestyle demonstrated their dependence on Him.

Luke 1:7
But they had no children, because Elizabeth was barren; and they were both well on in years.

Their marriage was childless. Elizabeth was a barren woman. In Jewish society this was a difficult status to accept. It was one of the bitterest of sorrows. Hannah, the mother of Samuel the prophet, also comes to mind in this connection (1 Samuel 1:10).

The Lord knew all about their longing for a child. It was enough for them that the matter rested in the wisdom and providence of God.

Thank You, Heavenly Father

For the ordinance and gift of marriage to mankind;
For the mutual help and comfort of husbands and wives;
For believing husbands and wives who have established Christian homes;
For biblical characters like Zechariah and Elizabeth whose example in marriage and godliness encourage us in modern times;
For believing parents who pray for their children before and after they are born;
For the gift of children who are truly a reward from the Lord;
For growth in grace and the knowledge of God through thoughtful Bible reading;
For medical expertise in the area of human fertility;
For those who campaign on a pro-life basis for the safety of the unborn child;
For those in government, both locally and nationally, who are unashamedly Christian and are endeavouring to promote godly standards and human decency in the land.
For sustaining your people in various countries of the world where governments are totalitarian and deny their citizens the most basic human rights;

In Jesus' Name, Amen

3. Luke 1:8-17
An Angel of the Lord appears to Zechariah.

Luke 1:8
Once when Zechariah's division was on duty and he was serving as priest before God, ⁹ he was chosen by lot, according to the custom of the priesthood, to go into the temple of the Lord and burn incense.

Zechariah's duty as an Aaronic priest was: '*serving as priest before God.*' His holy office could easily have become commonplace. There is not a hint that he had lapsed into that frame of mind. On the contrary we shall find that he was conscientious in the discharge of his duty to burn incense in the morning and in the evening (Exod. 30:7-8). There were so many priests that the opportunity to offer the incense may have occurred as rarely as twice in a priest's lifetime. Lots were cast in order to select the priest who would serve on a particular day.

Luke 1:10
And when the time for the burning of incense came, all the assembled worshippers were praying outside. ¹¹ Then an angel of the Lord appeared to him, standing at the right side of the altar of incense. ¹² When Zechariah saw him, he was startled and was gripped with fear.

While Zechariah was inside the temple the assembled worshippers were outside. When they saw the smoke of incense ascending they were ready to offer their supplications. On this particular day God had a surprise for his servant. An angel appeared to him standing on the right side of the altar. Zechariah was utterly astonished and filled with fear.

Luke 1:13
But the angel said to him: "Do not be afraid, Zechariah; your prayer has been heard. Your wife Elizabeth will bear you a son, and you are to give him the name John. ¹⁴ He will be a joy and delight to you, and many will rejoice because of his birth, ¹⁵ for he will be great in the sight of the Lord. He is never to take wine or other fermented drink,

and he will be filled with the Holy Spirit even from birth. ¹⁶ *Many of the people of Israel will he bring back to the Lord their God.* ¹⁷ *And he will go on before the Lord, in the spirit and power of Elijah, to turn the hearts of the fathers to their children and the disobedient to the wisdom of the righteous—to make ready a people prepared for the Lord."*

There is a surprise here for all believers. God sometimes answers our prayers long after we offer them. We may have forgotten them! It is not for us to prescribe the time or the way our prayers are to be answered.

This was an answer to prayer far beyond the asking and thinking of Zechariah and Elizabeth. Advancing age seemed to indicate that they were past having a child of their own. The purposes of God in the birth of John the Baptist were not hindered by the age of his parents.

He was to be a special child with a special name. Even more surprising the child would be regenerate from birth! His life would have a divine purpose: *many of the people of Israel will he bring back to the Lord their God.*

John would also have a prophetic unction in his ministry: *And he will go on before the Lord, in the spirit and power of Elijah, to turn the hearts of the fathers to their children and the disobedient to the wisdom of the righteous—to make ready a people prepared for the Lord."*

THANK YOU, HEAVENLY FATHER:

For Luke's careful attention to detail in the research and writing of his gospel;
For the ongoing, living relationship with God that marked the lives of Zechariah and Elizabeth;
For Your providential ordering of events in the everyday lives of your people;
For Your wise answering of prayer, doing more for us than we ask or think;
For the gift of pregnancy and childbirth;

For the joy and delight that the birth and growth of a baby brings;
For Your special purpose in the birth of a child;
For using humble, godly parents to fashion the lives of future leaders in the Church and in the world;
For Your believing people who uphold Your ministers in their holy service through their reciprocal service of prayer and intercession;
For the unseen ministry of angels whom You send to minster to those who are the heirs of salvation.

IN JESUS' NAME, AMEN

4. Luke 1:18-25
The Angel of the Lord has a Message for Zechariah

Luke 1:18
Zechariah asked the angel, "How can I be sure of this? I am an old man and my wife is well on in years." [19] The angel answered, "I am Gabriel. I stand in the presence of God, and I have been sent to speak to you and to tell you this good news. [20] And now you will be silent and not able to speak until the day this happens, because you did not believe my words, which will come true at their proper time." [21] Meanwhile, the people were waiting for Zechariah and wondering why he stayed so long in the temple. [22] When he came out, he could not speak to them. They realised he had seen a vision in the temple, for he kept making signs to them but remained unable to speak.

The angel Gabriel had Zechariah's full attention! He told the old priest that he had come from the presence of God and had been sent to speak to him specifically with the message: *'Your wife Elizabeth will bear a son' (v. 13)*. God only knows how many times Zechariah had breathed a prayer for a child to complete his family. Now that the moment had come when God was answering his prayer he responded with incredulity, because by his logic he could see an impediment: *'How can I be sure of this? I am an old man and my wife is well on in years" (v. 18)*.

A further imprimatur was added by the angel: *And now you will be silent and not able to speak until the day this happens, because you did not believe my words, which will come true at their proper time.*

After what seemed to the people like an unusually long service Zechariah emerged from the temple. Having been rendered speechless, he could not share his experience in so many words. The worshippers were correct in concluding that their priest had seen a vision in the temple. He tried to communicate to them with signs, but his dumbness remained.

Luke 1:23

When his time of service was completed, he returned home. [24] *After this his wife Elizabeth became pregnant and for five months remained in seclusion.* [25] *"The Lord has done this for me," she said. "In these days he has shown his favour and taken away my disgrace among the people."*

It may have been easier for Zechariah and Elizabeth to believe that Isaac, Samson and Samuel in olden times were conceived *'out of time'* than to accept that what God had done several times in the past He could do again. Zechariah ran the angel's message through the sieve of human reason and came to a full stop! Does his reaction surprise us?

Zechariah's dumbness persisted but Elizabeth found voice and immediately praised the Lord: *"The Lord has done this for me,"* she said. *"In these days he has shown his favour and taken away my disgrace among the people."*

I wonder if an artist has ever depicted Zechariah's homecoming that evening. It would make a good subject and has all the materials for producing a masterpiece. The elderly couple were discovering that 'God works in a mysterious way, His wonders to perform.' I imagine they reminisced about this particular evening for as long as they lived.

THANK YOU, HEAVENLY FATHER:

For your patience with us when our human logic gets in the way of our trusting you with all our hearts;

For communicating your will to us in plain language;

For the balancing influence of a husband or wife or close friend whose relationship with the Lord exposes our unbelief, strengthens our faith and encourages us through praise and prayer;

For the fact that Your ways are higher than our ways, and Your thoughts than our thoughts;

For encouraging Your servants in their ministries by revealing Yourself to them, renewing their spiritual vision and increasing their knowledge of the God whom they serve;

For raising up choice servants of the word in succeeding generations despite the context of increasing ungodliness in society;
For the manifold ministries of the Holy Spirit in all creation, including the lives of men, women and children.

IN JESUS' NAME, AMEN

5. Luke 1:26-33
The Angel Gabriel visits the Virgin Mary

Luke 1:26
In the sixth month, God sent the angel Gabriel to Nazareth, a town in Galilee, [27] to a virgin pledged to be married to a man named Joseph, a descendant of David. The virgin's name was Mary.

Later the angel Gabriel told Mary that her elderly cousin Elizabeth was in the *'sixth month'* of her pregnancy (v. 36). In either case the phrase had this connotation within the extended family circle.

The angel Gabriel was sent from God, this time to the city of Nazareth in the region of Galilee, the hometown of a young unmarried woman named Mary.

Luke is careful to explain that Mary was a virgin i.e. an unmarried chaste young woman. It is likely that she was still in her teens, but in her culture this was regarded as the age at which young women were considered ready for marriage. This is why Luke records that she was *'pledged to be married to a man named Joseph'* who belonged to the family of David.

What we call *'engagement'* in Western culture is not quite the equivalent of a Jewish espousal or betrothal. The couple did not live together as husband and wife until a year had passed. During that time they were 'as good as married' in the sight of the local people, because it was public knowledge that they were promised to each other. To break the contract was unthinkable, except in the case of unfaithfulness on the part of either of them. In such an unhappy event a formal divorce was necessary to dissolve the engagement.

Luke 1:28
The angel went to her and said, "Greetings, you who are highly favoured! The Lord is with you." [29] Mary was greatly troubled at his words and wondered what kind of greeting this might be.

That was to put it mildly. Young single women are not used to having angelic visitors come to their homes. The angel's greeting was introductory to the message he had been entrusted with. Whatever words he might have used, Mary was not prepared for them: *"Greetings, you who are highly favoured! The Lord is with you."*

She was speechless and somewhat confused. Gabriel continued speaking.

Luke 1:30
But the angel said to her, "Do not be afraid, Mary, you have found favour with God. ³¹ You will be with child and give birth to a son, and are to give him the name Jesus. ³² He will be great and will be called the Son of the Most High. The Lord God will give him the throne of his father David, ³³ and he will reign over the house of Jacob for ever; his kingdom will never end."

As Mary meditated on the angel's message did she recall the prophecy of Isaiah where he told King Ahaz about a remarkable future event?

Isa 7:14 *Therefore the Lord himself will give you a sign: The virgin will be with child and will give birth to a son, and will call him Immanuel.*

Would the memory of this scripture have comforted her? Could she have seen herself as the virgin referred to in the prophecy?

THANK YOU, HEAVENLY FATHER:

For Your faithful servants who, like Gabriel, are ever ready to receive and deliver Your Word to those to whom you send them;
For the extensive prophetic preparation for the incarnation of your son Jesus;
For His miraculous conception in the womb of the virgin Mary;
For Mary's chastity and purity so that she was a vessel fit for the Master's use;
For the privilege that was given to Mary of being the mother of the Son of God;

For Jesus' birth in humble circumstances so that He who was rich, for our sakes became poor, that we through His poverty might become rich;
For the glorious names and offices of Your Son, so that He is no less than the King of Kings and Lord of Lords;
For the worship that is due to Him, as very God of very God;
For the beautiful name Jesus that means so much to all believers
For Jesus, the one and only mediator between God and men, who is at once both human and divine, who perfectly represents God to us and now represents us in the presence of God;
For the truth that we do not kneel *before* Mary and worship her, but kneel *beside* her in love and gratitude to worship her Son.

IN JESUS' NAME, AMEN

6. Luke 1:34-38
Mary's Acceptance of Gabriel's Message

Luke 1:34
"How will this be," Mary asked the angel, "since I am a virgin?" [35] The angel answered, "The Holy Spirit will come upon you, and the power of the Most High will overshadow you. So the holy one to be born will be called the Son of God."

If we compare the responses of Zechariah and Mary to Gabriel's messages there is a different meaning in each of them. Zechariah's response *'How can I be sure of this?'* (v. 18) expressed unbelief. Mary's response *'How will this be, since I am a virgin?'* seems to indicate acceptance. Setting aside all that she did not know of this mystery, she began wondering about the method. She did not reject the possibility, but accepted it. Unlike Zechariah, Mary required no sign. She surrendered her body to the Almighty, such was the calibre of her faith. It was simple and it was strong.

The Holy Spirit, the third Person of the Holy Trinity, was involved in the miracle of the Virgin Birth of Jesus. He had a major function in that the body of Jesus was a fresh creation from the hand of God made possible by the Holy Spirit. Jesus' paternity was neither Jewish nor Gentile because He was the God-man. Gabriel had said: *'the holy one to be born will be called the Son of God.'*

Luke 1:36
Even Elizabeth your relative is going to have a child in her old age, and she who was said to be barren is in her sixth month. [37] For nothing is impossible with God." [38] "I am the Lord's servant," Mary answered. "May it be to me as you have said." Then the angel left her.

Mary's condition was helped when Gabriel told her of Elizabeth's pregnancy, now in her sixth month. Zechariah and Elizabeth had despaired of ever having a child of their own. What made it possible? Gabriel's assurance *'For nothing is impossible with God'* was a satisfactory and sufficient imprimatur for Mary. The acceptance of that great principle gave Mary inward peace. It will do the same for us.

Mary's acceptance of the will of God for her shows her to be a woman of faith. If I had to write an epitaph for Mary's life of service four words would be adequate: *'God made her willing.'*

THANK YOU, HEAVENLY FATHER:

For all that was revealed about Your Son in the message that Gabriel brought to Mary: we are still unpacking its meaning for Mary and for ourselves;

For the ministry of the Holy Spirit to Mary, delivering her from sinful pride because of the privilege given to her as the mother of God's Son and giving her a spirit of faith and humility to accept Your will for her life;

For the ministry of the Holy Spirit within us that causes our minds to hurry on down the years of history so that we anticipate that day on which every knee shall bow before Jesus, and every tongue confess that He is Lord;

For Mary's example and encouragement to women everywhere, especially to those who are believers;

For your selection of Mary, a young woman of low estate to be the mother of Jesus, demonstrating that You frequently choose the lowly things of this world and the despised things to nullify the things that are, so that no one may boast before You.

For the over-arching assurances that Gabriel conveyed to Mary: *'The Lord is with you'* (v.28) and *'nothing is impossible with God'* (v.37).

IN JESUS' NAME, AMEN

7. Luke 1:39-45
Mary visits Elizabeth

Luke 1:39
At that time Mary got ready and hurried to a town in the hill country of Judea, ⁴⁰ where she entered Zechariah's home and greeted Elizabeth.

Was there anyone else who would believe Mary's story more readily than her cousin Elizabeth? Perhaps not. It is reckoned by some commentators that Mary's journey may have taken three days. No doubt she was thinking deep thoughts as she walked, anticipating the response of Elizabeth.

Elizabeth's overwhelming welcome and her glad cry of joy would have dispelled any reserve that Mary may have felt. Elizabeth too had needs and the Holy Spirit would use Mary to minister to her.

Luke 1:41
When Elizabeth heard Mary's greeting, the baby leaped in her womb, and Elizabeth was filled with the Holy Spirit.

Here is an example of how older women and younger women can minister to each other. Their difference in age was not a barrier. Of course, both these women were pregnant, and in both cases God had miraculously intervened in their lives and both were willing for the will of God.

Luke 1:42
In a loud voice she (Elizabeth) exclaimed: "Blessed are you among women, and blessed is the child you will bear!

Elizabeth's exclamation was comforting and encouraging to Mary. The Holy Spirit within her gave her this insight into Mary's condition and the special character of the child she would bear

Luke 1:43
But why am I so favoured, that the mother of my Lord should come to me?

Elizabeth used words that only the Holy Spirit could give her. The phrase *'the mother of my Lord'* is exemplary in its brevity, adequate in meaning and immeasurable in its ministry to Mary.

Luke 1:44
As soon as the sound of your greeting reached my ears, the baby in my womb leaped for joy.

This time assurance is ministered to Elizabeth. Her child (who would be John the Baptist) leaped in her womb. We recall that she was in the sixth month of her pregnancy.

Luke 1:45
Blessed is she who has believed that what the Lord has said to her will be accomplished!"

What a beautiful beatitude! It confirmed Mary's grasp of the angel Gabriel's message and her acceptance of her unique pregnancy.

We might ask:
What if Mary had not made that visit to Elizabeth?

Elizabeth might never have been filled with the Holy Spirit and Mary might never have blessed us with her Magnificat, which has been described as one of the most important hymns in the history of the church.

WE THANK YOU, HEAVENLY FATHER:

For the multi-faceted ministry of the Holy Spirit; we look forward to learning more about his *'blessed ways'*;

For the spiritual health of these two women, Elizabeth and Mary, who were sensitive to the ministry of the Holy Spirit in their own and each other's lives;

For the gift of faith, by which both women looked for their coming Saviour and the blessings that he would bring;

For their humility before God, in which they accepted the privilege of motherhood;

For their love and respect for each other and their understanding of each other's condition and needs;

For the inspiration of the Holy Scriptures by the Holy Spirit, and the rich legacy of hymnody and song which flows from them;

IN JESUS' NAME, AMEN

8. Luke 1:46-56
Mary's Song

Luke 1:46
And Mary said: "My soul glorifies the Lord [47] and my spirit rejoices in God my Saviour, [48] for he has been mindful of the humble state of his servant.

From now on all generations will call me blessed, [49] for the Mighty One has done great things for me—holy is his name.

[50] His mercy extends to those who fear him, from generation to generation.

[51] He has performed mighty deeds with his arm; he has scattered those who are proud in their inmost thoughts.

[52] He has brought down rulers from their thrones but has lifted up the humble.

[53] He has filled the hungry with good things but has sent the rich away empty.

[54] He has helped his servant Israel, remembering to be merciful [55] to Abraham and his descendants forever, even as he said to our fathers."

The first observation on reading Mary's Song is that her mind was well-stocked with the Scriptures. The biblical scenes that came to her mind's eye and the biblical language she used are evidence of this.

More than two thousand years later modern congregations can sing Mary's Song with the voice and with understanding. The hymn, *'Tell out, my soul, the greatness of the Lord'* is a modern rendering of Mary's Song and by this time, may well be known universally. Individuals may use the hymn as a prayer of worship. It's good to find Scriptures and hymns that express what we want to say to the Lord in praise and prayer.

Mary and her cousin Elizabeth were filled with the Holy Spirit. Elizabeth's home must have seemed like the gate of heaven as they worshipped together.

It is appropriate for us to kneel beside Mary and worship God.

She worshipped the God of the Scriptures; she glorified Him in her personal circumstances; like her we see ourselves as sinners in His sight and rejoice in God our Saviour; with her we testify that He exalts the humble; that He does great things; that we have been recipients of His mercy throughout many generations; that He is the God of history; and that He is faithful to His promises.

In Mary's mind the promises that God had made to the patriarch Abraham so long ago were as fresh as the morning dew.

Luke 1:56
Mary stayed with Elizabeth for about three months and then returned home.

We are left wondering about the fellowship that Elizabeth and Mary shared in the following three months. We had a sample of it in the record of their first day together!

THANK YOU, HEAVENLY FATHER:

For the experience that Elizabeth and Mary had when *'heaven came down and glory filled their souls.'*
For the Holy Spirit's inspiration filling their hearts with praise;
For the clarity that was given them as they discussed their pregnancies and pondered the purposes of God for the children they had been promised;
For the spirit of humility in both of them, not thinking great things about themselves but confessing their lowly circumstances; they *'gloried in the Lord'*;
For their grasp of God's attributes: his mercy, his greatness, his might, his sovereignty in the affairs of men and nations, his wise providence, his faithfulness to his promises;
For their certainty of the good things that they believed God would yet do in their lives.

For their confidence in the Holy Scriptures: so evident in their thinking and speaking and praising.

In Jesus' Name, Amen

9. The Birth of John the Baptist
Luke 1:57-66

Luke 1:57
When it was time for Elizabeth to have her baby, she gave birth to a son.
[58] Her neighbours and relatives heard that the Lord had shown her great mercy, and they shared her joy.
[59] On the eighth day they came to circumcise the child, and they were going to name him after his father Zechariah, [60] but his mother spoke up and said, "No! He is to be called John."

Traditions, good and bad, can be far-reaching. The tradition of giving a first-born son the same name as his father was the one that Elizabeth was up against. Normally this would have been acceptable, except that God had already named her son. So at the circumcision of the boy when he was eight days old, Elizabeth had to speak up to ensure that God's will in this matter was done, and seen to be done.

In v. 59 we wonder who *'they'* were. First, *'they'* refers to Zechariah and Elizabeth, who had to arrange for the boy's circumcision. Next, *'they'* were her friends and neighbours. However *'they'* were overstepping their place in taking an active part in naming the child. It may have been traditional, but Elizabeth could not go along with it and have peace of mind.

'Well done, Elizabeth! It may have seemed a small matter in the sight of others, but you were intent on naming your boy 'John' as God had said.'

Luke 1:61
They said to her, "There is no-one among your relatives who has that name."[62] Then they made signs to his father, to find out what he would like to name the child.
[63] He asked for a writing tablet, and to everyone's astonishment he wrote, "His name is John."[64] Immediately his mouth was opened and his tongue was loosed, and he began to speak, praising God.
[65] The neighbours were all filled with awe, and throughout the hill country of Judea people were talking about all these things.

⁶⁶ Everyone who heard this wondered about it, asking, "What then is this child going to be?" For the Lord's hand was with him.

Zechariah, like his wife, knew not to disobey what God had revealed to him about his son's name. Someone obtained a writing tablet and Zechariah wrote on it *'His name is John.'* God honours those who honour him and Zechariah was honoured when God restored his speech. His first words were an expression of praise to God.

The impact on the neighbours was awesome. That is to say that they were aware that God was present and active among them. When neighbours gossip, they can sometimes be malicious, but here they gossiped about what the Lord had done for Zechariah and his wife. The neighbours also surmised correctly that the baby John was going to be an extraordinary child. Right from his earliest days it was said that *'the Lord's hand was with him'.*

THANK YOU, HEAVENLY FATHER:

For your faithfulness to humble believers such as Zechariah and Elizabeth;

For Elizabeth's safe delivery in childbirth, in view of her advanced age;

For their witness to their neighbours in their determination to do the will of God in the naming of their son;

For Your providence in entrusting John, who was to have such an important ministry as the fore-runner of Jesus, to two humble and godly parents;

For continually surprising us in how you prepare future leaders in the ministry of your word, in the leadership of your church and in national and local governments. Their tutors were humble parents and their seminary was the familiar surroundings of their homes.

For the fact that we can entrust our children to your loving providence as they grow up, leave home and find their places in your will for their lives;

For the superintendence of your Holy Spirit in our lives, and in the lives of our children and grandchildren;

For the encouragement of the Scriptures in the matter of training our children in godliness;
For your gift of saving faith that distinguishes your people throughout all generations.

IN JESUS' NAME, AMEN

10. Luke 1:67 – 80
Zechariah's Song

The Holy Spirit had a major role in the infancy narratives of John the Baptist and Jesus.

The son of Zechariah and Elizabeth would be filled with the Holy Spirit from his birth (v. 15). The special child in Mary's womb would be born by the power of the Holy Spirit (v. 35). When Mary entered the home of Elizabeth she was greeted with a benediction inspired by the Holy Spirit (v. 41-45). When John the Baptist was born his father Zechariah was filled with the Spirit and praised God in the inspired words of his *'Benedictus' (vv. 67-79).*

67 His father Zechariah was filled with the Holy Spirit and prophesied:

In such passages as this the layout of modern Bible versions is very helpful in enabling us to distinguish between prose and poetry, and recognise the parts of a psalm, or a song – such as those of Mary and Zechariah. His song is laid out in verse, just like the Song of Mary (vv. 46-55).

It has two parts: vv. 68 – 75 are addressed to *'The Lord, the God of Israel';* and vv. 76 – 79. are about Zechariah's son and his future ministry.

Luke 1:68 – 75
"Praise be to the Lord, the God of Israel, because he has come and has redeemed his people.

69 He has raised up a horn of salvation for us in the house of his servant David 70 (as he said through his holy prophets of long ago),

71 salvation from our enemies and from the hand of all who hate us—

72 to show mercy to our fathers and to remember his holy covenant, 73 the oath he swore to our father Abraham:

74 to rescue us from the hand of our enemies and to enable us to serve him without fear 75 in holiness and righteousness before him all our days.

Various Scriptures were in Zechariah's mind: Psalm 106:10; Isaiah 9:1-2; 40:3; & 57:19-21. The inspiration of the Holy Spirit is clearly seen in his song.

Notice the themes mentioned by Zechariah: redemption (v. 68); salvation (v.69); prophecy (v. 70); the Abrahamic covenant (vv.72-73); deliverance from the oppression of enemies (v.74); personal holiness and righteousness (v.75).

Zechariah was deeply thankful for the prospect of Messiah's appearing and kingdom and was completely confident of God's fulfilment of his covenant with Abraham. In the birth of his son John the Baptist, and the near approach of Christ, Zechariah saw the Messiah's kingdom close at hand.

A prayer at the heart of Zechariah's song reminds the Lord of his covenant with Abraham (vv. 72-73). On that basis the saintly old priest asks that God will enable his people to serve him without fear in holiness and righteousness before him all our days (vv. 74-75). The ministries of John the Baptist and Jesus will usher in a kingdom of holiness and righteousness.

Luke 1:76 - 79

And you, my child, will be called a prophet of the Most High; for you will go on before the Lord to prepare the way for him,

[77] to give his people the knowledge of salvation through the forgiveness of their sins,

[78] because of the tender mercy of our God, by which the rising sun will come to us from heaven [79] to shine on those living in darkness and in the shadow of death, to guide our feet into the path of peace."

Zechariah addresses his son John and prophecies that he shall *'go before the Lord to prepare the way for him'* (Isa. 40:3); and *'give his peoplethe knowledge of salvation through the forgiveness of their sins'* (Luke 3:3); a salvation characterised by *'the tender mercy of God'*.

As a result *people who were in darkness shall see a great light'* (Isa. 9:1-2). Their lives shall have the light of life and they shall walk in paths of peace.

Zechariah saw clearly what we, centuries later, are still seeking to understand about the ways and works of God.

Luke 1:80
And the child grew and became strong in spirit; and he lived in the desert until he appeared publicly to Israel.

This is the report of a boy, a youth, an adult developing a strong constitution and sterling character in order to respond to God's direction when his ministry will commence.

THANK YOU, HEAVENLY FATHER:

For the way you entrust and enable godly parents in the raising of their children with a view to your service;
For the Holy Scriptures and the direction and comfort they bring to conscientious believers;
For your faithfulness to your covenant with Abraham through whom all families of the earth are blessed;
For the gospel of Jesus Christ, the power of God unto salvation to all who believe, both Jews and Gentiles;
For the inspirational ministry of the Holy Spirit in our daily lives;

IN JESUS' NAME, AMEN

11. Luke 2:1-7
The Birth of Jesus

Luke 2:1-3
In those days Caesar Augustus issued a decree that a census should be taken of the entire Roman world. ² *(This was the first census that took place while Quirinius was governor of Syria.)* ³ *And everyone went to his own town to register.*

These verses introduce the narrative of Jesus' birth in order to explain that Mary and Joseph were obliged to comply with the decree of Caesar Augustus (he reigned from 27BC until 14AD), although for them this involved travelling to Bethlehem to be included in the census. This shows that they were responsible citizens.

Luke 2:4-5
So Joseph also went up from the town of Nazareth in Galilee to Judea, to Bethlehem the town of David, because he belonged to the house and line of David. ⁵ *He went there to register with Mary, who was pledged to be married to him and was expecting a child.*

The journey was long for a woman heavy with child. Nevertheless they trusted themselves to the providence of God, undertook the journey and arrived safely in Bethlehem.

Luke 2:6-7
While they were there, the time came for the baby to be born, ⁷ *and she gave birth to her firstborn, a son. She wrapped him in cloths and placed him in a manger, because there was no room for them in the inn.*

Luke has a wonderful economy with words, yet the details he includes are meaningful; for example Jesus was *'her firstborn son'*, she *'placed him in a manger'* and there was *'no room for them in the inn.'* A manger was an animal feeding trough (a large stone with a hollow in it) built into a stable wall.

We recall that Luke was writing the story of Jesus to build up the faith of his Roman friend, Theophilus (1:1-4). He anchors Jesus' birth to the census authorised by Caesar Augustus (vv. 1-2), and included details of the Jewish world to which Joseph and Mary belonged (vv. 4-5).

In a BBC broadcast on Christmas Day in the 1960s a veteran Irish Baptist preacher summarised the leading details of this section as follows: 1st The Inn was Crowded; 2nd The Host was Ignorant; and 3rd The Travellers were Poor. In other words the inn-keeper didn't know who it was he was turning away!

Another preacher remarked *'When Christ first came among us we pushed him into an outhouse, and we have done our best to keep him there ever since.'*

When Jesus was born the Roman empire extended itself further than ever before or since, including Parthia (Mesopotamia) one way, and Britain another way. It was called *'the empire of the whole earth'*, in Luke 1:1 it is called *'the entire Roman world.'*

The Roman government had a long reach – stretching all the way to Nazareth in Palestine. Biblical prophecy had a longer reach – stretching over centuries since Isaiah, Micah and other prophets had predicted Jesus' birth in Bethlehem. However, God's love had the longest reach of all - when he sent his Son into the world to be born of the virgin Mary in Bethlehem.

God overruled the time that Augustus decreed the taxing; he directed the enforcement of the decree in such a way that Mary must go to Bethlehem. Little did the Roman Emperor, and his official Quirinius in Syria, think that they were instruments in the hand of the God of Israel, and were carrying out the purposes of the King of kings.

THANK YOU, HEAVENLY FATHER:

For your sovereign providence ordering all things in heaven above and on the earth beneath for the fulfilling of your purposes;
For sending your Son in the fulness of time, born of a woman, born under the law, to redeem those who were under the law (Gal. 4:4);

For your indescribable gift, your Son Jesus Christ (2 Cor. 9:15);
For the fact that He who was rich for our sakes became poor, so that we through his poverty might become rich (2 Cor. 8:9);
For Mary and Joseph's attention to civil duties at a stressful time in their lives, and your honouring of them in this matter (Luke 20:25);
For the miracle of the incarnation of Jesus Christ, so that he became the God-man, the one and only mediator between God and men.

IN JESUS' NAME, AMEN

12. Luke 2:8-20
The Shepherds and the Angels

There are four parts to this chapter:(1) the visit of the angel of the Lord to the shepherds (vv. 8ff) and their visit to Bethlehem to see Jesus, (2) the presentation of Jesus in the temple and his recognition by the old man Simeon and Anna the prophetess (vv. 21ff), (3) the boy Jesus at the Temple at 12 years of age (vv. 41ff). and (4) the return of the family to Nazareth (vv. 51ff).

Luke 2:8-15
And there were shepherds living out in the fields nearby, keeping watch over their flocks at night.

⁹ An angel of the Lord appeared to them, and the glory of the Lord shone around them, and they were terrified.

¹⁰ But the angel said to them, "Do not be afraid. I bring you good news of great joy that will be for all the people.

¹¹ Today in the town of David a Saviour has been born to you; he is Christ the Lord.

¹² This will be a sign to you: You will find a baby wrapped in cloths and lying in a manger."

¹³ Suddenly a great company of the heavenly host appeared with the angel, praising God and saying, ¹⁴ "Glory to God in the highest, and on earth peace to men on whom his favour rests."

¹⁵ When the angels had left them and gone into heaven, the shepherds said to one another, "Let's go to Bethlehem and see this thing that has happened, which the Lord has told us about."

Why were humble shepherds the first visitors that Mary and Joseph and the baby had on the night that Jesus was born?

The answer is that they had been visited and spoken to by an angel of the Lord who not only told them about the birth of Jesus but also explained the significance of his birth (vv. 10-12).

Furthermore they had witnessed a great company of angels praising God for the events of that night (v. 14). The effect on the shepherds was moving, to say the least, and so a group of them arrived in Bethlehem to where the family was sheltering for the night (v. 15).

Luke 2:16–20
So they hurried off and found Mary and Joseph, and the baby, who was lying in the manger.
¹⁷ When they had seen him, they spread the word concerning what had been told them about this child, ¹⁸ and all who heard it were amazed at what the shepherds said to them.
¹⁹ But Mary treasured up all these things and pondered them in her heart.
²⁰ The shepherds returned, glorifying and praising God for all the things they had heard and seen which were just as they had been told.

We imagine that Mary and Joseph were comforted by the shepherds; especially by the news they brought about the message of the angels: *'Today in the town of David a Saviour has been born to you; he is Christ the Lord.'*

But soon the shepherds had to return to their flocks and so the news of Jesus' birth spread rapidly in the environs of Bethlehem (vv.17, 18 & 20). Mary however, drew immense comfort and strength and assurance by meditating on all that had taken place that night. Only God knew the secret and worshipful thoughts of Mary's soul.

THANK YOU, HEAVENLY FATHER:

For the trustworthy record of the miraculous incarnation and virgin birth of your son Jesus; thoroughly researched by Luke and written under the supervision of the Holy Spirit;
For the faith and fortitude of Mary and Joseph in coping with the stresses of that night;
For providing mutual encouragement for them by sending the shepherds to visit the family in Bethlehem;
For the *'evangelising zeal'* of the shepherds who told those whom they met about the Saviour's birth;

For Mary's private and precious thoughts as she nursed and bonded with her special Son; and meditated on his identity and destiny.

IN JESUS' NAME, AMEN

13. Luke 2:21-39
The Presentation of Jesus in the Temple

Luke 2:21-24
On the eighth day, when it was time to circumcise him, he was named Jesus, the name the angel had given him before he had been conceived.
²² When the time of their purification according to the Law of Moses had been completed, Joseph and Mary took him to Jerusalem to present him to the Lord ²³ (as it is written in the Law of the Lord, "Every firstborn male is to be consecrated to the Lord"), ²⁴ and to offer a sacrifice in keeping with what is said in the Law of the Lord: "a pair of doves or two young pigeons".

Throughout Jesus' life he was faithful to keep all of God's law. His parents were his example in this important matter. Luke is precise in recording the naming of Mary's child: *His name was called JESUS, the name given by the angel before He was conceived in the womb*. Of course, their child being a male, the rite of circumcision was necessary when he was eight days old. Circumcision made Jesus part of the covenant people of God and placed him under the Mosaic covenant (Gal. 4:4) and also connected him to the Abrahamic covenant.

A second ceremony is recorded in v. 22 *'when the time of their purific-ation according to the Law of Moses was completed Joseph and Mary took him to Jerusalem to present him to the Lord.'* It seems that they had gone home to Nazareth (after v. 21) and then about 40 days later they travelled to Jerusalem and the Temple. Notice the word *'their'* before *'purification'* in v.22. It refers to the fact that Mary and Joseph abstained from sexual relations during this time.

Their offering at the Temple consisted of *'a pair of turtledoves or two young pigeons'*. It signified that the family had slender resources. These offerings were not made on Jesus' behalf; they were for the sinfulness of Joseph and Mary.

Luke 2:25 – 32
Now there was a man in Jerusalem called Simeon, who was righteous and devout. He was waiting for the consolation of Israel, and the Holy Spirit was upon him.
²⁶ It had been revealed to him by the Holy Spirit that he would not die before he had seen the Lord's Christ.
²⁷ Moved by the Spirit, he went into the temple courts. When the parents brought in the child Jesus to do for him what the custom of the Law required, ²⁸ Simeon took him in his arms and praised God, saying:
²⁹ "Sovereign Lord, as you have promised, you now dismiss your servant in peace.
³⁰ For my eyes have seen your salvation, ³¹which you have prepared in the sight of all people, ³² a light for revelation to the Gentiles and for glory to your people Israel."

Simeon was on duty when Joseph and Mary and Jesus entered the Temple. It was clear why they had come. They handed their baby son to Simeon who immediately prophesied by the inspiration of the Holy Spirit (vv. 29-32). Simeon was *'righteous and devout. He was waiting for the consolation of Israel. It had been revealed to him that he would not die before he had seen the Lord's Christ.'* Simeon's prayer song is known as the *'Nunc dimittis'*.

Luke 2:33-35
And Joseph and His mother marvelled at those things which were spoken of Him.
Then Simeon blessed them, and said to Mary His mother, "Behold, this Child is destined for the fall and rising of many in Israel, and for a sign which will be spoken against ³⁵ (yes, a sword will pierce through your own soul also), that the thoughts of many hearts may be revealed."

Did Mary and Joseph understand the words of Simeon, in particular his prophecy about the child? Simeon used plain words, but they had a profound meaning that would only be clarified in the fulness of time. The heart of Mary, his mother, would be pierced painfully by the suffering of her Son.

An epitaph for Simeon might be *'God made him content!'* Life could give him nothing more, now that he had seen God's salvation. Notice the superintendence of the Holy Spirit throughout the narrative. A detail such as Simeon's time of entering the temple was controlled by the Holy Spirit. Simeon had a working knowledge of the prophecy of Isaiah; for example, he had 52:10; 42:6; and 49:6 in mind when he spoke his hymn of blessing.

Luke 2:36-38
There was also a prophetess, Anna, the daughter of Phanuel, of the tribe of Asher. She was very old; she had lived with her husband seven years after her marriage, ^{37} and then was a widow until she was eighty-four.

She never left the temple but worshipped night and day, fasting and praying. ^{38} Coming up to them at that very moment, she gave thanks to God and spoke about the child to all who were looking forward to the redemption of Jerusalem.

Clearly God had a remnant of faithful Israelites who maintained a godly witness as they lived in Jerusalem and worshipped at the Temple despite its corrupted leadership and commercialism. Anna was a prophetess and, depending how we calculate it, may have been getting close to 100 years of age! The Spirit filled her heart and mind with thoughts of her Redeemer and Saviour – and she could not keep silent. An appropriate epitaph for Anna could be *'She spoke of Him!'*

Luke 2:39-40
When Joseph and Mary had done everything required by the Law of the Lord, they returned to Galilee to their own town of Nazareth.

^{40} And the child grew and became strong; he was filled with wisdom, and the grace of God was upon him.

The family returned to their home in Nazareth. Living there would be a welcome change after so much travelling with a very young baby. Luke doesn't mention a visit to Egypt as we find in Matthew 2:13-22, but such a visit would have to be placed between vv. 38 and 39. Jesus' childhood years were spent in Nazareth where people referred to him as *'the carpenter's son.'*

We are indebted to Luke for this brief cameo of Jesus' childhood. Compare the clause *'and the grace of God was upon him'* (v. 40) with John's mature reminiscence in the preface to his gospel: *'We have seen his glory, the glory of the One and Only, who came from the Father, full of grace and truth* (1:14).'

THANK YOU, HEAVENLY FATHER:

For believing souls whose confidence in the Scriptures enabled them to live hopefully as they waited for the advent of Jesus;
For a faithful remnant of godly folk who maintained their spiritual glow despite the prevailing unbelief of the times in which they lived.
For Jesus' experience growing up as a child, a boy and a young man; and his ability to sympathise with us at every stage of our lives from the cradle to the grave;
For the sure and certain hope of believers today who are waiting for the Second Advent of our Lord Jesus Christ.

IN JESUS' NAME, AMEN

14. Luke 2:41-52
The Boy Jesus at the Temple

Luke 2:41-46
Every year his parents went to Jerusalem for the Feast of the Passover.
⁴² When he was twelve years old, they went up to the Feast, according to the custom. ⁴³ After the Feast was over, while his parents were returning home, the boy Jesus stayed behind in Jerusalem, but they were unaware of it.
⁴⁴ Thinking he was in their company, they travelled on for a day. Then they began looking for him among their relatives and friends. ⁴⁵ When they did not find him, they went back to Jerusalem to look for him.
⁴⁶ After three days they found him in the temple courts, sitting among the teachers, listening to them and asking them questions.

The annual Passover involved another journey to Jerusalem and home again. Jesus was aged twelve at this time, and in Jewish reckoning was about to become a man. Luke recorded his fulfilling the law of Moses by his circumcision (v.21). Here Jesus is portrayed as trained in the law (v. 46-47).

All too soon it was time for the homeward journey and so, in company with many other friends and acquaintances from Nazareth who together made up a caravan of pilgrims, Joseph and Mary began the journey. But did anyone know where Jesus was? His parents enquired among their relatives, but they searched in vain. They decided to turn back hoping they would find him in Jerusalem.

After three days they found Jesus in the Temple courts, *'sitting among the teachers, listening to them and asking them questions,'* completely absorbed in the discussion that was going on. The onlookers were amazed (v. 47), not least Mary and Joseph (v. 48).

Luke 2:47-50
Everyone who heard him was amazed at his understanding and his answers. ⁴⁸ When his parents saw him, they were astonished. His mother said to him, "Son, why have you treated us like this? Your

father and I have been anxiously searching for you." ⁴⁹ "Why were you searching for me?" he asked. "Didn't you know I had to be in my Father's house?" ⁵⁰ But they did not understand what he was saying to them.

Mary, in motherly fashion, spoke out of anxiety for Jesus' well-being: *"Son, why have you treated us like this? Your father and I have been anxiously searching for you."*

Here we have the first spoken words of Jesus recorded in the gospels: *"Why were you searching for me?" he asked. "Didn't you know I had to be in my Father's house?"* He was not being unmannerly to his mother, but was speaking respectfully and honestly to her about a growing awareness within himself of his identity and destiny.

We all feel for Mary and Joseph in their anxiety. We also feel for Jesus who had to share something very special with them, probably for the first time, and in public: *'I had to be in my Father's house?'*

The initial amazement of Mary and Joseph remained, and Jesus' answer was filed away in their minds until understanding would come in due time.

Luke 2:51-52

Then he went down to Nazareth with them and was obedient to them. But his mother treasured all these things in her heart. ⁵² And Jesus grew in wisdom and stature, and in favour with God and men.

Jesus was a model son. We may be sure that he looked on his parents with respect. Luke remarks on his filial obedience to them. We may presume that He learned Joseph's trade alongside him in the workshop in Nazareth. Verse 52 shows that Jesus was also an ideal teenager: growing in wisdom (intellectually), in stature (physically), in favour with God (spiritually), and with men (socially).

THANK YOU, HEAVENLY FATHER:

For these glimpses into the childhood and boyhood of Jesus. We are grateful for what this narrative revealed, and readily understand that his parental relationships and personal development during his teenage years are private matters;

For the part that biblical faith and instruction played in Jesus' all-round development as a child, a boy, a youth and an adult;

For the comfort that is ours when we commit our sons and daughters and grandchildren to your loving providence and fatherly care as they leave home to make their way in the world;

For Joseph and Mary – we know that only eternity will reveal the calibre of their spiritual lives, their humble service and the contribution they made to the development of their special Son.

IN JESUS NAME, AMEN

15. Luke 3:1-20
John the Baptist Prepares the Way

Luke 3:1 – 2
In the fifteenth year of the reign of Tiberius Caesar—when Pontius Pilate was governor of Judea, Herod tetrarch of Galilee, his brother Philip tetrarch of Iturea and Trachonitis, and Lysanias tetrarch of Abilene—² during the high priesthood of Annas and Caiaphas, the word of God came to John son of Zechariah in the desert.

The list of those who were in local government and who held office in the sanctuary at that period reads like *'a rogues' gallery.'* They were all infamous for wickedness: we know little or nothing about them but evil. What must have society been like? What a time for God to raise up a preacher! God doesn't make a man for the job; He has a man for the job. In this case, the man was John the Baptist, the cousin of Jesus. John's ministry began when it did because *'the word of God came to him.' (v.2)*

Luke 3:3-6
He went into all the country around the Jordan, preaching a baptism of repentance for the forgiveness of sins. ⁴ As is written in the book of the words of Isaiah the prophet: "A voice of one calling in the desert, 'Prepare the way for the Lord, make straight paths for him. ⁵ Every valley shall be filled in, every mountain and hill made low. The crooked roads shall become straight, the rough ways smooth. ⁶ And all mankind will see God's salvation.'"

John was without equal for forthrightness and bluntness. He preached repentance and called on all who repented to be baptised. He was aware that his ministry was heaven sent, and he knew that heaven would bless it.

Luke 3:7-9
John said to the crowds coming out to be baptised by him, "You brood of vipers! Who warned you to flee from the coming wrath? ⁸ Produce fruit in keeping with repentance. And do not begin to say to

yourselves, 'We have Abraham as our father.' For I tell you that out of these stones God can raise up children for Abraham. ⁹ The axe is already at the root of the trees, and every tree that does not produce good fruit will be cut down and thrown into the fire."

John's preaching was direct and powerful. Listening to him was like being interrogated in a court of law. He left guilty consciences no hiding places – *'produce fruit in keeping with repentance'*, he thundered.

Luke 3:10-14 *"What should we do then?" the crowd asked. ¹¹ John answered, "The man with two tunics should share with him who has none, and the one who has food should do the same." ¹² Tax collectors also came to be baptised. "Teacher," they asked, "what should we do?" ¹³ "Don't collect any more than you are required to," he told them. ¹⁴ Then some soldiers asked him, "And what should we do?" He replied, "Don't extort money and don't accuse people falsely—be content with your pay."*

John knew the people's secret sins and exposed them. He not only demanded inward repentance but changed lives as well. What was wrong in people's lives had to be put right (vv. 10-14). What was more, he warned them of the coming Messiah who would baptise the truly repentant with the Holy Spirit and would punish the unrepentant with the hell-fire (vv. 15-18). John exhorted his hearers by every means.

Luke 3:15—20
The people were waiting expectantly and were all wondering in their hearts if John might possibly be the Christ. ¹⁶ John answered them all, "I baptise you with water. But one more powerful than I will come, the thongs of whose sandals I am not worthy to untie. He will baptise you with the Holy Spirit and with fire. ¹⁷ His winnowing fork is in his hand to clear his threshing-floor and to gather the wheat into his barn, but he will burn up the chaff with unquenchable fire." ¹⁸ And with many other words John exhorted the people and preached the good news to them. But when John rebuked Herod the

tetrarch because of Herodias, his brother's wife, and all the other evil things he had done, [20] Herod added this to them all: He locked John up in prison.

Not even King Herod was immune to John's searching preaching. The King was an adulterer, never to mention other evil things he had done. John denounced Herod – and was imprisoned by the king.

THANK YOU, HEAVENLY FATHER:

For Your blessing on preaching as a major means of communicating the Gospel; thank You for sending Jesus, the prince of preachers, whose all-round ministry met a world of need;

For raising up preachers (such as John the Baptist) at times of deep spiritual darkness so that kings and commoners were awakened to the day of salvation and had opportunity to flee from the wrath to come;

For the diligent work of Bible translators in spreading the gospel around the world so that previously unreached people-groups can have your word in their native languages;

For all those who this day heard the Gospel in their own language for the first time, and became believers in Jesus.

IN JESUS' NAME, AMEN

16. Luke 3:21-23
The Baptism of Jesus

Luke 3:21 – 22
When all the people were being baptised, Jesus was baptised too.
And as he was praying, heaven was opened [22] *and the Holy Spirit descended on him in bodily form like a dove.*
And a voice came from heaven: "You are my Son, whom I love; with you I am well pleased."

Luke has a beautiful economy with words – this cameo of Jesus' baptism is a case in point. He used only three crisp sentences to paint his word-picture and tells the story so authentically that we feel as if we were there among the crowd watching the event.

Luke makes the connection between the ministries of John and Jesus by recording Jesus' baptism (See also Matthew 3:13-and Mark 1:9-11).

John's baptism signified repentance on the part of the candidate. Therefore it is natural and legitimate for us to ask the question:

Why did Jesus want to be baptised by John?

Part of the reason was that the moment had come in His Father's plan for the Son of God to step into public view. In the past thirty years Jesus had grown to manhood (his age is noted in v.23). They had been comparatively hidden years: learning, submitting to his parents, forging relationships within and without his increasing family circle.

Yet all the while he was conscious of going about 'his Father's business' – just as he had been at 12 years of age.

Let's refer to Matthew's account of the Baptism.

Matt 3:13
Then Jesus came from Galilee to the river Jordan to be baptised by John.

¹⁴ But John tried to deter him, saying, "I need to be baptised by you, and do you come to me?"

¹⁵ Jesus replied, "Let it be so now; it is proper for us to do this to fulfil all righteousness." Then John consented.

It's easy to imagine them, standing in the River Jordan: a hesitant John and an insistent Jesus. John had no option but to baptise Jesus. He could not disobey Him.

This first act of Jesus on the threshold of His ministry was important and significant. He was baptised:(1) *to fulfil all righteousness; (2) to identify himself with sinners whom He had come to save;* and *(3) in anticipation of His later death, and burial and resurrection.*

His baptism signified His commitment to His later death, and burial and resurrection. In baptism Jesus was **buried** in the likeness of His coming death; and was **raised** in the likeness of His coming resurrection. Baptism cannot be a thing of slight importance, if Christ himself was baptised. However, believers in their baptism are looking back on Christ's death, burial and resurrection, identifying with their Saviour and rising to waLuke in newness of life thereafter.

Jesus' baptism was significant for another major reason:

Luke 3:21 - 23
When all the people were being baptised, Jesus was baptised too.

And as he was praying, heaven was opened ²² and the Holy Spirit descended on him in bodily form like a dove.

And a voice came from heaven: **"You are my Son, whom I love; with you I am well pleased."**

²³ Now Jesus himself was about thirty years old when he began his ministry. He was the son, it was thought, of Joseph

God the Holy Spirit descended silently and rested on Jesus, like a dove; in addition the voice of God the Father was heard speaking words that could not be mistaken: ***"You are my Son, whom I love;***

with you I am well pleased." There was no doubt and no ambiguity about the identity of Jesus Christ from that day forward.

THANK YOU, HEAVENLY FATHER:

For this clear and beautiful record of the baptism of Jesus at the hands of John the Baptist;

For the long years of preparation that you invested in the life of your Son before showing him to Israel;

For the clear imprimatur that you placed on the life of your Son Jesus in his baptism, by sending your Holy Spirit visibly and identifying him audibly before all who were present on that occasion;

For *'the John the Baptist figures'* whom you have used in the work of the gospel through the centuries who were *'finger-posts'* pointing the way to Jesus.

For the assurance that if we believe in Jesus there is nothing in us that you cannot pardon for His sake and glory.

IN JESUS' NAME, AMEN

17. Luke 3:23-38
The Genealogy of Jesus

We are pausing long enough in these readings to notice that Luke included a family genealogy in his gospel. He had a purpose for doing so.

We remember that Matthew began his gospel with a similar genealogy of Jesus (Matthew 1:1-17). His list began with Abraham (v. 2), then on to King David (v. 6), and on to the Babylonian Exile (v. 11-12), and so on until Joseph is mentioned, *'the husband of Mary, of whom was born Jesus, who is called Christ'* (v.16).

Matthew's genealogy (1:1-17) relates to Joseph's family

Matthew set out his list in chronological order. The list demonstrates that Jesus was a son of Abraham (*'a true son of Abraham'*: an expression that became a religious and legal term) and a son of David (*he was of royal blood*).

Matthew wrote his gospel for the benefit of the Jewish people, hence the emphases just mentioned in the previous paragraph.

Luke's genealogy (3:23-38) relates to Mary's family.

Luke 3:23–24 *Now Jesus himself was about thirty years old when he began his ministry. He was the son, (so it was thought,) of Joseph, the son of Heli,* [24] *the son of Matthat, the son of Levi*

The comment about Jesus being the son of Joseph, *'so it was thought'* is a reference to how the local people thought and spoke of him. Joseph and Mary knew differently (as do Bible readers to this day).

Luke 3:31-32 *The son of David,* [32] *the son of Jesse, the son of Obed, the son of Boaz* Recall the Book of Ruth.

Luke 3:34 *The son of Isaac, the son of Abraham, the son of Terah, the son of Nahor Recall Genesis 11:27 etc.*

Luke 3:38 *The son of Seth, the son of Adam, the son of God Recall Genesis 4:25 & 26*

Luke constructed his list in reverse order. However, in the above references it is easy to recognise such names as **David** and his father **Jesse,** his grandfather **Obed** and great-grandfather **Boaz.**

Notice also **Jacob**, his father **Isaac**, his grandfather **Abraham** and his great-grandfather **Terah.**

This list is exhaustive because it goes right back to **Seth** and his father **Adam** and his creator, **God.**

The list demonstrates that Mary also was descended from Abraham and from David.

Genealogical documents were highly prized among the Jews, indeed as in some nomadic tribes in Africa, for example, genealogies could be memorised, and recited on demand, far down the generations.

Thousands of such family documents were destroyed with the demise of the Jewish state and the destruction of Jerusalem by the Roman armies in 70 AD.

Between them, Matthew and Luke published the two family histories, and in doing so placed beyond doubt the descent of Jesus from King David. Had this not been the case the Jewish authorities would have challenged any claim to Messianic authority made by him, or by others on his behalf.

That these denials were never forthcoming bears adequate testimony to the value of the documents recorded in the New Testament of our Lord and Saviour Jesus Christ.

So Luke had at least two purposes for the genealogy:(1) to show the place of Jesus in the family of Israel and (2) to reveal how he is a member of the human race.

Jesus is not simply one with *the whole Jewish race*: he is one with the *whole human race*, for he is a son of Adam (apart from Adam's sin).

THANK YOU, HEAVENLY FATHER:

For the clear evidence of the superintendence of the Holy Spirit in the gathering and preservation of the family documents of Joseph and Mary and their inclusion in the New Testament scriptures;

For your grace to individuals in every generation, men and women from every walk of life, both saints and sinners, kings and commoners, who appear in the two genealogies;

For Matthew's evidence that Jesus belonged to Israel, and for Luke's evidence that Jesus belonged to humanity, being born of a woman, born under the law, that he might redeem those under the law, that we might receive the full rights of sons (Gal 4:4-5);

For the fact that while we live in a world in which everyone will die, we have a living Saviour: *'as in Adam all die, so in Christ all will be made alive'* (1 Cor. 15:22).

IN JESUS' NAME, AMEN

18. Luke 4:1-13
The Temptation of Jesus

Luke 4:1 - 2
Jesus, full of the Holy Spirit, returned from the Jordan and was led by the Spirit in the desert, ² where for forty days he was tempted by the devil. He ate nothing during those days, and at the end of them he was hungry.

Immediately following Jesus' baptism, with its eloquent testimony to Jesus as the Son of God, the devil mounted a full-scale attack on him. He waited 40 days, until Jesus' human reserves were at their lowest due to his prolonged fast. The devil's objective was to drive a wedge of disobedience between Jesus and his Father in heaven. For all his wiles, he might have known that it would be an exercise in futility. We must remember that Jesus was led by the Spirit into the wilderness. We presume that the wilderness referred to was in Judea (not Sinai).

Luke 4:3 – 4
The devil said to him, "If you are the Son of God, tell this stone to become bread." ⁴ Jesus answered, "It is written: 'Man does not live on bread alone.'"

Notice the focus of the devil's attack: 'If you are the Son of God.' The first temptation was like the one faced by Adam and Eve in the Garden of Eden – it focussed on 'forbidden fruit'. Jesus could have made bread from the stones of the desert floor. The litmus-test was *'Is this my Father's will?'* The second Adam didn't yield to the temptation; instead he remembered a scripture in **Deuteronomy 8:3**. It was the word that he needed in that moment of temptation and so he answered the devil effectively and finally. The phrase *'It is written'* was fail-safe. *'Man does not live on bread alone.'* The devil was silenced.

Luke 4:5 - 8
The devil led him up to a high place and showed him in an instant all the kingdoms of the world.

⁶ And he said to him, "I will give you all their authority and splendour, for it has been given to me, and I can give it to anyone I want to. ⁷ So if you worship me, it will all be yours."

⁸ Jesus answered, "It is written: 'Worship the Lord your God and serve him only.'"

It is not necessary for us to know how the devil transported Jesus from place to place for each temptation. Did he have to? The power of temptation is largely the power of suggestion. Is there a spot in Judea from which all the kingdoms of the world can be seen? One thing we are sure of: the devil is a liar. Think about what he said to Jesus in v.6. The claims he made were bogus.

Nevertheless the suggestion was made, and a powerful one at that. Literally, *'if you will worship me, all the kingdoms of the world will be yours!'* Jesus didn't have to think about his answer for very long. Here is that phrase again (v.8): *'It is written'*. This time Jesus thought about **Deuteronomy 6:13** *'Worship the Lord your God and serve him only.'* As before, the devil was silenced.

Luke 4:9 - 13
The devil led him to Jerusalem and had him stand on the highest point of the temple. "If you are the Son of God," he said, "throw yourself down from here.

¹⁰ For it is written: "'He will command his angels concerning you to guard you carefully; ¹¹ they will lift you up in their hands, so that you will not strike your foot against a stone.'"

¹² Jesus answered, "It says: 'Do not put the Lord your God to the test.'"

¹³ When the devil had finished all this tempting, he left him until an opportune time.

Notice again the focus of the temptation: *'If you are the son of God.'* This time the action suggested is a temptation to attempt the reckless and ridiculous. There are those who say 'the devil can quote Scripture'. That's not quite right – the devil can mis-quote Scripture.

Defeated by Jesus in temptations one and two the devil thinks he will use the Scriptures also. He mis-quoted Psalm 91:11-12 by taking the assurance of God's protection out of context and making it applicable to reckless and suicidal behaviour. Jesus' answer was brief, powerful and to the point. This time he was thinking about **Deuteronomy 6:16**. *"It says: 'Do not put the Lord your God to the test.'"* The devil was silenced for the third time and left Jesus – until another time.

THANK YOU, HEAVENLY FATHER:

For the inspired record of Jesus' temptations and for his victory over Satan in every instance;
For the reality of Jesus'; temptations, that he was tempted in every way, just as we are – yet without sin (Hebrews 4:15);
For the fact that there are biblical answers to the devil's temptations;
For the *'character-reference'* that Jesus gave the devil: John 8:44, so that we are well-warned about listening to him on any subject.

IN JESUS' NAME, AMEN

19. Luke 4:14-30
Jesus Rejected at Nazareth

Luke 4:14 – 20
Jesus returned to Galilee in the power of the Spirit, and news about him spread through the whole countryside. [15] He taught in their synagogues, and everyone praised him.

[16] He went to Nazareth, where he had been brought up, and on the Sabbath day he went into the synagogue, as was his custom. And he stood up to read. [17] The scroll of the prophet Isaiah was handed to him. Unrolling it, he found the place where it is written:

[18] "The Spirit of the Lord is on me, because he has anointed me to preach good news to the poor. He has sent me to proclaim freedom for the prisoners and recovery of sight for the blind, to release the oppressed, [19] to proclaim the year of the Lord's favour."

[20] Then he rolled up the scroll, gave it back to the attendant and sat down. The eyes of everyone in the synagogue were fastened on him,

Everything that Jesus said and did was *'in the power and/or the fulness of the Holy Spirit.'* He had been anointed for service by the descent of the Holy Spirit upon him at his baptism (3:1-18). Here he is back in Nazareth, his hometown, and at first people enthused about him as rural people do: *'one of our own boys is a preacher.'* He was praised everywhere.

He arrived in Nazareth on the Sabbath day, and in keeping with the custom of his family since his childhood, went into the synagogue. In accordance with synagogue custom he stood up to read the Scripture appointed for the day (he may have done this many times previously). The attendant handed him the scroll of Isaiah. Unrolling it he turned to (what we know as) **Isaiah 61:1-2** and began reading aloud. He returned the scroll to the attendant and sat down. We can imagine the strange silence that followed. Every eye was fastened on him as they waited for him to speak.

We wonder how much of Isaiah's prophecy of the Messiah's advent and ministry they understood. Take, for instance, the final clause of the reading, [19] *"to proclaim the year of the Lord's favour."*

That should have rung bells in their memories. It was a reference to the Year of Jubilee which occurred in Israel once every fifty years. After seven time seven years the fiftieth year was a Jubilee. (Read about its introduction in Leviticus 25.)

Amazing things took place and joy filled the nation. It brought rest to the land which was allowed to lie fallow. Therefore no crops were sown and none were harvested, and in preparation for this, God always granted a triple harvest. Slaves were liberated, and the land returned to former owners. Without question the year of Jubilee was the greatest event in the lifetime of a Hebrew. Only against the year of Jubilee is it possible to appreciate the forcefulness of what Jesus was announcing in the synagogue in Nazareth.

He was introducing a year of Jubilee such as Israel had never seen! What a description of his ministry! This was the Messiah's manifesto.

Luke 4:21 – 22
He began by saying to them, "Today this scripture is fulfilled in your hearing."
²² All spoke well of him and were amazed at the gracious words that came from his lips. "Isn't this Joseph's son?" they asked.

His first sentence must have electrified the congregation. No preacher had ever said such a thing before after reading a scripture portion. In the scripture reading the prophet Isaiah had foretold the nature of the ministry of the Messiah. His hearers could not find any flaw in the exposition he gave them. *"Isn't this Joseph's son?"* they asked, as their amazement increased.

Luke 4:23 – 24
Jesus said to them, "Surely you will quote this proverb to me: 'Physician, heal yourself! Do here in your home town what we have heard that you did in Capernaum.'" ²⁴"I tell you the truth," he continued, "no prophet is accepted in his home town.'

Jesus knew there was a barrier preventing them accepting his teaching. Simply because he had dwelt among them for 30 years and his every feature was familiar to them, they would not receive his teaching. This was why Jesus challenged their attitude by reminding them of the proverb *'Physician, heal yourself!'*

Then, if any were still in doubt about his meaning he added *'Do here in your home town what we have heard that you did in Capernaum.'* He concluded with the statement *"no prophet is accepted in his home town."*

Luke 4:25 – 29

"I assure you that there were many widows in Israel in Elijah's time, when the sky was shut for three and a half years and there was a severe famine throughout the land. [26] Yet Elijah was not sent to any of them, but to a widow in Zarephath in the region of Sidon.

[27] And there were many in Israel with leprosy in the time of Elisha the prophet, yet not one of them was cleansed—only Naaman the Syrian." [28] All the people in the synagogue were furious when they heard this. [29] They got up, drove him out of the town, and took him to the brow of the hill on which the town was built, in order to throw him down the cliff. [30] But he walked right through the crowd and went on his way.

Jesus told the story of Elijah and the widow of Zarepath and the story of the cleansing of Naaman the Syrian. What was his point?

Jesus knew that his hometown people wanted an exhibition of his miraculous powers – but he was not of a mind to *'entertain'* them.

They got the point clearly when he pointed out that in Elijah's time God met the need of the widow of Zarephath in Sidon – *but there were many widows in Israel whose needs were not met.*

In Elisha's time God healed Naaman the leper, the army commander in Syria – *but there were many lepers in Israel whose needs were not met.*

Now that Jesus was expounding on the sovereign mercies of God the people of Nazareth didn't like it at all. Instances of God's grace to Gentiles made them furious..

In their fury they rose up as one body and drove Jesus out of the town to the edge of a cliff where they were determined to throw him down and murder him. We should beware of *'democratic religion!'*

The incident is a strong indication of how far away the Jewish people were from God. The shadow of the cross hung over Jesus' ministry from the very beginning.

In the providence of God *he walked right through the crowd and went on his way.* 'His hour had not yet come.' It was impossible either for demons or men to terminate his ministry. 'He had come to his own home, and his own people received him not.'

THANK YOU, HEAVENLY FATHER:

For the numerous Messianic prophecies in the Book of Isaiah, none of which shall fail in their fulfilment;

For the ever-present ministry of the Holy Spirit in the life of Jesus your beloved Son;

For Jesus' ministry in word and deed, preaching, teaching and healing - an all-round ministry;

For every blessing of every kind that the Messiah's advent and ministry brought to Israel and to the world;

For the help and inspiration of the Holy Spirit as we read the Scriptures: enabling us to read, to understand and to obey your will, as it is revealed to us;

For the fact that this is still the year of the Lord's favour;

For all the people of the world who have the Word of God available to them in their own language;

For all who are working daily to make your Word available to people groups who are still without your Word in their own language;

For all who are being persecuted for righteousness' sake, whom you are upholding by your Holy Spirit and whose witness for Jesus is unstoppable.

IN JESUS' NAME, AMEN

20. Luke 4:31-37
Jesus Drives Out An Evil Spirit

Lk 4:31-32

Then he went down to Capernaum, a town in Galilee, and on the Sabbath began to teach the people. ³² They were amazed at his teaching, because his message had authority.

The next sentence discloses that Jesus was visiting the synagogue in Capernaum. Jesus was a faithful Jew in his attendance at worship. Here, as in Nazareth, he must have been invited to speak. The people were *'amazed'* at his teaching. The word has the meaning *'struck by a blow'* or *'being dumbfounded'*. Imagine listening to Jesus that morning.

Lk 4:33-35

In the synagogue there was a man possessed by a demon, an evil spirit.

He cried out at the top of his voice, ³⁴ "Ha! What do you want with us, Jesus of Nazareth? Have you come to destroy us? I know who you are—the Holy One of God!"

³⁵ "Be quiet!" Jesus said sternly. "Come out of him!" Then the demon threw the man down before them all and came out without injuring him.

What consternation there must have been when the demon, yelling at the top of his voice, disrupted the synagogue service! The evil spirit that possessed the unfortunate man, being one of the devil's minions, knew the identity of Jesus of Nazareth and addressed him as *'the Holy One of God'*. The local people had never heard Jesus addressed like this before, nor had they seen or heard him cast out a demon with such authority. The expression *'be quiet!'* was similar to the words of Jesus when he stilled the stormy sea (Mark 4:39).

The demons know who Jesus is, but that knowledge doesn't make them believers: they are devils still (James 2:19).

Jesus silenced the demon and commanded it to come out of the man. With a final attempt at harming its victim the demon threw him down. Luke records that this did not cause him further serious injury.

Lk 4:36-37
All the people were amazed and said to each other, "What is this teaching? With authority and power he gives orders to evil spirits and they come out!" ³⁷ *And the news about him spread throughout the surrounding area.*

As we meditate on this miracle it appears that the hub around which everything took place was Jesus' teaching in the synagogue (v. 31).

The people reacted to Jesus with amazement at his authority, but the demon, speaking from within the man it possessed, reacted with venomous language (v. 34).

It would appear also that more than one demon had possessed the man: *What do you want with us, Jesus of Nazareth? Have you come to destroy us?* The demon used the plural personal pronoun 'us'.

Why did the demons challenge Jesus during the synagogue service? The demons were opposed to the Word of God. They knew they were threatened by Jesus' words – and so they attacked him. It was their final fling of defiance. Their casting-out only served to glorify Jesus. It does not surprise us at all that *'news about him spread throughout the surrounding area.'*

Jesus placed a premium on preaching and teaching throughout his ministry. We need to give preaching and teaching their rightful place in Christian work today.

THANK YOU, HEAVENLY FATHER:

For the authority of Jesus' words as he preached and taught in the
    synagogue in Capernaum;
For the power of his words in rousing the demons to challenge him;
For the power of his words in casting out the demons and setting
    their victim free;

For the premium that Jesus placed on preaching and teaching, both by his words and example;

For the power of the Gospel: we believe it is the power of God to salvation to everyone that believes, to the Jew first, and also to the Greek. (Romans 1:16);

For the ministry of the Holy Spirit attending the word preached and taught by Jesus;

For all who are your servants in the work of the gospel; those who, like Jesus, have given themselves to the work of preaching, teaching and healing; and for their skills and dedication placed at the service of Jesus Christ;

IN JESUS' NAME, AMEN

21. Luke 4:38-44
Jesus Heals Many

Luke 4:38-39
Jesus left the synagogue and went to the home of Simon. Now Simon's mother-in-law was suffering from a high fever, and they asked Jesus to help her.
³⁹ So he bent over her and rebuked the fever, and it left her. She got up at once and began to wait on them.

We imagine that this was not the first time that Jesus visited this home. It was Peter's house and his mother-in-law lived there also. She happened to be ill with a high fever. Her family had no hesitation in asking Jesus to help her. Jesus *'rebuked'* the fever, writes Luke, *'and it left her'* (just as he had rebuked the demon in v. 35.) This time Jesus rebuked a disease, not a demon. Her healing was instantaneous. She felt so well and so refreshed that she began preparing food for Jesus and his disciples.

Luke 4:40-41
When the sun was setting, the people brought to Jesus all who had various kinds of sickness, and laying his hands on each one, he healed them.
⁴¹ Moreover, demons came out of many people, shouting, "You are the Son of God!"
But he rebuked them and would not allow them to speak, because they knew he was the Christ.

Imagine the scene somewhere in the vicinity of Peter's home. It is the end of day and the sun is setting. People are bringing their loved ones and friends to be healed by Jesus. He healed them simply by laying his hands on each of them (v. 40). What wholeness followed that touch!

However, there were those present who were demon-possessed. When the demons were confronted by Jesus they came out of people yelling ' *"You are the Son of God!"* – but He silenced them immediately. *'His hour had not yet come'* (John 13:1) and therefore Jesus did not want his identity to be widely known. It was not because the demons were shouting an untruth; he did not need the testimony of demons.

Luke 4:42-44
At daybreak Jesus went out to a solitary place. The people were looking for him and when they came to where he was, they tried to keep him from leaving them.
⁴³ But he said, "I must preach the good news of the kingdom of God to the other towns also, because that is why I was sent."
⁴⁴ And he kept on preaching in the synagogues of Judea.

The previous day had been a busy one – no wonder then that Jesus began the next day by seeking a lonely place to prepare for what the new day might bring. Jesus had a rhythm of work and rest. It was upset occasionally but this was his habit. He not only needed solitude, he needed to pray.

The local people were not attuned to his habits and therefore they were up early looking for him, and having found him did their best to persuade him to stay in their area for a longer period.

His ministry was always on his mind. He gave them a truthful answer when he said: *"I must preach the good news of the kingdom of God to the other towns also, because that is why I was sent."* So he continued going from town to town and from synagogue to synagogue preaching as he went. Our hearts respond: *'Your kingdom come.'*

THANK YOU, HEAVENLY FATHER:

For these instances of Jesus' power to deliver from the bondage of demon-possession and from illness;

For these glimpses into the work-ethic of Jesus, also his rhythm of work and rest; and for the refreshment he found in solitude and prayer;

For his sense of mission when he said: *"I must preach the good news of the kingdom of God to the other towns also, because that is why I was sent."*

For your faithfulness to your Son and to all who have gone forth in his name to preach the gospel to those who are lost and perishing;
For all who will experience the saving power of Jesus today;
For all who will experience the healing power of Jesus today;
For all who will engage in your service today, in the fullness of health and of the Holy Spirit.;
For the extension of your kingdom, throughout the world;

In Jesus' Name, Amen

22. Luke 5:1-11
Jesus Calling Disciples

Lk 5:1-3
One day as Jesus was standing by the Lake of Gennesaret, with the people crowding round him and listening to the word of God, [2] he saw at the water's edge two boats, left there by the fishermen, who were washing their nets.

[3] He got into one of the boats, the one belonging to Simon, and asked him to put out a little from shore. Then he sat down and taught the people from the boat.

Jesus had keen powers of observation and concentration. Imagine: he is addressing a large crowd of people, who are pressing around him at the water's edge. While he is speaking he is also thinking: how can I address these people from a better vantage point? He spots a solution.

Why not ask Peter, who owned one of the boats, to anchor it a few yards offshore? When this was done, seated in the boat and no longer standing, he taught the people. Both he and his hearers could see each other much better.

Lk 5:4-7
When he had finished speaking, he said to Simon, "Put out into deep water, and let down the nets for a catch."

[5] Simon answered, "Master, we've worked hard all night and haven't caught anything. But because you say so, I will let down the nets."

[6] When they had done so, they caught such a large number of fish that their nets began to break.

[7] So they signalled to their partners in the other boat to come and help them, and they came and filled both boats so full that they began to sink.

What had Jesus in mind when he asked Peter to go fishing again? A matter of hours previously the men had tied up the boats after fishing all night – and it had been a fruitless night because no fish had been caught.

We cannot help but detect some hesitation in Peter's response to Jesus' direction. Was he thinking *'I'm an experienced fisherman – what does Jesus know about fishing?'* Lending Jesus his boat to use as a pulpit was easy, but obeying his directions and going fishing in broad daylight was quite another thing.

Here is where Jesus' purpose is revealed. Peter, James and John had never seen such a large catch before – it took their combined efforts to haul the catch to shore! The boats were dangerously overloaded and were close to sinking. They would never forget it.

Lk 5:8-11

[8] When Simon Peter saw this, he fell at Jesus' knees and said, "Go away from me, Lord; I am a sinful man!"

[9] For he and all his companions were astonished at the catch of fish they had taken, [10] and so were James and John, the sons of Zebedee, Simon's partners. Then Jesus said to Simon, "Don't be afraid; from now on you will catch men."

[11] So they pulled their boats up on shore, left everything and followed him.

Peter was crushed with a sense of unworthiness. He regretted his begrudging obedience to Jesus' request to go fishing. He felt unfit to be in the immediate presence of Jesus.

Notice the impact on the whole group. *He and all his companions were astonished at the catch of fish they had taken, and so were James and John, the sons of Zebedee, Simon's partners.* The word for *'astonished'* (v. 10) has several shades of meaning that go all the way from *'emotionally shaken'* to *'absolutely terrified'*

Jesus had Peter's full attention when he said to him: *"Don't be afraid; from now on you will catch men."*

Jesus' call, and the prophecy it contained, would be etched on Peter's memory as one of his most unforgettable moments.

THANK YOU, HEAVENLY FATHER:

For the many points in our lives where we have fresh encounters with Jesus, when our trust in him is strengthened and our service to him is renewed;
For times when obedience in a simple matter is the gateway to increasing knowledge of Jesus and the discovery of our lifework;
For the encouragement that friends and colleagues may receive through devotion to Jesus on our part;
For the astonishing ways in which Jesus can use everything we possess when it is yielded to him;
For the fulfilment that was predicted in Jesus' call to the disciples – and to us, when we obey his call.

IN JESUS' NAME, AMEN

23. Luke 5:12-16
The Man with Leprosy

Luke 5:12-15

While Jesus was in one of the towns, a man came along who was covered with leprosy. When he saw Jesus, he fell with his face to the ground and begged him, "Lord, if you are willing, you can make me clean."

13 Jesus reached out his hand and touched the man. "I am willing," he said. "Be clean!" And immediately the leprosy left him.

14 Then Jesus ordered him, "Don't tell anyone, but go, show yourself to the priest and offer the sacrifices that Moses commanded for your cleansing, as a testimony to them."

15 Yet the news about him spread all the more, so that crowds of people came to hear him and to be healed of their sicknesses.

There is ongoing discussion about whether what is called *'leprosy'* in the Gospels is the equivalent of the disease that is known as *'leprosy'* today. The term *'leprosy'* in the Bible covers a variety of skin complaints. Most common forms of what is called *'leprosy'* today are more technically known as Hanson's Disease, and on the whole are not contagious.

Here there is no doubt that this man's leprosy was at an advanced stage because Luke writes *'he was covered with leprosy.'* His body would have been deformed by the ravages of the disease. The man was not just ill; he was an outcast.

This leper must have heard of Jesus and his ability to heal, so when the opportunity presented itself he gathered his courage and went in among the crowd to where Jesus was and fell on the ground before him saying, *"Lord, if you are willing, you can make me clean."* The leper's action would have horrified all who were near him. His disease was regarded as highly contagious.

The man knew that his leprosy was at an advanced stage. He also knew that Jesus was able to help him. His plea to Jesus was made with total confidence in his ability.

Contrary to local custom, Jesus reached out his hand and touched the man and by doing so, in the eyes of fastidious people, he had made himself *'unclean'*. Jesus simply spoke two words *'Be clean!'* and the leper was cleansed. It was a mighty miracle.

In v. 14 Jesus is not binding the man to secrecy about his healing. He is directing the healed man to follow the biblical directions in his circumstances: *"Don't tell anyone, but go, show yourself to the priest and offer the sacrifices that Moses commanded for your cleansing, as a testimony to them"* (Leviticus 14:2-32). In Biblical times it was the priest's responsibility to look after the hygiene of the people.

In other words the miracle that Jesus had performed for this leper would stand up to scrutiny. Consequently the priest would have to declare that the leper was clean. That would be eloquent testimony to the reality of Jesus' power to heal.

It doesn't surprise us that the healing instantly became a talking point far and wide, nor does the public's response to the news: *'Yet the news about him spread all the more, so that crowds of people came to hear him and to be healed of their sicknesses' (v. 15).*

Luke 5:16
But Jesus often withdrew to lonely places and prayed.

Sometimes we wonder how Jesus sustained such a demanding ministry. Another instance of healing comes to mind: when the woman who touched the hem of Christ's garment was healed. Jesus asked an astonishing question (he was in the midst of a crowd of people) *'Who touched me?'* Why? He knew that power had gone out of him (Luke 8:46).

The answer to our question is in v. 16. Jesus sustained his ministry with his rhythm of work and withdrawal for privacy and prayer. Would to God that we, who call ourselves by his name and seek to follow his example, had the same holy discipline in our Christian service.

THANK YOU, HEAVENLY FATHER:

For the gift of faith such as the leper had when he called on Jesus;
For the fact that a true work of Jesus' power will always stand up to examination;

For the power of Jesus to meet human need in all its manifestations, not least in our need to know You, the living and true God;
For refreshment such as Jesus found in withdrawal from the pressure of work and people so that he was alone with You;
For all whose medical skills are dedicated to relieving the world's suffering by promoting health and hygiene among those who are poor and vulnerable;
For every manifestation of Jesus' power to save and to heal;
For the fact that Jesus Christ is the same, yesterday, today and forever;

IN JESUS' NAME, AMEN

24. Luke 5:17-26
Jesus Heals a Paralytic

Luke 5:17
One day as he was teaching, Pharisees and teachers of the law, who had come from every village of Galilee and from Judea and Jerusalem, were sitting there. And the power of the Lord was present for him to heal the sick.

We are not told exactly where Jesus was on this occasion. It must have been a central location somewhere between Galilee and Jerusalem because He had some distinguished company sitting before him.

Two features are important. First, the presence of the Pharisees and teachers of the law: *who had come from every village of Galilee and from Judea and Jerusalem*. These were the professional theologians of Judaism. The leading theological minds were gathered to hear the teaching of Jesus. Second, a note inserted in the narrative by Luke: *the power of the Lord was present for him to heal the sick*. Suddenly, there was an interruption.

Luke 5:18-19
Some men came carrying a paralytic on a mat and tried to take him into the house to lay him before Jesus. ¹⁹ When they could not find a way to do this because of the crowd, they went up on the roof and lowered him on his mat through the tiles into the middle of the crowd, right in front of Jesus.

We admire these men for several things. They had a friend who was physically handicapped and could not walk. They were determined to gain access to the building where Jesus was and nothing was going to be allowed to stand in their way. Entrance through the doorway was impossible because of the crowd. Then they had an idea: they understood the construction of the house and went up to the roof using the exterior staircase. Once up there, they began to remove some tiles to make an opening '*and lowered their friend on his mat through the tiles into the middle of the crowd, right in front of Jesus.'* How's that for determination and for ingenuity? At that point Jesus noticed something about the four friends that no one else could see. *'He saw their faith.'*

Luke 5:20-24
When Jesus saw their faith, he said, "Friend, your sins are forgiven."
²¹ The Pharisees and the teachers of the law began thinking to themselves, "Who is this fellow who speaks blasphemy? Who can forgive sins but God alone?"
²² Jesus knew what they were thinking and asked, "Why are you thinking these things in your hearts? ²³ Which is easier: to say, 'Your sins are forgiven,' or to say, 'Get up and walk'?"
²⁴ But that you may know that the Son of Man has authority on earth to forgive sins. . . ." He said to the paralysed man, "I tell you, get up, take your mat and go home."

If we concentrate for a moment we may get an insight into the mind of Jesus. Luke says that Jesus saw the faith of the friends (v. 20), he knew the thoughts of the Jewish leaders (v. 22), he exercised his divine right and ability to forgive sins (v. 20), and then he demonstrated his power to heal by asking the paralytic man to get up and walk (v. 24). At one and the same time he was forgiving sins, reading men's thoughts and healing a paralytic!

If the Jewish leaders had never been in the presence of Jesus before they received the full shock treatment in what Jesus said and did. They grumbled about his words in his presence (v. 21) – and we may be sure that the story would lose nothing in the telling when they reported to their colleagues.

The paralytic man needed healing. He also needed to have his sins forgiven. Jesus took the initiative and spoke the word of forgiveness: *"Friend, your sins are forgiven."* Of course the Jewish leaders were annoyed, as Jesus knew they would be. *"Who is this fellow who speaks blasphemy? Who can forgive sins but God alone?"* Had they followed their own logic they might have reached a logical conclusion: 'This man forgives sins, this man must be God!' But not one of them was prepared to say so.

Jesus questioned them: 'Which is easier: to say *'Your sins are forgiven'*, or to say *'Get up and walk'*? He answered the question by his words and actions: *"that you may know that the Son of Man has authority on earth to forgive sins...."* He said to the paralysed man, *"I tell you, get up, take your mat and go home."* Notice the name that Jesus used of himself because of the presence of the Jewish leaders. It was a name that was rooted in the Old Testament scriptures, particularly in the Book of Daniel (Daniel 7:13-14). Every rabbi present would have caught the inference.

Luke 5:25-26

Immediately he stood up in front of them, took what he had been lying on and went home praising God.
²⁶ Everyone was amazed and gave praise to God. They were filled with awe and said, "We have seen remarkable things today."

The miracle touched everyone who witnessed it. A great sense of 'awe' – *'godly fear in the presence of God's power'* came over the crowd. The healed man and those whose hearts were in harmony with the ministry of Jesus *'gave praise to God.'*

THANK YOU, HEAVENLY FATHER:

For the witness of Jesus' words and works: the Word of God had indeed become flesh and dwelt among us;
For the compassion and kindness of Jesus to the handicapped man expressed in his words of forgiveness and of power;
For the fact that only Jesus has the prerogative to forgive sins;
For the place of the Holy Spirit in the ministry of Jesus: *'the power of the Lord was present to heal the sick'* (v. 17);
For the determined faith of the four men who were concerned about their handicapped friend and brought him to Jesus;
For the challenge their initiative is to us who, with all our modern facilities, are much less enterprising in gospel work, if at all;
For Jesus' perfect knowledge of the thoughts of men, he can never be deceived by sinners;

For the name by which Jesus revealed himself to the rabbis who were present; he declared himself to be the Son of Man, the One sent from heaven, who had been given all authority on heaven and earth, including the authority to forgive sins;

For the spirit of awe – or reverence in the presence of God's power - that came over the crowd. May we also know it as we meditate on the many aspects of this miracle;

For the outburst of praise that followed the miracle, from the man who was healed, and also from the crowd.

In Jesus' Name, Amen

25. Luke 5:27- 32
The Calling of Levi

Luke 5:27-28
After this, Jesus went out and saw a tax collector by the name of Levi sitting at his tax booth. "Follow me," Jesus said to him, [28] and Levi got up, left everything and followed him.

Did Levi (his other name was Matthew) respond to Jesus' call as promptly as he did because news about his teaching, preaching and healing had reached him? Possibly; recall 5:15 & 26, for example.

Jesus' call consisted of two words that Matthew believed he had to obey: *'Follow me.'* It would appear that ignoring or disobeying the call never occurred to him. He was possibly pondering in his heart, 'Is this the Messiah?'

His instant response may tell us that he was on the verge of such an action. *'Levi got up left everything and followed him'*. Matthew wasn't a simpleton, easily swayed by any and every influence or fad that came along. He had a responsible position in the Roman Imperial Service as the tax officer (possibly in Capernaum, which was a busy town where two great trade routes crossed).

Matthew appears to have had a fertile mind, in keeping with his employment. He now uses it with fresh initiative to reach his peers, tax collectors and others 'seedy characters' i.e. those who were off-handedly referred to by the Pharisees as *'sinners'*.

Luke 5:29
Then Levi held a great banquet for Jesus at his house, and a large crowd of tax collectors and others were eating with them.

Is this the first instance of 'hospitality evangelism' in the Gospels? He must have had sufficient means to lay on a great banquet and, if so, was prepared to use his money to pay for it. His friends accepted his invitation and we get the impression that they were treated to an enjoyable meal. The banquet was held in Levi's house, which means that he had adequate accommodation for his guests.

Amid the conversation going on around the table Jesus was meeting individuals who may never have gone to hear him preach. Matthew knew what their souls needed, for he had been one of them. A converted soul desires the conversion of others

²⁹ But the Pharisees and the teachers of the law who belonged to their sect complained to his disciples, "Why do you eat and drink with tax collectors and 'sinners'?"

V. 30 begins with the word *'but'*. The *'religious police'* and their ilk are present looking in on the banquet with critical eyes. They direct their criticism to Jesus' disciples: *"Why do you eat and drink with tax collectors and 'sinners'?"*

The word *'complained'* (NIV) or *'murmured'* (NKJV) sounds like the buzzing of bees. What a vivid description of the buzz of criticism made by the Pharisees and their followers. Jesus deflected the criticism to himself and took up the challenge immediately.

Luke 5:31-32
Jesus answered them, "It is not the healthy who need a doctor, but the sick. ³² I have not come to call the righteous, but sinners to repentance."

The Pharisees and their kind believed in *'salvation by segregation'*, which is to say they kept themselves apart from anyone that was considered a sinner. If one kept away from such people, somehow one would be able to avoid any kind of contamination, any kind of guilt by association.

Jesus comes and not only does he associate with the lepers, the outcasts, the sinners, but he goes to dinner at a house full of tax-gatherers!

'It is not the healthy who need a doctor, but the sick,' said Jesus. *'I have not come to call the righteous but sinners to repentance'*.

He was not declaring the Pharisees *'righteous'*. They were righteous in their own estimation; but their self-righteousness blinded them to any need for personal repentance. No one needed Jesus more than they did. They did not know how sick they were.

THANK YOU, HEAVENLY FATHER;

For the gracious initiative of Jesus in calling disciples to follow him; otherwise we might not have followed at all;
For the fact that when we *'left all and followed him'*, it was not to our loss; we had become spiritually rich for the first time;
For the evangelising zeal of Matthew who devised a way for his former companions to meet and eat with Jesus;
For the readiness of Jesus to mix with people: He sought people because they were sinners, they had a need and he had a cure.

IN JESUS' NAME, AMEN

26. Luke 5:33-39
Jesus Questioned about Fasting

Luke 5:33
They said to him, "John's disciples often fast and pray, and so do the disciples of the Pharisees, but yours go on eating and drinking."

We need to bear in mind that Luke's gospel was written and circulated years after the earthly ministry of Jesus ended, in which case his book could be consulted for guidance on various matters. Here the question is about fasting. Nowhere did Jesus lay down any requirement about fasting as part of the Christian faith.

However, it was something of a mystery to the Pharisees and the Scribes that the disciples of John the Baptist fasted but, in complete contrast, Jesus' disciples didn't fast but just *'go on eating and drinking.'* The critics were holding up John's disciples in a favourable light, in an effort to turn Jesus against John and John against Jesus.

Luke 5:34
Jesus answered, "Can you make the guests of the bridegroom fast while he is with them?

It was a strange answer, using the illustration of a Jewish wedding feast. But, in fact It is was a very revealing and penetrating statement. Before a wedding you fast in preparation for the wedding feast until the groom comes. Then the cake is cut, the food is brought out, the wine is served, it is a time of celebration. Jesus is implying that *'the groom had come.'* He was speaking about himself as the long-awaited Messiah of the Jews. It was not a time for fasting.

Luke 5:35
But the time will come when the bridegroom will be taken from them; in those days they will fast."

Realistically, Jesus could look ahead to his suffering and death, events about which his disciples were hardly aware and about which the Pharisees knew nothing, even though it would be they would hound him to death. Those would be days of mourning and not feasting. Fasting and mourning were frequently found together in eastern cultures.

Luke 5:36 – 39

He told them this parable: "No-one tears a patch from a new garment and sews it on an old one. If he does, he will have torn the new garment, and the patch from the new will not match the old.

37 And no-one pours new wine into old wineskins. If he does, the new wine will burst the skins, the wine will run out and the wineskins will be ruined.

38 No, new wine must be poured into new wineskins. 39 And no-one after drinking old wine wants the new, for he says, 'The old is better.'"

Whatever did he mean? Jesus is telling the Pharisees that a new era is breaking through. They needed to understand that some of their customs from the ancient days of fasting didn't fit the presence of the Messiah on earth. He had put his finger on their problem. The Pharisees were resisting change; they weren't ready for the newness of the kingdom of God which had come among them.

To take up Jesus' illustrations: he hadn't come to patch up Judaism with a new piece of material, for the simple reason that the old and the new would not be compatible.

Nor had he come to try to fill the old wineskins of Judaism with new wine because the new wine would burst the old wineskins.

As far as the Pharisees were concerned their attitude to Jesus and his ministry was *'the old is good enough.'*

THANK YOU, HEAVENLY FATHER:

For the breaking through of the kingdom of God in history;
For the joy of Matthew after his conversion, and his initiative in
       gathering his former colleagues to meet and talk with Jesus;
For Your wisdom in making all things new, and not patching up
       what had become obsolete;

For the teaching methods of Jesus who could illustrate the most profound truths using commonplace illustrations such as patches and wineskins;

For the breaking through of the kingdom of God in the lives of all believers; we are miracles of saving grace. New wine needs new wineskins!

IN JESUS' NAME, AMEN

27. Luke 6:1 - 11
Lord of the Sabbath

Luke 6:1-4(ANIV)
One Sabbath Jesus was going through the cornfields, and his disciples began to pick some ears of corn, rub them in their hands and eat the grain.

² Some of the Pharisees asked, "Why are you doing what is unlawful on the Sabbath?"

³ Jesus answered them, "Have you never read what David did when he and his companions were hungry? ⁴ He entered the house of God, and taking the consecrated bread, he ate what is lawful only for priests to eat. And he also gave some to his companions."

This section is a tale of two Sabbath days. Sabbath rules could be brutal, and they were for the most part not biblical. Almost any action that would appear normal or necessary was against the law. A false tooth could not be worn. Spitting would be interpreted as *'a work'* (and there was to be no labour on the Sabbath!). If a wall fell on a man on the Sabbath day it was lawful to remove enough debris to find out if he was a Jew or a Gentile. If he was a Jew it was lawful to help him, but if he was a Gentile you were not obliged to do anything, except to wait until Sunday! The purpose of the Sabbath had been lost. The Lord God had given it through Moses as a blessing to the Jewish people, and it had been made into a burden.

Isn't it ironic that the Pharisees were never too busy that they hadn't time to follow Jesus to watch his every move and catch his every word?

Even when Jesus and his disciples were walking through a cornfield they were there, dogging his footsteps with an ulterior motive. Some of the Pharisees asked, *"Why are you doing what is unlawful on the Sabbath?"*

They objected to Jesus and his disciples plucking and eating a few ears of corn as they walked through the cornfield. In the estimation of the Pharisees, Jesus and his men were guilty of working on the Sabbath day because they rubbed the ears in their hands to get at the nourishing grain. In other words they were reaping and threshing the grain!

Jesus answered them, "Have you never read what David did when he and his companions were hungry?' (v. 3)

Jesus gave them a biblical answer by quoting the behaviour of King David when he and his companions entered the house of God (the tabernacle – not Solomon's Temple), *and taking the consecrated bread, he ate what is lawful only for priests to eat. And he also gave some to his companions.*

The account of this is in 1 Samuel 21:1-6 and does not mention whether this took place on a Sabbath. For Luke, the issue here was not about rabbinical rules for the Sabbath but about Jesus' authority over it.

Jesus justified their *'working'* on the Sabbath day by appealing to the necessity of eating. His men were hungry. This may have been a new experience for the disciples, since they had forsaken all to follow Jesus.

In David's case, Ahimelech, who was the priest on duty in the tabernacle, gave him permission to take the used showbread (it was now stale, and had been replaced by freshly baked bread) to feed his men. Only priests were permitted to eat this bread, hence David had violated a commandment (see Leviticus 24:5-9). This was not disputed.

Luke 6:5
Then Jesus said to them, "The Son of Man is Lord of the Sabbath."

In Jesus' case, a greater than David was here! Jesus' declaration must have been like a body-blow to the Pharisees. He ruled and properly interpreted the Sabbath.

Luke 6:6-7
On another Sabbath he went into the synagogue and was teaching, and a man was there whose right hand was shrivelled.

⁷ The Pharisees and the teachers of the law were looking for a reason to accuse Jesus, so they watched him closely to see if he would heal on the Sabbath.

As dutiful Jews (and Pharisees) the opposition was present in the synagogue on the Sabbath day. But they were not in worshipping mode. They were in fault-finding mode. Jesus is several thoughts ahead of them.

Luke 6:8-9
But Jesus knew what they were thinking and said to the man with the shrivelled hand, "Get up and stand in front of everyone." So he got up and stood there.
⁹ Then Jesus said to them, "I ask you, which is lawful on the Sabbath: to do good or to do evil, to save life or to destroy it?"

Jesus was aware of their every thought. He knew what was in man (Jn. 2:25)

Luke 6:10
He looked round at them all, and then said to the man, "Stretch out your hand." He did so, and his hand was completely restored.

Jesus didn't wait for an answer because he knew it would not be forthcoming. Instead, he commanded the man, *"Stretch out your hand."* He did so, and his hand was completely restored. Jesus had given the Pharisees a positive illustration about the proper use of the Sabbath day. We wonder did they notice that he had also made a man whole.

Luke 6:11
But they were furious and began to discuss with one another what they might do to Jesus.

They were beside themselves with rage and blinded by hatred.
Thankfully, the Christian attitude to the Sabbath was determined by the example and teaching of Jesus, the Lord, and not by the

strictures of the Pharisees. His teaching, when compared with traditional Jewish belief, was like a new garment which will replace an old, or new wine which will burst old wineskins (5:36-37).

THANK YOU, HEAVENLY FATHER:

For the new wine of the kingdom of God;
For the life and ministry, teaching and example of Jesus - His truth sets us free;
For all those to whom the coming of the Gospel has brought deliverance from sin's bondage and glorious freedom in Christ;
For enlightening our minds so that we may discern your will on any matter and what are the traditions of men, and enabling us to live accordingly;
For the infallible ministry of the Holy Spirit whom You have given to indwell us forever, and also to lead us into all truth;

IN JESUS' NAME, AMEN

28. Luke 6:12 - 16
The Twelve Apostles

Luke 6:12-16
One of those days Jesus went out to a mountainside to pray, and spent the night praying to God.
¹³ When morning came, he called his disciples to him and chose twelve of them, whom he also designated apostles:
¹⁴ Simon (whom he named Peter), his brother Andrew, James, John, Philip, Bartholomew, ¹⁵ Matthew, Thomas, James son of Alphaeus, Simon who was called the Zealot, ¹⁶ Judas son of James, and Judas Iscariot, who became a traitor.

We might ask the question: *'What does it take to make an apostle?'* A convenient answer could be *'A man chosen specifically for the position by Jesus Christ.'* We can fill out that answer by recalling the qualifications there were required when the infant Church was electing a successor to Judas Iscariot after the resurrection and ascension.

Acts 1:21 - 22
Therefore it is necessary to choose one of the men who have been with us the whole time the Lord Jesus went in and out among us, ²² beginning from John's baptism to the time when Jesus was taken up from us. For one of these must become a witness with us of his resurrection."

Therefore the settled criteria for an apostle were that *he had been with Jesus all the way from John's baptism until his resurrection and ascension to heaven.*

We might also ask: *By what criteria did Jesus select these twelve men?* He selected them following a night of prayer, and on the basis of whatever insight he had into the character of each of them. Otherwise they were untried men because they had been with him such a short time. And in the back of our minds is the end-note about Judas Iscariot *'who became a traitor'*.

Four of them we know were fishermen. One of them, at least, had been a tax-collector. Probably most of them were Galileans. Not one was a Pharisee, or priest, or ruler, or an elder among the people. At a later date all were regarded by the Jewish hierarchy as *'unschooled, ordinary men'* (Acts 4:13). None was great, or rich, or noble, or highly connected.

Jesus had more than twelve disciples by this time – we recall him sending out seventy at another time, two by two. From the many he chose twelve for special service. As *'disciples'* they were learners in the school of Christ; as *'apostles'* they were his ambassadors, men who were sent. Jesus' action on that morning brought a measure of organisation to his followers.

What did it mean for their future lives? Already Jesus had made it clear that he was beginning a new society and not improving an old one! He had already announced himself as Lord of the Sabbath Day. Even the day of rest would be different because the New Testament churches would observe the resurrection day as their holy day, and thus the break with the old regime would be complete.

The twelve sons of Jacob, from whom the whole Israelite nation had grown, were to be replaced by these twelve apostles, who would stand at the head of a new people of God. Within the framework of the church, the twelve apostles would be responsible, under the guidance of the Holy Spirit, to interpret the mind of Christ and lead the saints in the conquest of a sinful world. They were the evangelists, preachers, teachers and missionaries of the early church. They were also the churches' leaders with authority to speak the word of Christ.

What happened to them? The New Testament features some of the apostles, others remain in relative obscurity. Tradition tells us that virtually every one of them met a dreadful and violent death, except for John, who suffered other shameful humiliations before being banished as an old man to the Isle of Patmos. Tradition also says that Bartholomew was crucified, that Thomas was thrust through with a spear and killed, that Simon Zelotes was crucified in the year 74 AD in Britain, and the rest of the apostles suffered various kinds of martyrdom.

The question still waiting for an answer is 'Why was Judas chosen?' Answers that have been put forward are unworthy of Jesus Christ. For instance here is a ridiculous explanation: *'better to say that Satan appointed Judas and not Jesus.'* The true answer lies in the wisdom of God, and He has not chosen to disclose it.

Judas was a traitor; the other eleven committed themselves to their lives' end and sealed the testimony of their faith in their own blood.

THANK YOU, HEAVENLY FATHER:

For the amazing structure that is emerging in the ministry of Jesus in Luke's careful writing of the story of salvation;
For the guidance Jesus received regarding his choice of apostles following his night of prayer alone with You;
For the sterling service that eleven of these men rendered to Christ and his Church for the remainder of their lives;

IN JESUS' NAME, AMEN

29. Luke 6:17 - 26
Blessings and Woes

Luke 6:17 – 19
He went down with them and stood on a level place.

A large crowd of his disciples was there and a great number of people from all over Judea, from Jerusalem, and from the coast of Tyre and Sidon, [18] who had come to hear him and to be healed of their diseases.

Those troubled by evil spirits were cured, [19] and the people all tried to touch him, because power was coming from him and healing them all.

There was no IT (Internet Technology) in those days, but news travelled fast. Reports of Jesus' ministry were spreading far and wide and people came *'to hear him and to be healed of their diseases'*.

Luke draws attention to another category of need: *'those troubled by evil spirits were cured.'* He also mentions the pressure of the crowd: *'and the people all tried to touch him, because power was coming from him and healing them all.'* We are reminded of 5:16 where Luke noted: *'The power of the Lord was present for him to heal the sick.'* While in many places Jesus did not heal every sick person he encountered, it seems that he did here. Luke writes that *'he was healing them all.'*

Our first impression is that Jesus felt deep concern as he looked at his (now numerous) disciples (v. 17). It is clear that as the message was given, it was for the ears of the disciples first, but also had immediate practical meaning for everyone present.

It's interesting that Luke is able to write that the people came *to hear him and to be healed of their diseases*. Luke stresses the importance of Jesus' preaching ministry over his healing ministry.

How are we to understand the blessings and woes that Jesus pronounced here?

The formula that Jesus used in his preaching was a traditional one that every Jew would understand. These sayings were known as oracles, reminiscent of the Old Testament prophets, with positive oracles being introduced by 'Blessed are you. . .' and negative oracles being introduced by 'Woe to you. . .'

Luke 6:20 – 23 The Positive Oracles

Looking at his disciples, he said: "Blessed are you who are poor, for yours is the kingdom of God.
²¹ Blessed are you who hunger now, for you will be satisfied.
Blessed are you who weep now, for you will laugh.
²² Blessed are you when men hate you, when they exclude you and insult you and reject your name as evil, because of the Son of Man.
²³ "Rejoice in that day and leap for joy, because great is your reward in heaven. For that is how their fathers treated the prophets.

The positive oracles seem to have been directed to the disciples. They are messages of assurance to those who are enduring hardship for the kingdom of God. There is a day of reckoning coming when earth's wrongs will be righted. (The Psalms have many similar messages.) It is certain that God is faithful and will fulfil his promises. If the world treats Jesus' disciples as it treated him, and the Old Testament prophets before him, then they are in following *'in prophetic succession'* (v. 23).

Luke 6:24 – 26 The Negative Oracles

"But woe to you who are rich, for you have already received your comfort."
²⁵ Woe to you who are well fed now, for you will go hungry.
Woe to you who laugh now, for you will mourn and weep.
²⁶ Woe to you when all men speak well of you, for that is how their fathers treated the false prophets.

The negative oracles seem to have been directed to the public, and particularly to people who seek only pleasure and lead frivolous lives, treating nothing seriously, including God's truth. Therefore these are warnings and are calls for mourning and sorrow for mistakes made.

THANK YOU, HEAVENLY FATHER:

For Jesus' words of blessing and woe, spoken from a pastor's heart about people and their relationship with You;
For the learning curve experienced by the newly-appointed apostles; preparing them for their future ministry;
For the growing interest of the common people who were prepared to travel great distances to hear the Word of God;
For the many men and women with medical skills who are busy in your service around the world, often working in situations where they lack so much basic equipment.

IN JESUS' NAME, AMEN

30. Luke 6:27 - 36
Love for Enemies

We noticed in a number of previous studies that a structure was emerging in the ministry of Jesus. Here are some 'laws of Christ'. These are Jesus' first direct commands in Luke's gospel. Here are his laws on human relationships. These are radical ethics.

Notice Jesus' authoritative words intended to catch the attention of all within the sound of his voice: "But I tell you who hear me:" which is the equivalent of Matthew's introductory phrase for Jesus' pronouncements in the Sermon on the Mount (which he reports at greater length), "You have heard that it has been said. . ." followed by "But I say unto you."

Luke 6:27 – 31
"But I tell you who hear me: Love your enemies, do good to those who hate you, ²⁸ bless those who curse you, pray for those who ill-treat you.

²⁹ If someone strikes you on one cheek, turn to him the other also. If someone takes your cloak, do not stop him from taking your tunic.

³⁰ Give to everyone who asks you, and if anyone takes what belongs to you, do not demand it back. 31 Do to others as you would have them do to you.

In vv. 27 & 28 there are four commands about loving one's enemies: we identify them by the verbs used. *Love. . . do good. . . bless. . . pray.*

In vv. 29 & 30 there are four examples of the commands; and in v. 31 there is a summary: *Do to others as you would have them do to you.*

Luke 6:32 – 36
"If you love those who love you, what credit is that to you? Even 'sinners' love those who love them.

³³ And if you do good to those who are good to you, what credit is that to you? Even 'sinners' do that.

³⁴ And if you lend to those from whom you expect repayment, what credit is that to you? Even 'sinners' lend to 'sinners', expecting to be repaid in full.
³⁵ But love your enemies, do good to them, and lend to them without expecting to get anything back."

In vv. 32-34 there are three further examples of the commands. They are not about loving / doing good / lending to those who love you / do good to you / who will lend to you. That would be unexceptional behaviour. Even 'sinners' love/ do good /and lend to those who love / do good/ and lend to them. Jesus commands that his disciples be Christ-like in their behaviour.

V.35a. repeats the three commands about how we relate to our enemies: *love. . . do good. . . lend without expecting anything back.*

In v. 35b there is a divine promise.

Luke 6:35b
Then your reward will be great, and you will be sons of the Most High, because he is kind to the ungrateful and wicked.

V. 36 is a concluding summary.

Luke 6:36
Be merciful, just as your Father is merciful.

The basis for all these commands is the character of God, and the fact that the believer while ungrateful and wicked has been the recipient of God's mercy. Jesus, the early church and the evangelists emphasised that the command to love lies at the heart of his ethical teaching. Jesus himself set the example.

Often the ability to will good for one's enemies may seem impossible, Luke believed that the same Spirit who empowered Jesus (Luke 4:14) dwells in believers and can empower them to choose love for enemies.

THANK YOU, HEAVENLY FATHER:

For the testimony of the created world to Your power and glory;
For the testimony of Your incarnate Son who revealed Your grace and truth;
For the conviction of sin that we experienced when studying this passage of Scripture and the assurance that when we confess our lack of Christ-likeness You will forgive our sins and cleanse us from all unrighteousness;
For reminding us that we *'once were strangers to grace and to God'* – but Jesus sought and found us;
For Your people who, in every generation, have proved the length, breadth, depth and height of Your love in Jesus Christ Your Son.

IN JESUS' NAME, AMEN

31. Luke 6:37 - 42
Judging Others

Luke 6:37 - 38
"Do not judge, and you will not be judged. Do not condemn, and you will not be condemned. Forgive, and you will be forgiven.
³⁸ Give, and it will be given to you. A good measure, pressed down, shaken together and running over, will be poured into your lap. For with the measure you use, it will be measured to you."

We need to keep in mind the conclusion to the previous section as we read vv. 37ff: *'Be merciful, just as your Father is merciful.'* Not one of us likes to be judged unkindly or harshly by others. Do not judge!

What is forbidden here is the tendency of criticising and finding fault with others, in other words *'censoriousness'*. It is easily done, for instance, by making oneself to look better by criticising others as worse.

In keeping this command we will not escape God's final judgment, but rather in the Day of Judgment one will be judged mercifully. We are not to be naïve. This command does not forbid us using our powers of discretion and altering our behaviour or involvement accordingly.,

The second sentence (v. 37b) is well-nigh synonymous with the first. 'Do not condemn *and you will not be condemned.*'

Forgive, and you will be forgiven (v. 37c). Believers cannot ignore the guilt of those who have sinned against them or proclaim that the guilty are innocent. Jesus commands us to forgive people who are indeed guilty of sinning against us.

Give and it will be given to you (v. 38). A good measure, pressed down, shaken together and running over, will be poured into your lap. For with the measure you use, it will be measured to you.

Imagine going into an old fashioned country grocery store to purchase several pounds of sugar. The shopkeeper picks up a paper bag, scoops up some sugar and pours it into the bag. Then he will lift the bag between the fingers and thumbs of both his hands and thump it on the countertop. This means that the sugar fills the bag and there are no unfilled corners. Next, he takes up his scoop again and adds more sugar until the bag is full completely.

If your local grocer was a niggardly man he wouldn't serve you so diligently – nor would you continue to be his customer. Jesus' point is very clear. In two words he commands us: 'Be generous.'

All these commands are a commentary on the Golden Rule: Luke 6:31 *Do to others as you would have them do to you*.

We need to think deeply about the sections that follow in order to find the connection that Jesus had in mind.

Luke 6:39 - 40

He also told them this parable: "Can a blind man lead a blind man? Will they not both fall into a pit? [40] *A student is not above his teacher, but everyone who is fully trained will be like his teacher.*

Talk about a teacher and his student (v. 40) may tell us that Jesus had the Pharisees in mind at this point. In Jesus' estimation they were blind leaders of the blind. How useless is a university which at best can only produce graduates as blind at its own professors. No one who attended the schools of the Pharisees ever graduated as a believer in Jesus!

Luke 6:41 -42

"Why do you look at the speck of sawdust in your brother's eye and pay no attention to the plank in your own eye?
[42] *How can you say to your brother, 'Brother, let me take the speck out of your eye,' when you yourself fail to see the plank in your own eye?*
You hypocrite, first take the plank out of your eye, and then you will see clearly to remove the speck from your brother's eye.

Here is another commonsense illustration. Jesus is not making fun of disabled people, but of hypocrites who are always telling other people what to do to sort out their lives – but they would need to sort themselves out first.

Jesus knew where he was going and throughout his ministry didn't hesitate to call people to follow him.

THANK YOU, HEAVENLY FATHER:

For the wisdom of Jesus and the clear leadership that he gave to his disciples, apostles and the people of Israel;
For the commonsense aspect of the laws of Christ; they make perfect sense;
For the inwardness of discipleship which means that disciples must examine themselves first of all, if they would minister to others;
For the outwardness of discipleship which means that people can see the principles we live by, whose we are, and whom we serve.

IN JESUS' NAME, AMEN

32a. Luke 6:43 – 45
A Tree and its Fruit

Luke 6:43 – 45
"No good tree bears bad fruit, nor does a bad tree bear good fruit.
⁴⁴ Each tree is recognised by its own fruit. People do not pick figs from thorn-bushes, or grapes from briers.
⁴⁵ The good man brings good things out of the good stored up in his heart, and the evil man brings evil things out of the evil stored up in his heart. For out of the overflow of his heart his mouth speaks."

There is no arguing with the principle that *'each tree is recognised by its own fruit.'* It is a self-evident truth. The same is true of people. There are *'good'* people and there are *'bad'* people. Jesus had been teaching laws of His Kingdom and those who were his disciples would be recognisable by their character: *'the good man brings good things out of the good stored up in his heart.'* It is only a matter of time until the motives of the heart become obvious. If the heart is right then the life will be right also. The image of fruit is irrefutable. The nature of a tree can be seen.

32b. Luke 6:46-49
The Wise and Foolish Builders

Luke 6:46 - 49(ANIV)
"Why do you call me, 'Lord, Lord,' and do not do what I say?
⁴⁷ I will show you what he is like who comes to me and hears my words and puts them into practice.
⁴⁸ He is like a man building a house, who dug down deep and laid the foundation on rock. When the flood came, the torrent struck that house but could not shake it, because it was well built.
⁴⁹ But the one who hears my words and does not put them into practice is like a man who built a house on the ground without a foundation. The moment the torrent struck that house, it collapsed and its destruction was complete."

This time Jesus is talking about foundations. Foundations are usually hidden out of sight – but they determine the security and stability of a building.

In the area where Jesus was teaching his audience could look around them and see deep ravines where winter floods had cut into the mountains. They may also have been able to see the ruins of houses that foolish builders had built on sand and not on a good foundation. These homes had been completely destroyed and swept away. Nothing remained. Storms test foundations. Solid foundations stand the test. The foundation corresponds with what a person does with Jesus' teaching, and the floods refer to divine judgment.

People could find themselves in agreement with Jesus' teaching: and being the good teacher that he was he challenged them to act on his teaching. *"Why do you call me, 'Lord, Lord,' and do not do what I say?"*

If they *'built'* on his teaching they would be like a house that was built on rock. If they did not act on his teaching they would be like a house that was built on sand. In the Day of Judgment they would perish.

These people had never heard teaching like this from the rabbis in the synagogues. The Pharisees and the teachers of the Law had not taught them like this, with such straightforward commonsense and ready application.

The solid rock is the word of Christ and not the commandments of Moses. Jesus was indeed initiating a new era.

THANK YOU, HEAVENLY FATHER:

For all that was new in the teaching of Jesus: it must have been like
    a drink of cold, refreshing water to those who received it;
For Jesus' illustrations drawn from everyday life, requiring no tech-
    nical or other specialised knowledge to understand them;
For the ready application of Jesus' teaching to every hearer's life;
For the enlightenment given by the Holy Spirit so that many believed
    on Jesus; they found life by believing his word.

IN JESUS' NAME, AMEN

33. Luke 7:1 - 10
The Faith of the Centurion

This is a narrative full of surprises. A Roman centurion is kindly disposed to the Jews to the extent that he had built them a synagogue in Capernaum. The centurion having heard of Jesus is convinced he should send for him to heal his servant who was ill. The centurion sent Jewish elders from the synagogue asking Jesus to come to his home. The Jewish elders did as he asked, even though it meant they had to come to Jesus with the request. Sometimes people were amazed at Jesus. Here Jesus was amazed at the faith of the centurion.

Lk 7:1 - 6
When Jesus had finished saying all this in the hearing of the people, he entered Capernaum. ² There a centurion's servant, whom his master valued highly, was sick and about to die.

³ The centurion heard of Jesus and sent some elders of the Jews to him, asking him to come and heal his servant. ⁴ When they came to Jesus, they pleaded earnestly with him, "This man deserves to have you do this, ⁵ because he loves our nation and has built our synagogue."

⁶ So Jesus went with them. He was not far from the house when the centurion sent friends to say to him: "Lord, don't trouble yourself, for I do not deserve to have you come under my roof.' So Jesus went with them.

This Roman centurion was an exceptional man. He had such a good working relationship with the elders of the synagogue that some of them carried an urgent message from him to Jesus asking him to come and heal a servant who was sick. The elders reciprocated the centurion's mutual feelings to the extent that they actually delivered a message to Jesus on his behalf, underlining their obligation to him for building them a synagogue (v. 5).

Lk 7:7 – 8
That is why I did not even consider myself worthy to come to you. But say the word, and my servant will be healed. ⁸ for I myself am a man

under authority, with soldiers under me. I tell this one, 'Go', and he goes; and that one, 'Come', and he comes. I say to my servant, 'Do this', and he does it."

Jesus was close to Capernaum and the centurion's house when he was met by friends of the centurion saying. *'Lord, don't come, I am unworthy of having you in my house; this is why I didn't come to you in the first place.'* The word *'unworthy'* says a lot about the man. Despite the rank that he had in the Roman army he was also a *'humble'* man *(vv. 6b & 7)*. Another thing about him is his *'thoughtfulness' (v. 8)*. He was a man in whom the Roman army had invested authority; he used it every day when issuing orders to his soldiers. He never yet had one who disobeyed him. Well then, Jesus is also a man who has authority, he has power to heal the sick, he has only to *'say the word'*, *'issue a command'*, and *'my servant will be healed.'*

Luke 7:9 – 10
When Jesus heard this, he was amazed at him, and turning to the crowd following him, he said, "I tell you, I have not found such great faith even in Israel."

10 Then the men who had been sent returned to the house and found the servant well.

Luke says that Jesus was *amazed*. He had been disappointed that his own people, the Jews, did not have faith in him such as this centurion had. In after days people would read the Gospel of Luke and point to this incident as evidence of the gospel spreading to the Gentile world..

Jesus was indeed the awaited Messiah! We wonder what impact this miracle had on the centurion's Jewish friends.

We can confidently presume that there was *amazement* in the home of the centurion when his friends returned and found the servant fully recovered. The affirmation of the centurion's faith served as support and encouragement for the acceptance of Gentiles into the church of Jesus Christ.

THANK YOU, HEAVENLY FATHER:

For the ministry of Jesus Christ which crossed religious and political lines bringing healing, blessing and salvation to Jews and Gentiles;

For the faith of this centurion and for the Holy Spirit enlightening him through the authority vested in him as a centurion, and directing his thoughts to the authority of Jesus;

For the authority of Jesus in every realm, vested in him by his Father in heaven and remaining so until time shall end;

For the fact that we do not believe in a Jesus who did things, *but in a Jesus who does things!*

For all who are engaged in world evangelisation at this time in history; it is a task fit for the Son of God;

IN JESUS' NAME, AMEN

34. Luke 7:11 - 17
Jesus Raises a Widow's Son

We need to remember that Luke's gospel was not available until years after the resurrection and ascension of Jesus. The reason for mentioning this again is because of the use of the title 'Lord' in the previous reading (vv. 1-11) and in this one. In v. 7 it was the centurion who used the title to address Jesus when expressing shyness, **'Lord,** *don't trouble yourself, for I do not deserve to have you come under my roof.'* Here Luke uses the title in v. 13 to describe Jesus' emotions when meeting the widow of Nain, *"When the* **Lord** *saw her, his heart went out to her and he said, 'Don't cry."* This should not surprise us because for Luke and his readers the Jesus of this story and the church's risen Lord were one and the same.

Luke 7:11 – 13
Soon afterwards, Jesus went to a town called Nain, and his disciples and a large crowd went along with him.
¹² As he approached the town gate, a dead person was being carried out—the only son of his mother, and she was a widow. And a large crowd from the town was with her.
¹³ When the Lord saw her, his heart went out to her and he said, "Don't cry."

Nain is located six miles south-southeast of Nazareth and is about twenty-five miles from Capernaum. As Jesus approached the town gate a funeral procession was coming out on its way to the local cemetery. It had a large attendance of local people. The whole scene touched the heart of Jesus deeply and he immediately spoke words of consolation to the widow who had sustained such a great loss in the death of her only son.

Luke 7:14 – 15
Then he went up and touched the coffin, and those carrying it stood still. He said, "Young man, I say to you, get up!" ¹⁵ The dead man sat up and began to talk, and Jesus gave him back to his mother.

Then Jesus did a most unexpected thing. He touched the coffin and the funeral procession stopped. He simply spoke a few words, *"Young man, I say to you, get up!"* With a marvellous economy of words Luke records the miracle (v. 15), *'The dead man sat up and began to talk, and Jesus gave him back to his mother.'*

Touching a dead body made one ceremonially unclean, but Jesus ignored this convention. In this healing no mention is made of anyone's faith, which shows that it was entirely the gracious initiative of Jesus and by his word alone that the sick were healed and the dead raised. The widow's joy was well nigh inexpressible. To have her only son restored to her in her old age was a blessing beyond calculation. Her darkness was turned to light and her mourning into joy.

Light began to dawn among some in the crowd. After a moment of shock, described as *'awe'*, they praised God, *'A great prophet has appeared among us'*, they said. *'God has come to help his people.'* We recall that Jesus referred to himself as a prophet in 4:24. The village of Nain had a visit from God that day.

Luke 7:16
They were all filled with awe and praised God. "A great prophet has appeared among us," they said. "God has come to help his people."

Widows without sons had no visible means of support, and were cast on the charity of others. Widows and orphans were two groups that God singled out as deserving special consideration by the church.

Luke 7:17 *This news about Jesus spread throughout Judea and the surrounding country.*

Conversation about the miracle and about Jesus who had raised a dead man to life would go on well into the night at hundreds of firesides in Judea.

THANK YOU, HEAVENLY FATHER:

For the *'tales of poor folk'* that are recorded in the gospels and the gracious intervention of Jesus in their lives;

For the faith of Luke himself that comes shining through in his reporting of the ministry of Jesus; it is clear that he knew Jesus as the Son of God and the Saviour of the world;

For the witness of all those who were involved in this miracle i.e. the widow and her son, those who carried the coffin, and the local population attending the funeral, all of whom spread the praise of Jesus abroad by word of mouth and from personal experience;

For how much good was accomplished by Jesus in his varied ministry simply because he walked in harmony with heaven as directed by his heavenly Father;

IN JESUS' NAME, AMEN

35. Luke 7:18 - 35
Jesus and John the Baptist

Luke 7:18 - 21
John's disciples told him about all these things. Calling two of them, [19] he sent them to the Lord to ask, "Are you the one who was to come, or should we expect someone else?" [20] When the men came to Jesus, they said, "John the Baptist sent us to you to ask, 'Are you the one who was to come, or should we expect someone else?'" [21] At that very time Jesus cured many who had diseases, sicknesses and evil spirits, and gave sight to many who were blind.

Did John the Baptist send two of his disciples to Jesus on his own behalf or for the benefit of the disciples? John, imprisoned by Herod, knew that his days were numbered and to the last he is sending men to Jesus. John wants his disciples to know beyond any doubt that Jesus is the Messiah, so that after his ministry is over they will follow Jesus. It seems that John's disciples arrived with Jesus when he was in the midst of a very busy programme of *'curing many who had diseases, sicknesses and evil spirits, and gave sight to many who were blind* (v. 21).'

Luke 7:22 - 23
So he replied to the messengers, "Go back and report to John what you have seen and heard: The blind receive sight, the lame walk, those who have leprosy are cured, the deaf hear, the dead are raised, and the good news is preached to the poor. [23] Blessed is the man who does not fall away on account of me."

John the Baptist knew that the mandate for his ministry was written in Isaiah 40:3-5. John also knew that the mandate for Jesus' ministry was written in Isaiah 61:1-2. John may have known about Jesus' exposition of that passage when preaching in the synagogue in Nazareth. Jesus gave John a reply that he would recognise (v. 22). The beatitude that Jesus added (v. 23) was warmly pastoral.

Luke 7:24 - 28
After John's messengers left, Jesus began to speak to the crowd about John: "What did you go out into the desert to see? A reed swayed by the wind? ^{25} If not, what did you go out to see? A man dressed in fine clothes? No, those who wear expensive clothes and indulge in luxury are in palaces. ^{26} But what did you go out to see? A prophet? Yes, I tell you, and more than a prophet. ^{27} This is the one about whom it is written: "'I will send my messenger ahead of you, who will prepare your way before you.' ^{28} I tell you, among those born of women there is no-one greater than John; yet the one who is least in the kingdom of God is greater than he."

Jesus decided it was time to challenge the people about their response to John the Baptist's ministry. Many lives had been transformed by it and were baptised as a sign of genuine repentance. But there were many others who had not benefitted at all. Jesus asked penetrating questions(v. 24ff): did you go out to see an odd-fellow?; a dandified individual oozing with wealth?; or did you go to hear a prophet? If you did, you don't know how right you were (v. 26). The prophet Isaiah wrote about John and his ministry (v. 27). The man you heard is the greatest human being who ever lived (v. 28), but to be least in the kingdom of God is to be greater than John. What a curriculum vitae!

Luke 7:29 - 30
(All the people, even the tax collectors, when they heard Jesus' words, acknowledged that God's way was right, because they had been baptised by John ^{30} But the Pharisees and experts in the law rejected God's purpose for themselves, because they had not been baptised by John.)

John's ministry yielded a great harvest of souls (v. 29). But the leaders of Judaism had rejected his ministry and had missed God's purpose for themselves (v. 30).

Luke 7:31 - 35

"To what, then, can I compare the people of this generation? What are they like? ³² They are like children sitting in the market-place and calling out to each other:" 'We played the flute for you, and you did not dance; we sang a dirge, and you did not cry.' ³³ For John the Baptist came neither eating bread nor drinking wine, and you say, 'He has a demon.' ³⁴ The Son of Man came eating and drinking, and you say, 'He is a glutton and a drunkard, a friend of tax collectors and "sinners".' ³⁵ But wisdom is proved right by all her children."

In the North of England there is a saying, *'There's nowt so queer as folk.'* It is saying that people sometimes behave in a very strange way. It is applicable to the situation being described by Jesus (v. 31).

He spoke about children arguing while at play: some wanted to play weddings and other wanted to play funerals (v. 32). John the Baptist was an austere man – *and people said he had a demon* (v.33). Jesus, on the other hand, behaved normally- *and people said he was a glutton and a drunkard, and a man who kept bad company' (v. 34).*

For Jesus the arrival of the kingdom of God was a time for celebration and joy.

THANK YOU, HEAVENLY FATHER:

For the ministry of John the Baptist preparing the way for Jesus;
For the ministry of Jesus to John the Baptist comforting him at a very difficult period of his life and ministry;
For the outlook of Jesus – the arrival of the kingdom of God was a time for celebration and joy;

IN JESUS' NAME, AMEN

36. Luke 7:36 - 50
Jesus Anointed by a Sinful Woman

Luke 7:36 – 38
Now one of the Pharisees invited Jesus to have dinner with him, so he went to the Pharisee's house and reclined at the table.
³⁷ When a woman who had lived a sinful life in that town learned that Jesus was eating at the Pharisee's house, she brought an alabaster jar of perfume, ³⁸ and as she stood behind him at his feet weeping, she began to wet his feet with her tears. Then she wiped them with her hair, kissed them and poured perfume on them.

Jesus did not share the outlook of the Pharisees with their *'salvation by segregation'* policy. This is why this section has him accepting the invitation of a Pharisee to have a meal with him at his house. As we already discovered (Matthew's banquet Study 25) these meals were not totally private. People could stand outside looking in the windows at the guests or even have managed to get inside without being thrown out. This may be how the woman with a sinful past came to be inside the house and got so close to Jesus as to stand behind him. Not only that, *she brought an alabaster jar of perfume, and as she stood behind him at his feet weeping, she began to wet his feet with her tears. Then she wiped them with her hair, kissed them and poured perfume on them.* (vv. 37-38). She was a brave soul. She had a reputation. She was a despised person. But, as we shall learn, she was also a forgiven and grateful soul who loved Jesus.

Luke 7:39 – 43
When the Pharisee who had invited him saw this, he said to himself, "If this man were a prophet, he would know who is touching him and what kind of woman she is—that she is a sinner."
⁴⁰ Jesus answered him, "Simon, I have something to tell you." "Tell me, teacher," he said.
⁴¹ "Two men owed money to a certain money-lender. One owed him five hundred denarii, and the other fifty. ⁴² Neither of them had

the money to pay him back, so he cancelled the debts of both. Now which of them will love him more?"

⁴³ *Simon replied, "I suppose the one who had the bigger debt cancelled." "You have judged correctly," Jesus said.*

The Pharisee may have thought that his thoughts were known only to himself. Jesus knew what Simon was thinking. *"Simon, I have something to tell you." "Tell me, teacher,"* he said.

Jesus told Simon the story of two men who were in debt to a money-lender to the tune of 500 pence and 50 pence respectively. But neither of them could pay. Both men were broke. They knew it – and the money-lender knew it also! To their great surprise, the money-lender forgave both of them their debts. It's a wonder Simon didn't ask for the name of the money-lender at once.

Then came the punch line. We doubt if Simon saw it coming. It was posed as a question: *"Now which of them will love him more?"* Without hesitation Simon answered: *"I suppose the one who had the bigger debt cancelled." "You have judged correctly,"* Jesus said.

Luke 7:44 – 50

Then he turned towards the woman and said to Simon, "Do you see this woman? I came into your house. You did not give me any water for my feet, but she wet my feet with her tears and wiped them with her hair. ⁴⁵ *You did not give me a kiss, but this woman, from the time I entered, has not stopped kissing my feet.* ⁴⁶ *You did not put oil on my head, but she has poured perfume on my feet.* ⁴⁷ *Therefore, I tell you, her many sins have been forgiven—for she loved much. But he who has been forgiven little loves little."*

⁴⁸ *Then Jesus said to her, "Your sins are forgiven."* ⁴⁹ *The other guests began to say among themselves, "Who is this who even forgives sins?"*

⁵⁰ *Jesus said to the woman, "Your faith has saved you; go in peace."*

Jesus caught Simon's attention again, and said to him, 'Simon, look at this woman.' While you are doing that, think about your behaviour towards me. *'I came into your house. You did not give me any water for my feet. . ., You did not give me a kiss. . ., You did not put oil on my head' (vv. 44-46).*

Now Simon, think of what she has done. *"She wet my feet with her tears and wiped them with her hair; this woman, from the time I entered, has not stopped kissing my feet; she has poured perfume on my feet (vv. 44-46).* Therefore, I tell you, her many sins have been forgiven—for she loved much. But he who has been forgiven little loves little." (v. 47)

Then Jesus said to her, *"Your sins are forgiven" (v. 48).*

[Naturally the guests wondered: *"Who is this who even forgives sins?"*]

⁵⁰ Jesus said to the woman, "Your faith has saved you; go in peace."

THANK YOU, HEAVENLY FATHER:

For the behaviour of Jesus in the house of Simon the Pharisee: he was direct, he was uncompromising, he revealed his authority to forgive sin; he upheld the dignity and honesty of the woman who came to show her loving gratitude to him for sins forgiven, so that she was not embarrassed or put to shame;

For the woman who had such a notorious past, who might have wished to go away and hide, but had the courage to confess Jesus Christ as her Saviour before many who possibly had known her past.

IN JESUS' NAME, AMEN

37. Luke 8:1 - 15
The Parable of the Sower

Luke 8:1 – 3
After this, Jesus travelled about from one town and village to another, proclaiming the good news of the kingdom of God. The Twelve were with him, ² and also some women who had been cured of evil spirits and diseases: Mary (called Magdalene) from whom seven demons had come out; ³ Joanna the wife of Chuza, the manager of Herod's household; Susanna; and many others. These women were helping to support them out of their own means.

This is an informative and interesting opening paragraph. It records Jesus' first missionary journey (v. 1 It names a number of women who travelled with Jesus and the disciples and provided for the material needs of the whole group from their private resources (vv. 2 – 3). It names Joanna, whose husband Chuza, was a steward of King Herod, who helped financially. It says that some of the women had been wonderfully delivered from evil spirits and diseases. One of them, Mary Magdalene, had been liberated from seven demons. Together, the Lord and his disciples plus the women made up a sizeable group.

Luke 8:4 - 8
While a large crowd was gathering and people were coming to Jesus from town after town, he told this parable:
⁵ "A farmer went out to sow his seed. As he was scattering the seed, some fell along the path; it was trampled on, and the birds of the air ate it up. ⁶ Some fell on rock, and when it came up, the plants withered because they had no moisture. ⁷ Other seed fell among thorns, which grew up with it and choked the plants. ⁸ Still other seed fell on good soil. It came up and yielded a crop, a hundred times more than was sown." When he said this, he called out, "He who has ears to hear, let him hear."

Jesus caught the crowd's attention by telling a story of a familiar rural scene. Perhaps there was a farmer sowing seed nearby, in full view of the crowd listening to Jesus.

Being largely an agricultural people the audience would understand the action of the farmer. He used only good seed. It fell on four types of soil. This determined the yield in each case. The punch line to the parable was a simple one: *"He who has ears to hear, let him hear" (v. 8).*

Luke 8:9 – 10
His disciples asked him what this parable meant. ¹⁰ He said, "The knowledge of the secrets of the kingdom of God has been given to you, but to others I speak in parables, so that, "'though seeing, they may not see; though hearing, they may not understand.'"

It was Jesus' disciples who asked the meaning of the parable. There was knowledge of the kingdom of God that was given to them. It was the public who were more likely to wonder about the meaning of Jesus' parables. Isaiah had made a prophecy about this (Isa. 6:9). It was a judgment on people who do not listen.

Luke 8:11 – 15
"This is the meaning of the parable: The seed is the word of God.
¹² Those along the path are the ones who hear, and then the devil comes and takes away the word from their hearts, so that they may not believe and be saved. ¹³ Those on the rock are the ones who receive the word with joy when they hear it, but they have no root. They believe for a while, but in the time of testing they fall away. ¹⁴ The seed that fell among thorns stands for those who hear, but as they go on their way they are choked by life's worries, riches and pleasures, and they do not mature. ¹⁵ But the seed on good soil stands for those with a noble and good heart, who hear the word, retain it, and by persevering produce a crop.

When the seed is sown in some hearts (those by the path through the field) *the devil comes and takes away the word from their hearts so that they may not believe and be saved* (v. 12). The devil is like the crows or seagulls that follow the farmer as he ploughs in order to steal the seed.

Those listeners who are like stony ground *receive the word with joy when they hear it, but they have no root. They believe for a while, but in time of testing fall away* (v. 13).

The seed that fell among thorns stands for *those who hear, but as they go on their way they are choked by life's worries, riches and pleasures, and they do not mature* (v. 14).

The seed that fell on good soil stands for *those with a noble and good heart, who hear the word, retain it, and by persevering produce a crop* (v. 15).

'Take heed how you hear,' said Jesus. *'What kind of soil are you?'* is a similar comment. *'Consider carefully how you listen,'* said Jesus (v. 18).

THANK YOU, HEAVENLY FATHER:

For the teaching methods of Jesus, even in our technological age, they still grip our imagination and challenge our attitude to hearing the Word of God;

For faithful pastors and evangelists who were (and are) diligent sowers of your word to us; God forbid that we should be careless hearers;

For the priceless gift of the word of God in its completeness that is available to us in our own language to read, believe and obey;

IN JESUS' NAME, AMEN

38a. Luke 8:16 - 18
A Lamp on a Stand

Luke 8:16 – 18
"No-one lights a lamp and hides it in a jar or puts it under a bed. Instead, he puts it on a stand, so that those who come in can see the light. ¹⁷ For there is nothing hidden that will not be disclosed, and nothing concealed that will not be known or brought out into the open.
¹⁸ Therefore consider carefully how you listen. Whoever has will be given more; whoever does not have, even what he thinks he has will be taken from him."

These verses are a further application of the parable of the sower: v. 18 shows the connection. *'Consider carefully how you listen.'*

This time the illustration is a domestic lamp which was a wick burning in a saucer of oil. It provided a dim light, and because of its low power was considered fairly safe.

Most people had beds that were mats which they rolled out on the floor every night. Some people had beds that were a wooden frame on short legs, much like a modern divan today. If you lit a lamp at night the last place you would put it would be under the bed!

That is not where light is needed. No, a lamp is set on a stand, where it can be seen. It is the purpose of light to reveal. It is a great help when looking for something. The lamp helps you find what you are looking for. You may come across things you didn't wish to find (v. 17)!

The disciples, who know the secrets of God's kingdom (vv. 9-10) are to let that light shine in order that others may believe and be saved. This is how souls in spiritual darkness and ignorance receive the light of the gospel. Jesus says to them, *'Consider carefully how you listen.'*

The second part of v. 18 is an expanded proverb. A modern counterpart might be *'The rich get richer and the poor get poorer'*. The subject here is not wealth or possessions but the knowledge of God. Careless hearing results in spiritual loss; careful hearing leads to growing knowledge of the gospel and of God. The proverb is correct: *'Whoever has will be given more, whoever does not have, even what he thinks he has will be taken from him."*

38b. Luke 8:19 – 21
Jesus' Mother and Brothers

Luke 8:19 – 21
Now Jesus' mother and brothers came to see him, but they were not able to get near him because of the crowd. ²⁰ Someone told him, "Your mother and brothers are standing outside, wanting to see you."
²¹ He replied, "My mother and brothers are those who hear God's word and put it into practice."

There is a delicacy to this section. Jesus was not only a public figure, he was the incarnate God, the Messiah and Saviour of the world. What was the appropriate way for him to relate to his family and for them to relate to him? The more the realisation of his real identity became known, family relationships could have become a problem. They didn't, because even on the cross Jesus made provision for the care of his mother Mary.

His mother and brothers came to see him (v. 19). That is a heart-warming piece of information. However they found it impossible to get anywhere near him because of the crowd that was around him.

Someone was thoughtful enough to pass a message to him (v. 20). *"Your mother and brothers are standing outside, wanting to see you."* We learn from this that Jesus belonged to an extended family. Whether Joseph was still alive at this time we do not know.

Jesus' reply was not unkind. He would always be Mary's son and a brother to his siblings.

This time he gave the words *'mother and brothers'* a new meaning. *'My real mother and brothers are not my physical kin but those who hear God's word and put it into practices'* (v. 21).

This is the first time that Jesus had spoken of his new family, the family of God. We do not enter the family of God by natural birth, but by the new birth of regeneration which is a work of the Holy Spirit. Its reality is seen in lives moulded by the word of God. Psalm 1 provides a good illustration.

THANK YOU, HEAVENLY FATHER:

For the support of our parents and siblings, and many of God's people who sacrificially minister to us in the service of the Gospel;
For the privilege of knowing You, the living and true God, and Jesus Christ whom You have sent;
For those who are new in the faith, and are discovering the warmth and the practical support of their new spiritual family;
For those whom the Holy Spirit is enlightening through hearing the gospel of Jesus Christ, and for the gift of saving faith that will be theirs when they come to him.
For the family of God in every nation, tribe, people and language;

IN JESUS' NAME, AMEN

39. Luke 8:22 - 25
Jesus Calms the Storm

Luke 8:22 - 23
One day Jesus said to his disciples, "Let's go over to the other side of the lake." So they got into a boat and set out. [23] *As they sailed, he fell asleep. A squall came down on the lake, so that the boat was being swamped, and they were in great danger.*

The demands that constant ministry made on Jesus were known only to him and his Father in heaven. The picture of him falling asleep in the boat is understandable, but for him to continue sleeping through a serious storm shows how much he needed restorative sleep. He was the God-man, but he had a human nature that was given to weariness just like ours.

Luke would have learned from the disciples who were with Jesus that day exactly how severe the storm really was: *A squall came down on the lake, so that the boat was being swamped, and they were in great danger.*

To this day the Sea of Galilee is renowned for its sudden and severe storms. Many people have lost their lives as a direct result of these storms.

The disciples were where they should have been; they were in a boat crossing Galilee, when they found themselves in great danger. What is more, their Master was with them, but he was asleep.

Luke 8:24 - 25
The disciples went and woke him, saying, "Master, Master, we're going to drown!" He got up and rebuked the wind and the raging waters; the storm subsided, and all was calm. [25] *"Where is your faith?" he asked his disciples.*

When professional fishermen are afraid for their safety it is time to be alarmed! The disciples had to waken Jesus because he was sound asleep: *"Master, Master, we're going to drown!"* Exactly what they expected him to do is not clear. In all their journeys they hadn't been with him in such an emergency before.

He got up and rebuked the wind and the raging waters; the storm subsided, and all was calm. The forces of nature submitted in instant obedience to the voice of their Creator. He is the Creator of heaven and earth and all the forces of nature are underneath his authority. We imagine the disciples were speechless, and perhaps somewhat embarrassed by their fear of a few moments ago.

"Where is your faith?" he asked his disciples (v. 25). It's easy to trust the Lord when it clear to see that everything is under control (*preferably under our control*). Some believers are vociferous and noisy about their faith in Jesus. When life takes a sudden turn, and control of everything is no longer in their hands (*was it ever?*) they can become as quiet as mice.

These professional fishermen were *'out of their comfort zone'*. The situation was outside their experience. The safety of the boat was no longer in their hands. That was how dire the situation was.

Jesus' question makes perfect sense with hindsight. Why didn't they trust him, whether he was asleep or awake? Did they think that he and they would all perish together? It seems like it. He asks us the same question when life's storms confound us*: 'Where is your faith?'*

Luke 8:25
In fear and amazement they asked one another, "Who is this? He commands even the winds and the water, and they obey him."

Their knowledge of Jesus was growing, sometimes gradually, sometimes phenomenally, as during and after the storm. 'Who is this?' indeed! *He commands even the winds and the water, and they obey him."* Yes!

He is the One '*by whom all things were made, and without him was not anything made that was made.*'

Thank You, Heavenly Father:

For Your power and wisdom displayed throughout the created universe, every whit of it declares Your glory;

For Your grace and truth revealed in Your Son Jesus, whom we believe upholds all things by the word of his power;

For all the storms of life through which You have brought us safely so that we may spend ourselves in Your glad service;

For the Operation Mobilisation ships that visit many nations (even closed countries) to distribute the Word of God and other related literature;

For the Hospital ships that visit many nations bringing surgical and medical help to those who are sick and dying for want of such resources in their own countries;

For vast numbers of volunteers who staff these ships and do it for love of their Saviour, Jesus Christ;

IN JESUS' NAME, AMEN

40. Luke 8:26 - 39
The Healing of a Demon-possessed Man

Luke 8:26 - 29
They sailed to the region of the Gerasenes, which is across the lake from Galilee. ²⁷ *When Jesus stepped ashore, he was met by a demon-possessed man from the town.*

For a long time this man had not worn clothes or lived in a house, but had lived in the tombs. ²⁸ *When he saw Jesus, he cried out and fell at his feet, shouting at the top of his voice, "What do you want with me, Jesus, Son of the Most High God? I beg you, don't torture me!"* ²⁹ *For Jesus had commanded the evil spirit to come out of the man.*

Many times it had seized him, and though he was chained hand and foot and kept under guard, he had broken his chains and had been driven by the demon into solitary places.

The disciples had survived a severe storm on Galilee in vv. 22-25, but here they are on another boat trip, this time to the south-eastern shore of the Sea of Galilee (vv. 26-27). Jesus was immediately confronted by a very strange person whom Luke describes as '*a demon-possessed man from the town*'.

His everyday behaviour was abnormal to say the least: '*for a long time this man had not worn clothes or lived in a house, but had lived in the tombs.*' He was so demented that he ran about in a state of nakedness, which for normal people would have been totally humiliating and disgraceful.

Seeing Jesus agitated the demons and he began shouting at the top of his voice: *"What do you want with me, Jesus, Son of the Most High God? I beg you, don't torture me!"* The evil spirit was so raucous because Jesus had ordered it to leave the man. The evil spirit had named Jesus with a superior and accurate title: '*Jesus, Son of the Most High God.*' Notice that the demonic world recognised Jesus immediately and were terrified because they knew he had authority over them and feared he would punish them.

Luke 8:30 - 31
Jesus asked him, "What is your name?" "Legion," he replied, because many demons had gone into him. ³¹ And they begged him repeatedly not to order them to go into the Abyss.

Jesus asked for the demon's name. The reply was startling: *"Legion," he replied, because many demons had gone into him.* The demons submit to Jesus by naming themselves, and bargain with him to minimise their punishment. They were terrified of the Abyss, the place where the Devil and his angels will be consigned to everlasting torment. Jesus did not send them to the Abyss, because in God's economy the appointed time for their final destiny had not yet come. Where would he send them?

Luke 8:32 - 33
A large herd of pigs was feeding there on the hillside. The demons begged Jesus to let them go into them, and he gave them permission. ³³ When the demons came out of the man, they went into the pigs, and the herd rushed down the steep bank into the lake and was drowned.

The demons are still bargaining with Jesus, wanting to enter a herd of pigs that were nearby. When they came out of the man they entered the pigs which immediately dashed headlong down a steep slope and were drowned in the sea. Jesus set the demon-possessed man free, even at the cost of a herd of pigs. The existence of pig-farming would suggest that this was a predominantly Gentile, rather than a Jewish area.

Luke 8:34 - 37
When those tending the pigs saw what had happened, they ran off and reported this in the town and countryside, ³⁵ and the people went out to see what had happened.

When they came to Jesus, they found the man from whom the demons had gone out, sitting at Jesus' feet, dressed and in his right mind; and they were afraid. ³⁶ Those who had seen it told the people how the demon-possessed man had been cured.

³⁷ Then all the people of the region of the Gerasenes asked Jesus to leave them, because they were overcome with fear. So he got into the boat and left.

The local people came to see what had happened. The pigs were nowhere to be seen, unless some carcases were floating in the sea. The focal point was the man who had been delivered from demon-possession. We imagine their surprise at the sight of him *'sitting at Jesus' feet, dressed and in his right mind'*. We don't know what people said about the change in the man but Luke says that their reaction to Jesus was one of fear. This was fear in the face of Jesus' power and holiness, and they asked him to leave the area. So Jesus got into the boat and left.

Luke 8:38 - 39
The man from whom the demons had gone out begged to go with him, but Jesus sent him away, saying, ³⁹ "Return home and tell how much God has done for you." So the man went away and told all over the town how much Jesus had done for him.

Notice that there was a 'before' and an 'after' in this man's life. He wanted to follow Jesus wherever he would lead. Jesus' will for him was that his witness was needed right where he lived. We say farewell to the man, happy in the service of Jesus, and witnessing to his own people.

THANK YOU, HEAVENLY FATHER:

For the wonderful change that Jesus works when he comes into our lives.

IN JESUS' NAME, AMEN

41. Luke 8:40 - 56
A Dead Girl and a Sick Woman

Luke 8:40 – 42a
Now when Jesus returned, a crowd welcomed him, for they were all expecting him. ⁴¹ Then a man named Jairus, a ruler of the synagogue, came and fell at Jesus' feet, pleading with him to come to his house ⁴² because his only daughter, a girl of about twelve, was dying.

The reason for the raised expectation of the crowd for Jesus' return from Gerasa is not given. Perhaps news from that area had travelled fast. Here is a strange sight: Jairus, a ruler of the synagogue no less, falls at Jesus' feet pleading with him to come and heal his twelve year old daughter who was close to dying. All barriers and prejudices were cast aside in the interest of his daughter's condition. Jesus immediately set out for Jairus' house.

Luke 8:42b – 46
As Jesus was on his way, the crowds almost crushed him. ⁴³ And a woman was there who had been subject to bleeding for twelve years, but no-one could heal her. ⁴⁴ She came up behind him and touched the edge of his cloak, and immediately her bleeding stopped. ⁴⁵ "Who touched me?" Jesus asked. When they all denied it, Peter said, "Master, the people are crowding and pressing against you." ⁴⁶ But Jesus said, "Someone touched me; I know that power has gone out from me."

The pressure of the crowd was suffocating. In the crowd a very sick woman who had a haemorrhage for some twelve years was doing her utmost to get near Jesus. He was her last hope. All the doctors she had consulted had failed to provide a cure for her condition. At last, she managed to stretch her arm between a few people and succeeded in touching the edge of Jesus' cloak. Her healing was immediate. To Peter's surprise Jesus asked what seemed like a silly question: 'Who touched me?' Peter learned the reason for Jesus' question when he said *"Someone touched me; I know that power has gone out from me."*

Luke 8:47 – 48
Then the woman, seeing that she could not go unnoticed, came trembling and fell at his feet. In the presence of all the people, she told why she had touched him and how she had been instantly healed. ⁴⁸ Then he said to her, "Daughter, your faith has healed you. Go in peace."

The woman, out of honesty and gratitude came before Jesus and fell at his feet. She told him why she had touched him and testified to her instant healing. Jesus' words were golden, *"Daughter, your faith has healed you. Go in peace."*

Luke 8:49 – 56
While Jesus was still speaking, someone came from the house of Jairus, the synagogue ruler. "Your daughter is dead," he said. "Don't bother the teacher any more." ⁵⁰ Hearing this, Jesus said to Jairus, "Don't be afraid; just believe, and she will be healed."
⁵¹ When Jesus arrived at the house of Jairus, he did not let anyone go in with him except Peter, John and James, and the child's father and mother. ⁵² Meanwhile, all the people were wailing and mourning for her. "Stop wailing," Jesus said. "She is not dead but asleep." ⁵³ They laughed at him, knowing that she was dead. ⁵⁴ But he took her by the hand and said, "My child, get up!" ⁵⁵ Her spirit returned, and at once she stood up. Then Jesus told them to give her something to eat. ⁵⁶ Her parents were astonished, but he ordered them not to tell anyone what had happened.

While Jesus and the woman were talking a messenger arrived from Jairus' home to say that the little girl was dead, and they were not to bother the teacher any more. Jesus had comforting words for Jairus: *"Don't be afraid; just believe, and she will be healed."*
Arriving at Jairus' home Jesus put the majority of people in the house outside, and admitted only Peter, James and John and the child's parents into the room. Outside the official mourners were making an unbearable amount of noise. *'Stop wailing,'* Jesus said, *'she is not dead but asleep.'* Those present responded with mocking laughter, *'knowing she was dead'*.

Jesus took the girl by the hand and said, *'My child, get up!' Immediately her spirit returned and at once she stood up.* Jesus directed that she be given some food. Her astonished parents appeared to be speechless, and Jesus ordered them not to tell anyone what had happened, *'his hour had not yet come'*. Meanwhile the little girl, whom Jesus dealt with so gently that she hardly knew she had died, was served some food.

THANK YOU, HEAVENLY FATHER:

For the power of Jesus over disease and death, two effects of sin's entrance into the world;

For the *'last-hope'* faith of the woman and the *'grief-stricken'* faith of Jairus, both of which Jesus honoured;

For Jesus' consideration and gentleness when raising the little girl, who in response to his words would open her eyes and sit up, hardly knowing she had died;

For the privilege of Peter, James and John who witnessed a clear revelation of Jesus' divinity (at the Transfiguration:9:28-36), of his humanity (in the Garden of Gethsemane:22:39-46) and of his power and compassion in the home of Jairus.

IN JESUS NAME, AMEN

42. Luke 9:1 - 9
Jesus Sends Out the Twelve

Luke 9:1 - 6
When Jesus had called the Twelve together, he gave them power and authority to drive out all demons and to cure diseases, ² and he sent them out to preach the kingdom of God and to heal the sick.
³ He told them: "Take nothing for the journey—no staff, no bag, no bread, no money, no extra tunic. ⁴ Whatever house you enter, stay there until you leave that town. ⁵ If people do not welcome you, shake the dust off your feet when you leave their town, as a testimony against them."
⁶ So they set out and went from village to village, preaching the gospel and healing people everywhere.

In study 28 we learned that Jesus engaged in a night of prayer after which he chose twelve of his disciples to be apostles. Here Jesus calls the Twelve (note the official title) together to commission them and endow them with power and authority to carry out a specific mission.

As an aide-memoire we might note that (1) *he called them together,* (2) *he gave them power and authority to drive out all demons and to cure diseases,* and (3) *he sent them out to preach the kingdom of God and heal the sick.*

What is happening here? Jesus is delegating his authority to his apostles. It was the same power by which Jesus healed people and performed miraculous feats. He entrusted his apostles with that power.

With regard to their material needs and support Jesus did not permit them to carry supplies with them: *'Take nothing for the journey – no staff, not bag, no bread, no money, no extra tunic.'* If they were offered hospitality in a home they were to stay there while they were in that town. If people were unwelcoming and inhospitable they were to shake off the dust off their feet when leaving the town, as a testimony against them. Some folk might ask: 'Were they living by faith or living off the faithful?' Jesus was telling them to *'travel light'*. There was urgency in their mission. They were neither to overstay their welcome anywhere nor spend time where they were not wanted. So off they went on a gospel blitzkrieg, *'preaching the gospel and healing everywhere.'*

Luke 9:7 - 9
Now Herod the tetrarch heard about all that was going on. And he was perplexed, because some were saying that John had been raised from the dead, ⁸ others that Elijah had appeared, and still others that one of the prophets of long ago had come back to life.

⁹ But Herod said, "I beheaded John. Who, then, is this I hear such things about?" And he tried to see him.

There was consternation in the palace of King Herod. News of the apostles' mission had reached him. Some of his informants said that John the Baptist had been raised from the dead. Others said that the prophet Elijah had appeared, and still others that one of the prophets had come back to life. Thinking aloud, he was heard to say. *'I beheaded John, Who, then, is this I hear such things about?' And he tried to see him.'* Herod couldn't find peace of conscience anywhere.

There is a very strong hint here that Herod was becoming upset; and depending on whether he can get to see Jesus or the apostles, the news that is reaching him may lead to grim circumstances for Jesus and the apostles in the not-too-distant future.

At this point in church history we are under apostolic authority when we read the words and teaching of the apostles in the pages of the New Testament. Their teaching is nothing less than the teaching of Christ. We must not neglect the authority and power of the apostolic word.

THANK YOU, HEAVENLY FATHER:

For the wisdom of Jesus' leadership in empowering his disciples, so that the potential benefits of his ministry were multiplied by twelve;

For the clear reflection of Jesus' ministry of preaching, teaching and healing, thus making the ministry of the apostles easily recognised;

For the ministry of the Holy Spirit working in Herod's conscience making him aware of his guilt and making him fearful in view of a possible meeting with Jesus or one of his apostles;
For the lasting ministry of the apostles of Jesus until this day and for as long as time shall last and the word of God still circulates;
For the ministry of the prophets of the Old Testament and the Apostles of the New Testament era, with Jesus Christ being the chief cornerstone.

In Jesus' Name, Amen

43. Luke 9:10 - 17
Jesus Feeds the Five Thousand

Luke 9:10 - 11
When the apostles returned, they reported to Jesus what they had done. Then he took them with him and they withdrew by themselves to a town called Bethsaida, [11] but the crowds learned about it and followed him.

He welcomed them and spoke to them about the kingdom of God, and healed those who needed healing.

It must have been an exciting reunion when the apostles returned from their mission work. How long did it take to give twelve oral reports?

It appears that Jesus decided that all of them needed a period of withdrawal and so the group went to the town of Bethsaida. Privacy and rest were difficult to come by because when their whereabouts became known the crowds followed them to Bethsaida. Jesus' reaction to this renewed pressure was to *'welcome them and speak to them about the kingdom of God, and heal those who needed healing.'*

Luke 9:12 – 14a
Late in the afternoon the Twelve came to him and said, "Send the crowd away so they can go to the surrounding villages and countryside and find food and lodging, because we are in a remote place here."

[13] He replied, "You give them something to eat." They answered, "We have only five loaves of bread and two fish—unless we go and buy food for all this crowd." [14] (About five thousand men were there.)

Time had been marching on and late afternoon soon came round. Perhaps the Twelve were feeling peckish themselves because they began to realise that the crowds were in need of refreshments. They suggested to Jesus that he should send the crowds away to surrounding villages and countryside and find food and lodging. There was none to be had in the remote location where they were.

Jesus had a challenge for the apostles, *'You give them something to eat,'* he said. 'We have only five loaves of bread (five small scones or cookies) and two fish (probably small sardine-like fish)'. Luke spares us the narrative of John's gospel at this point, so there is no mention of the boy who gave his lunch to Jesus. It is perfectly legitimate for us to recall it. The disciples suggested that they *'go and buy food for all this crowd.'* Again Luke omits discussion of the cost involved.

Luke 9:14b - 17
But he said to his disciples, "Make them sit down in groups of about fifty each." ¹⁵ The disciples did so, and everybody sat down.
¹⁶ Taking the five loaves and the two fish and looking up to heaven, he gave thanks and broke them. Then he gave them to the disciples to set before the people.
¹⁷ They all ate and were satisfied, and the disciples picked up twelve basketfuls of broken pieces that were left over.

The problem was solved on the initiative of Jesus, who before any food materialised ordered the disciples to have the people sit down in groups of fifty.

Taking the loaves and the two fish Jesus looked up to heaven, gave thanks for the food and broke it into small portions. Then the food was given to the disciples for distribution to the crowds. *They all ate and were satisfied, and the disciples picked up twelve basketfuls of broken pieces that were left over.* There was more food left than Jesus had to start with. All four gospels include this miracle.

Little is much when God is in it. After a few words of thanksgiving the blessing of God was added to the initial quantity of food. The result was that everyone ate, and the disciples filled twelve baskets with broken pieces.

Whatever unbelief has had to say about this miracle, Jesus did something here that only God has the power to do.

THANK YOU, HEAVENLY FATHER:

For Your hands that provided manna and quails in the wilderness of Sinai during Israel's wanderings; for the same hands that multiplied bread and fish late one afternoon at Bethsaida;
For the apostles' growing knowledge of Jesus: that he who ruled the wind and water was also Lord of bread and fish;
For the priority in Jesus' ministry, as on this occasion, firstly '*he spoke to them about the kingdom of God, and* secondly *healed those who needed healing;*'
For Jesus' infinite resourcefulness; able to do exceeding abundantly above all that we ask or think.

IN JESUS' NAME, AMEN

44. Luke 9:18 - 27
Peter's Confession of Christ

Luke 9:18 - 19
Once when Jesus was praying in private and his disciples were with him, he asked them, "Who do the crowds say I am?"
[19] They replied, "Some say John the Baptist; others say Elijah; and still others, that one of the prophets of long ago has come back to life."

Jesus is leading his disciples into a deeper and secure knowledge of his identity. It was of the utmost importance that they were sure of who he was. On this occasion he was praying in private. His disciples were nearby. Possibly his prayer prompted him to stop and talk to them about this important matter: *"Who do the crowds say I am?"*

The disciples answered as helpfully as they could: *"Some say John the Baptist; others say Elijah; and still others, that one of the prophets of long ago has come back to life."* (Recall what Herod had heard:9:7-8)

The reason for Jesus' question was that he had reached a turning point in his ministry. From this point onward he would begin teaching his disciples the necessity of his death (9:21; 9:44-45; 9:51; 18:31-34; 19:28; until he was nailed to the cross at Calvary 23:33-34).

Jesus wanted more from the disciples than a repetition of the current opinions of the people. They should have a better understanding than the crowds.

Luke 9:20 – 21
"But what about you?" he asked. "Who do you say I am?" Peter answered, "The Christ of God." [21] Jesus strictly warned them not to tell this to anyone.

Peter gave an inspired answer - that is not saying too much. Refer to Matthew 16:16 – 17.

Simon Peter answered, "You are the Christ, the Son of the living God." ¹⁷Jesus replied, "Blessed are you, Simon son of Jonah, for this was not revealed to you by man, but by my Father in heaven.

Be sure to catch Jesus' emphasis. Such knowledge of Jesus is God-given. It is the equivalent of the statement made by Paul in 1 Corinthians 12:*3 'No one can say 'Jesus is Lord,' except by the Holy Spirit.'*

Jesus accepted Peter's confession of faith and then immediately *'strictly warned them not to tell this to anyone.'* This was not because Peter's confession was false but precisely because it was true. The confession was not inappropriate, but the proclamation of it was dangerous. Such a proclamation could have precipitated any number of attempts on Jesus' life by the Jewish leaders. Neither they nor their people understood the implications of the words, *"You are the Christ, the Son of the living God."*

Jesus' name 'Christ/Messiah' meant suffering and death as God's anointed, whereas among the people it signified the Anointed King who would throw off the Roman yoke, smite the Gentiles and bring political independence and greatness to Israel. The public proclamation of Jesus as the Christ could have brought about an immediate confrontation between Jesus and Rome!

Another aspect of this was that Peter had to learn something more about his Lord. Christ's future included the suffering he was about to mention to the disciples in v. 22.

Luke 9:22
And he said, "The Son of Man must suffer many things and be rejected by the elders, chief priests and teachers of the law, and he must be killed and on the third day be raised to life."

Note Jesus' use of the title *'Son of Man'*. Note his deliberate and detailed prophecy: *'Suffer', 'be rejected', 'be killed', 'on the third day be raised to life.'*

Luke 9:23 – 27

Then he said to them all: "If anyone would come after me, he must deny himself and take up his cross daily and follow me. ²⁴ For whoever wants to save his life will lose it, but whoever loses his life for me will save it.

²⁵ What good is it for a man to gain the whole world, and yet lose or forfeit his very self?

²⁶ If anyone is ashamed of me and my words, the Son of Man will be ashamed of him when he comes in his glory and in the glory of the Father and of the holy angels. ²⁷ I tell you the truth, some who are standing here will not taste death before they see the kingdom of God."

In view of what lay ahead for Jesus, he emphasised the cost of discipleship. To follow him would mean self-denial, the bearing of a cross and following him closely. If some were to draw back in an effort to save their lives, they would in fact lose them. If some should succeed in gaining the whole world, and lost their own souls, what would be their gain? If we confess Christ courageously here below then he will recognise and honour us when he comes again. Between then and the coming of Christ some of the folk standing there would be privileged to see the kingdom of God breaking through in history: for example the transfiguration, the death of Jesus, his resurrection and ascension and the day of Pentecost.

THANK YOU, HEAVENLY FATHER:

For Peter's confession of Christ, knowledge which You revealed to him;
For Jesus' revelation of his suffering, he did not keep it as a secret from his disciples: they needed to know;
For all that the future holds for Jesus in your sovereign will, and for his people;

IN JESUS' NAME, AMEN

45. Luke 9:28 – 36
The Transfiguration of Christ

Luke 9:28 – 31
About eight days after Jesus said this, he took Peter, John and James with him and went up onto a mountain to pray. ^{29} *As he was praying, the appearance of his face changed, and his clothes became as bright as a flash of lightning.* ^{30} *Two men, Moses and Elijah,* ^{31} *appeared in glorious splendour, talking with Jesus. They spoke about his departure, which he was about to bring to fulfilment at Jerusalem.*

The apostles had been granted a remarkable insight into the real identity of Jesus in the previous study. Here Peter, James and John are privileged to have sight of the glory of Jesus – this event is known as the Transfiguration. It is breathtaking even to read about it. Jesus had taken the three apostles with him to a mountain to pray. We wonder when they noticed the change in Jesus' appearance.

As he was praying the appearance of his face changed, and his clothes became as bright as a flash of lightning. That was not all, two men whom they recognised as Moses and Elijah, representative of the Old Testament law and the prophets, appeared in glorious splendour, talking with Jesus. What a sight! Luke writes that the conversation of the three glorious persons was about Jesus' departure (*literally: his exodus i.e. his death*) that we would bring to fulfilment at Jerusalem.

Moses and Elijah had unusual departures from the earth: Moses was buried by God and Elijah was translated to heaven in a chariot of fire. Their roles on earth had been important. Moses was the mediator of the Old Covenant: it was through him that the Law was given by God to Israel. Elijah was one of the most important of the Old Testament prophets. Both the Law and the Prophets had prepared the way for the coming of the Messiah.

At the time of his death God did not permit Moses to enter the Promised Land along with the children of Israel (Deut. 34:1-4) but, in a far more wonderful way, he did get there. Many hundreds of years later he stood within the Promised Land and spoke personally with the Messiah.

Luke 9:32 - 33
Peter and his companions were very sleepy, but when they became fully awake, they saw his glory and the two men standing with him. ³³ *As the men were leaving Jesus, Peter said to him, "Master, it is good for us to be here. Let us put up three shelters—one for you, one for Moses and one for Elijah." (He did not know what he was saying.)*

Probably because Peter noticed that Moses and Elijah were leaving the scene, he suggested that the three apostles erect three shelters (or booths) to prolong the meeting of the three glorious persons. What happened next silenced Peter and cancelled his proposal.

Luke 9:34 - 35
While he was speaking, a cloud appeared and enveloped them, and they were afraid as they entered the cloud. ³⁵ *A voice came from the cloud, saying, "This is my Son, whom I have chosen; listen to him."*

What kind of cloud was this? It was the cloud of God's presence; recall this phenomenon in the Old Testament scriptures. The apostles were terrified as the cloud enveloped them. Then the voice of God was heard saying, *"This is my Son, whom I have chosen; listen to him."* Jesus was not Moses or Elijah risen from the dead. He is God's Son.

Luke 9:36
When the voice had spoken, they found that Jesus was alone. The disciples kept this to themselves, and told no-one at that time what they had seen.

Moses and Elijah were figures of the past, but from now on Jesus, the Son of God was the church's Lawgiver and Prophet. When the apostles looked up Moses and Elijah had gone and Jesus alone remained. As in 9:21, they were not permitted to tell anyone what they had seen. Some verses in John 1:14 and 2 Peter 1:18-19, also 1 John 3:2, show that two of the three apostles never forgot the sight of Jesus' glory for as long as they lived. Whatever unbelief might say about the transfiguration in succeeding centuries, for the apostles it was a real event.

Thank You, Heavenly Father:

For Your witness to the identity of Your Son Jesus, and Your affirmation of his supremacy as Your Appointed Spokesman;
For the fact that Jesus, as Your one and only Son has greater authority that the greatest of Your servants;
For the evidence of the appearance of Moses and Elijah talking with Jesus: clearly You are not the God of the dead, but of the living;
For allowing us these glimpses of the pre-incarnate glory of Jesus, his post-resurrection and ascension and *parousia* glory;
For departed believers who are already in Your immediate presence, seeing Jesus *'as he is'*.

In Jesus' Name, Amen

46. Luke 9:37 - 45
Healing a Boy with an Evil Spirit

Luke 9:37 – 41
The next day, when they came down from the mountain, a large crowd met him. [38] A man in the crowd called out, "Teacher, I beg you to look at my son, for he is my only child. [39] A spirit seizes him and he suddenly screams; it throws him into convulsions so that he foams at the mouth. It scarcely ever leaves him and is destroying him. [40] I begged your disciples to drive it out, but they could not."

[41] "O unbelieving and perverse generation," Jesus replied, "how long shall I stay with you and put up with you? Bring your son here."

[42] Even while the boy was coming, the demon threw him to the ground in a convulsion. But Jesus rebuked the evil spirit, healed the boy and gave him back to his father. [43] And they were all amazed at the greatness of God.

Returning from the Mount of Transfiguration Jesus and the disciples were met by a large crowd of people. In the crowd there was a very anxious man whose only child, a boy, was demon-possessed. He begged Jesus to come to the help of the boy. The father described the symptoms of the boy's condition very clearly: '*A spirit seizes him and he suddenly screams; it throws him into convulsions so that he foams at the mouth. It scarcely ever leaves him and is destroying him.*' Perhaps the apostles had met the family on their missionary tour, but they were unable to cure the child. There are those who think the boy had epilepsy – perhaps the diagnosis was not as straightforward as that because there was clear evidence of demon-possession.

Jesus' statement about the unbelief and perversity of the public (v. 41) leaves us wondering what he meant, and to whom he was speaking.

Luke 9:42 - 43
Even while the boy was coming, the demon threw him to the ground in a convulsion. But Jesus rebuked the evil spirit, healed the boy

and gave him back to his father. ⁴³ And they were all amazed at the greatness of God. Everyone was marvelling at all that Jesus did.

Jesus bade the evil spirit, *'Be gone,'* healed the boy and gave him back to his father.

We need to remember when we read (as in v. 43) about everyone marvelling at all that Jesus did, he was saying quite frankly that no amount of amazement and wonder equals faith. He found the prevailing unbelief a poor response to his ministry of preaching, teaching and healing. He had not come to win men's approval, but to save their souls for time and for eternity. He had only a limited time to preach the gospel to that generation.

Luke 9:43 – 45
And they were all amazed at the greatness of God. While everyone was marvelling at all that Jesus did, he said to his disciples, ⁴⁴ "Listen carefully to what I am about to tell you: The Son of Man is going to be betrayed into the hands of men."
⁴⁵ But they did not understand what this meant. It was hidden from them, so that they did not grasp it, and they were afraid to ask him about it.

Verse 44 carries a second Passion Announcement (the first was in vv. 21-22). Clearly Jesus' suffering and death and all that it involved filled his thoughts. The disciples needed to learn to think like this also. V. 45 is a sad commentary on their mind set, *'they did not understand what this meant.'*

There may also have been a divine check on their awareness of what lay ahead for Jesus for reasons known only to the wisdom of God, *'It was hidden from them, so that they did not grasp it, and they were afraid to ask him about it.'* They could have asked but chose not to.

THANK YOU, HEAVENLY FATHER:

For Your great patience with us when unbelief dulls our faculties so that our response to the glory, the words and works of Your Son are lack lustre; we acknowledge our carnality;
For the gracious actions of Jesus when pursuing his earthly ministry, such as when he responded to the pathetic plea of this man whose child was so very ill;
For the contrasting inability of the apostles to heal the boy and the father's belief that Jesus could heal his son; faith was working in an unlikely heart and mind;
For the urgency in Jesus' words in v. 41; they signified that he had only a limited time to bring the gospel to his generation;

IN JESUS' NAME, AMEN

47. Luke 9:46 - 50
The Disciples Argue over Position

Luke 9:46 - 48
An argument started among the disciples as to which of them would be the greatest. ⁴⁷Jesus, knowing their thoughts, took a little child and made him stand beside him.

⁴⁸Then he said to them, "Whoever welcomes this little child in my name welcomes me; and whoever welcomes me welcomes the one who sent me. For he who is least among you all—he is the greatest."

I think we need to realise that the disciples did not have the Holy Spirit indwelling them, because the Spirit was not yet given. Therefore some of their carnality (in this case egos as high as the Eiffel Tower!) ought not to surprise us. Nevertheless, it disappoints us. They were not perfect men even though they lived in the company of Jesus.

These grown men started to argue which of them would be the greatest. This kind of behaviour following Jesus' renewed prophecy about his approaching suffering and death seems entirely out of place. It would appear that Jesus ignored the argument, though he knew their thoughts.

Instead he simply took a little child who was nearby and made the child stand beside him. He said to the disciples, *"Whoever welcomes this little child in my name welcomes me; and whoever welcomes me welcomes the one who sent me. For he who is least among you all—he is the greatest."* Greatness in the kingdom of God is not calculated in the way the world estimates it.

Jesus showed the disciples a child, who stood by his side without fear, without any sense of its own importance, not puffed up with knowledge or any idea of superiority. It wasn't concerned in the least about where it came in the pecking order. Every child is important and has value in God's sight, but that was not how society valued children.

In v. 48 Jesus is asking the disciples to learn from the weakest member of society. *What value do you place on this child? The way you treat this child is the way you treat me. The way you treat me is the attitude you have to the Father who sent me.* It is easy to be busy for Jesus and have no time for a child. It is important receive a child in God's name.

In that circle of men probably the child was regarded as *'least'*. From the child Jesus turned to the disciples and said, *'For he who is least among you all—he is the greatest."* He had rebuked their inner selfishness. It was a powerful lesson in humility.

Luke 9:49 - 50

"Master," said John, "we saw a man driving out demons in your name and we tried to stop him, because he is not one of us." ⁵⁰ "Do not stop him," Jesus said, "for whoever is not against you is for you."

To add to the embarrassment of the disciples, who had been unable to cast out a demon from a boy, John said that they had seen an exorcist casting out demons and doing it in the name of Jesus! John had to admit that the disciples had tried to stop him.

John considered this man to be a fraud because he was not a disciple. Was this man a non-Christian exorcist, or a believer who was simply outside the circle of the disciples?

To their surprise Jesus said, *"Do not stop him, for whoever is not against you is for you."* Jesus didn't make an issue of it.

Here is a man who is involved in exorcism and in doing it he is promoting Jesus' ministry. Whatever else the man lacked, he knew that if there was any power to relieve demon possession it was associated with the power of Jesus. The man was not undermining the ministry of Jesus. He was not against him; in fact, he was for him. There is no neutral ground. One is either for Christ, or he is against Christ.

There we leave John to his thoughts. Soon he will have another problem to solve, as we shall see (vv. 51-56).

THANK YOU, HEAVENLY FATHER:

For the leadership of Jesus in that he silenced the disciples' argument about greatness by calling a child to demonstrate its complete lack of any idea of self-importance;
For the expansiveness of Jesus' leadership when he did not condemn an unknown man who was casting out demons in his (Jesus') name;
For the lesson that You have other servants in addition to us who are ministering in Jesus' name, even if we do not know them;
For those who are working for the glory of Jesus by pulling down the strongholds of Satan using gospel weapons;

IN JESUS' NAME, AMEN

48. Luke 9:51-56
Samaritan Opposition

Luke 9:51 - 56
As the time approached for him to be taken up to heaven, Jesus resolutely set out for Jerusalem.
⁵² And he sent messengers on ahead, who went into a Samaritan village to get things ready for him; ⁵³ but the people there did not welcome him, because he was heading for Jerusalem.
⁵⁴ When the disciples James and John saw this, they asked, "Lord, do you want us to call fire down from heaven to destroy them?"
⁵⁵ But Jesus turned and rebuked them, ⁵⁶ and they went to another village.

Recall 9:21-22, 44, and then read this section vv. 51-56. Jerusalem and what will happen there fills Jesus' thoughts and shapes his plans. A new angle on his future is in the clause, *'As the time approached for him to be taken up to heaven.'* Jesus knew that he had to die, but he also knew that he would return to his Father in heaven.

His route lay through Samaria, but when he sent some disciples to get things ready for him in the first village they would come to, the people there made it clear that they were not keeping a welcome for him, because he was heading for Jerusalem.

The Samaritans were used to Jewish pilgrims taking the short-cut through their country, but did not look on them with any favour. It took about three days for the pilgrims to walk from one end of Samaria to the other. The Samaritans hated the Jews who believed that the spiritual centre of Judaism was the Temple in Jerusalem. The Samaritans had erected a rival Temple at Mount Gerizim and believed that was where God ought to be worshipped.

It seems that Jesus made no comment about the Samaritans' attitude, but the brothers James and John had plenty to say. Their attitude went far beyond v. 5 of this chapter.

Little wonder that Jesus had nicknamed them 'Sons of Thunder'. They were explosive characters. (Recall John's previous complaint in this chapter: v. 49). Here, nothing short of fire from heaven would be adequate retribution on the Samaritans for not welcoming Jesus!

Possibly an incident from the life of Elijah prompted the thought (2 Kings 1:10ff).

In rejecting Jesus' messengers the Samaritans were rejecting him. They rejected him because they knew nothing of his coming passion and its necessity. Jesus rebuked the two brothers for their attitude. The KJV includes vv.55 & 56:

Luke 9:55 (KJV)
But he turned, and rebuked them, and said, 'Ye know not what manner of spirit ye are of. [56] For the Son of man is not come to destroy men's lives, but to save them.'

[The above sentences are regarded by modern bible translators as scribal insertions.]

The brothers were willing to use force to promote respect for Jesus. This is not how room for Jesus is made in men's lives. And why wipe out a whole village for the mistakes of a few of its inhabitants?

The two men were not thinking straight. Their zeal had overridden their knowledge of Jesus and his way of doing things. In Jesus' economy the time for judgment was not yet, this was *'the year of the Lord's favour'* (Luke 4:19).

When Jesus would next visit the Samaritans, through his apostles' preaching, the word would bear good fruit (Acts 8:1, 4-25; 9:31; 15:3). On this occasion they simply moved on to another village.

THANK YOU, HEAVENLY FATHER:

For Your ways are higher than our ways and Your thoughts than our thoughts;
For Your longsuffering toward us: You are not willing that any should perish but that all should come to repentance;
For the patient working of the Holy Spirit in our hearts and minds so that we learn to think and behave as Jesus would;
For Jesus' command that we should pray for our enemies and for those who persecute us;

For the transforming work of the Holy Spirit in John who came to be known as the 'beloved disciple' and whose N.T. Letters have so much to say about living in the love of God;
For the fact that You are not finished with any of your people yet! You are getting us ready to meet Your Son.

IN JESUS' NAME, AMEN

49. Luke 9:57 - 62
The Cost of Following Jesus

In a copy of the KJV that I have the section heading for these verses is:

MANY DESIRE TO FOLLOW JESUS, BUT ONLY ON THEIR OWN CONDITIONS

If you like to use a Bible that is helpfully outlined perhaps you will agree that this title captures what is going on in this section. We are following the NIV outline. The title is shorter and more precise.

THE COST OF FOLLOWING JESUS

The first man came to Jesus on his own volition, only to be told that he would be embarking on a life of no fixed abode (vv. 57-58).

The second man came to Jesus at his invitation, but there was a condition in his response. His father was not yet dead, but was an elderly man. The would-be disciple wanted to remain at home until after his father's death. Then he would follow Jesus. (vv. 59-60).

The third man also came on his own volition, but he too added a condition. He wanted permission to say farewell to his family. Jesus seemed to hint that there was a slim chance of him coming back afterwards (vv. 61-62).

Luke refers to *'a man'*, *'another man'* and *'still another'*. He adds nothing to give us a clue about their general circumstances, or whether they were Jews, Samaritans or Gentiles. Therefore we need to meditate on the responses of Jesus to these men.

Luke 9:57 - 58
As they were walking along the road, a man said to him, "I will follow you wherever you go." ⁵⁸ Jesus replied, "Foxes have holes and birds of the air have nests, but the Son of Man has nowhere to lay his head."

These encounters took place as Jesus journeyed to Jerusalem. Jesus used the Old Testament title *'the Son of Man'* of himself, a title used in Daniel 7:13-14. Jesus was calling this man to deny himself the security of hearth and home. Jesus did not have a home. Jesus didn't know where his next meal was coming from. Jesus did not know where he would sleep that night. Did the man know that Jesus was going to Jerusalem to die? It seems unlikely; otherwise he might have curbed his initial enthusiasm. If this man was to make good his professed willingness *to follow Jesus wherever he would go'* he needed to know that the 'job' carried no prospects but hardship.

Luke 9:59 – 60
He said to another man, "Follow me." But the man replied, "Lord, first let me go and bury my father." ⁶⁰ Jesus said to him, "Let the dead bury their own dead, but you go and proclaim the kingdom of God."

Jesus personally invited this man to follow him. However, the man had a condition which sounds reasonable, but possibly involved a lengthy period of time. The point was not that his father had died, but was growing old and the man wanted to stay at home until after his father's death. His intention was that he would follow Jesus then.

Jesus' reply requires some thinking about. Family traditions notwithstanding, Jesus was not prepared to accept this man's condition. Other members of the family could look after the old man's funeral arrangements when the time came. There was urgency to the call that Jesus had issued which took precedence over everything else. You are needed to proclaim the kingdom of God. There was only one place that Jesus required the man to be and that was on the front line of the kingdom.

Luke 9:61 – 62
Still another said, "I will follow you, Lord; but first let me go back and say good-bye to my family." ⁶² Jesus replied, "No-one who puts his hand to the plough and looks back is fit for service in the kingdom of God."

The third man might have needed half an hour, or half a day, or half a week to say farewell to his family circle. Who knows how long? The longer he would be back at home the harder it would be to cut his ties at home and return to follow Jesus. Remember that this man had volunteered (v. 61). I think Jesus saw into the man's heart and his home situation and raised the bar that he had to jump a little higher, for emphasis' sake. The man was like a ploughman, who with his hands on the plough, keeps looking back. You can imagine the result. In the kingdom this man's mind would not be on his work.

THANK YOU, HEAVENLY FATHER:

For supplying the needs of all who have answered the call of Jesus to work in his kingdom;
For undertaking for the parents, sisters and brothers of those who left home to enter the service of Jesus;
For Your complete honesty when calling men and women into the service of Jesus, and for honouring us for honouring You;

IN JESUS' NAME, AMEN

50. Luke 10:1-16
Jesus Sends Out the Seventy-two

Luke 10:1 – 2
After this the Lord appointed seventy-two others and sent them two by two ahead of him to every town and place where he was about to go. ² He told them, "The harvest is plentiful, but the workers are few. Ask the Lord of the harvest, therefore, to send out workers into his harvest field."

Jesus sent out Twelve whom he designated apostles in Luke 9:1-9. Here he sends out a further seventy-two disciples. There is no doubt that these missions point forward to the post-resurrection universal mission of the Christian Church. John the Baptist's mission to prepare the way for the Lord ended with his martyrdom. The seventy-two were sent ahead of Jesus to every town and place where he was about to go.

There are similarities in the instructions Jesus gave both groups. This time he gave them a new law: *The harvest is plentiful, but the workers are few. Ask the Lord of the harvest, therefore, to send out workers into his harvest field.* Sometimes churches and mission societies behave as if Jesus had never given this command. The modern way of finding new recruits for the Lord's work is to advertise in the religious and local press, or set up a missionary exhibition with application forms available on which to request an interview and so on. What was wrong with the Lord's method? Did it fail?

Luke 10:3 - 4
Go! I am sending you out like lambs among wolves. ⁴ Do not take a purse or bag or sandals; and do not greet anyone on the road.

Jesus did not stress the perks, because there were none. He honestly and realistically set out the hardships that prospective candidates might meet. They were to be cast wholly on Jesus to protect them when in danger and supply their materials needs as he saw fit when these arose. They were not to be easily diverted from the work he was sending them to do, for example Oriental type greetings which were long and time-consuming were best avoided.

Luke 10:5 - 9

"When you enter a house, first say, 'Peace to this house'. [6] If a man of peace is there, your peace will rest on him; if not, it will return to you. [7] Stay in that house, eating and drinking whatever they give you, for the worker deserves his wages. Do not move around from house to house.' [8] When you enter a town and are welcomed, eat what is set before you. [9] Heal the sick who are there and tell them, 'The kingdom of God is near you."

'Peace' (Shalom) was a typical Jewish greeting. It became Christianised to *'grace and peace'* and *'grace, mercy and peace'*. If the home they called at was where a Christian lived, then they would meet a man of peace, who would understand their greeting. Words like *'grace'*, *'mercy'* and *'peace'* all carried a Christian connotation being closely allied to the saving mission of the Messiah. If faith was not present in a home, then the greeting would not be effective. On the other hand the believer might invite the two evangelists who were standing at his front door to enter and make that house their home for as long as their work required. In which case, they would not need to look elsewhere for accommodation. The food they were served would be their wages (v. 7). Their ministry in that town would be to *"heal the sick who are there and tell them, 'The kingdom of God is near you."*

Luke 10:10 - 12

"But when you enter a town and are not welcomed, go into its streets and say, [11] 'Even the dust of your town that sticks to our feet we wipe off against you. Yet be sure of this: The kingdom of God is near.' [12] I tell you, it will be more bearable on that day for Sodom than for that town."

However in a town where they were not welcomed their duty was to go into its streets and say. *'Even the dust of your town that sticks to our feet we wipe off against you. Yet be sure of this: The kingdom of God is near.'* The unwelcoming town would hear the message in brief, as the evangelists were leaving.

Jesus added some instruction here so that the evangelists would know how to regard those who rejected their presence and message (v. 12). The judgment of Sodom was proverbial. It was less severe than the judgment awaiting those towns where the evangelists were not welcome.

Luke 10:13 - 15

"Woe to you, Korazin! Woe to you, Bethsaida! For if the miracles that were performed in you had been performed in Tyre and Sidon, they would have repented long ago, sitting in sackcloth and ashes. [14] But it will be more bearable for Tyre and Sidon at the judgment than for you. [15] And you, Capernaum, will you be lifted up to the skies? No, you will go down to the depths."

Cities like Korazin, Bethsaida and Capernaum who had the privilege of having Jesus perform miracles in them would face very severe judgment on the last day because of their unbelief. (See Matthew 11:20-24)

Luke 10:16

"He who listens to you listens to me; he who rejects you rejects me; but he who rejects me rejects him who sent me."

People would either receive/listen or not receive/not listen. No distinction is made between

THANK YOU, HEAVENLY FATHER:

For sending workers into Your harvest in answer to prayer.

IN JESUS' NAME, AMEN

51. Luke 10:17 - 24
The Seventy-two Return with Joy.

Luke 10:17 - 20
The seventy-two returned with joy and said, "Lord, even the demons submit to us in your name." [18] He replied, "I saw Satan fall like lightning from heaven. [19] I have given you authority to trample on snakes and scorpions and to overcome all the power of the enemy; nothing will harm you. [20] However, do not rejoice that the spirits submit to you, but rejoice that your names are written in heaven."

The seventy-two disciples returned over-flowing with joy at what they had seen and done on their mission. It may have taken quite a while for 72 men (possibly 36 reports) to describe their experiences. Did Jesus' response surprise them?

"I saw Satan fall like lightning from heaven." He seems to be describing their onslaught against the devil and his works very graphically. But is he speaking about what the disciples had done?

Jesus is speaking in the past tense. Away in eternal ages Satan had been cast out of heaven, thrown down from his exalted position of power. Jesus had witnessed Satan's rebellion against the Most High. Like a blinding flash of lightning disappearing into the darkness of night, Satan had fallen. Therefore, in the mind of Jesus it was not surprising that the demons had submitted to the disciples in his name.

Jesus' pastoral spirit was sensitive to dangers that the disciples faced because they had wielded such power. Therefore he warned them in vv.18-20 *"do not rejoice that the spirits submit to you, but rejoice that your names are written in heaven."* The power entrusted to them by Jesus was safe only in the hands of humble men.

Luke 10:21
At that time Jesus, full of joy through the Holy Spirit, said, "I praise you, Father, Lord of heaven and earth, because you have hidden these things from the wise and learned, and revealed them to little children. Yes, Father, for this was your good pleasure."

Jesus shared the disciples' joy. This is the only time in the gospels that Jesus is said to be joyful. The Holy Spirit was filling him with real joy so that the Son of God lifted his thoughts to his Father's throne in worshipful prayer. He praised his Father for granting divine power and gospel success to his disciples who were very ordinary men, and thanked Him for their experiences. For Jesus, his Father's pleasure was of the utmost importance.

Luke 10:22
"All things have been committed to me by my Father. No-one knows who the Son is except the Father, and no-one knows who the Father is except the Son and those to whom the Son chooses to reveal him."

In the economy of God the Father everything has been in the hands of His Son. Jesus' relationship to his Father is unique. Therefore the only way to knowing God is through Jesus the Son.

Luke 10:23 - 24
Then he turned to his disciples and said privately, "Blessed are the eyes that see what you see. ²⁴ For I tell you that many prophets and kings wanted to see what you see but did not see it, and to hear what you hear but did not hear it."

These are moments of great intimacy between Jesus and his disciples. They must understand that a new era has come and they are unspeakably privileged to witness and experience God's saving rule in the world. Others, also God's servants, had longed for these days but had been denied the privilege.

THANK YOU, HEAVENLY FATHER:

For the unique identity of Jesus as the Son of the Father, a relationship without parallel;
For the privilege of living in the days of God's power and Satan's defeat;
For the fact that the law and the prophets were until John, but now the kingdom had come;

For the fact that the kingdom was not coming to the wise and powerful but to those who received it like children;
For Mary's prophetic praise in the Magnificat, now being accomplished as God brought down the proud and exalted the humble (1:51-53)

In Jesus' Name, Amen

52. Luke 10:25 - 37
The Parable of the Good Samaritan

Luke 10:25 - 29
On one occasion an expert in the law stood up to test Jesus. "Teacher," he asked, "what must I do to inherit eternal life?" 26 "What is written in the Law?" he replied. "How do you read it?" 27 He answered: "'Love the Lord your God with all your heart and with all your soul and with all your strength and with all your mind'; and, 'Love your neighbour as yourself.'"

28 "You have answered correctly," Jesus replied. "Do this and you will live." 29 But he wanted to justify himself, so he asked Jesus, "And who is my neighbour?"

This lawyer who was a highly trained expert in the legal affairs of the nation thought he had framed the perfect question to trap Jesus in argument: *"Teacher,"* he asked, *"what must I do to inherit eternal life?"*

Jesus turned the question back on the questioner: *"What is written in the Law?" he replied. "How do you read it?"* Perhaps the lawyer had compromised himself by his question. It would show that he was not such an expert after all if he did not know the answer to his question. He answered: *"'Love the Lord your God with all your heart and with all your soul and with all your strength and with all your mind'* (Deut. 6:5); *and, 'Love your neighbour as yourself'* (Lev. 19:18).

"You have answered correctly," Jesus replied. *"Do this and you will live."*

The answer given by the lawyer in v. 27 is read in Jewish synagogues by the whole congregation both in their morning and evening prayers and is called *'The Shema.'* They omit the clause: *'Love your neighbour as yourself.'* For most Jews a neighbour was another Jew, not a Samaritan or a Gentile. The Pharisees and the Essenes (the Qumran sect of Dead Sea Scrolls fame) did not even include all Jews.

Jesus' acceptance of the lawyer's answer affirms that Deut. 6:5 is indeed the way to eternal life. It seems that all that is required of you to live eternally is to love the Lord your God with all your heart, soul, strength and mind. Nothing could be simpler. However, think about that and you will find that no-one, not one person, has kept the force of this commandment for the past five minutes, let alone for their entire lives. To make such a claim is really to say that you never sin, because it would be impossible to sin if you loved God in this way. However, it is one thing to give the answer; it is another thing to do it. *'Do this'* said Jesus, 'and you will live.'

The lawyer wanted the upper hand in this exchange. *He wanted to justify himself,* so he asked Jesus, *"And who is my neighbour?"*

Luke 10:30 - 35
In reply Jesus said: "A man was going down from Jerusalem to Jericho, when he fell into the hands of robbers. They stripped him of his clothes, beat him and went away, leaving him half-dead.

³¹ A priest happened to be going down the same road, and when he saw the man, he passed by on the other side.

³² So too, a Levite, when he came to the place and saw him, passed by on the other side.

³³ But a Samaritan, as he travelled, came where the man was; and when he saw him, he took pity on him. ³⁴He went to him and bandaged his wounds, pouring on oil and wine. Then he put the man on his own donkey, brought him to an inn and took care of him. ³⁵ The next day he took out two silver coins and gave them to the innkeeper. 'Look after him,' he said, 'and when I return, I will reimburse you for any extra expense you may have.'"

The lawyer is beginning to feel the pressure of Jesus' comments. He knows that he and Jesus will be diametrically opposed in their answers to this question. This time Jesus decided to answer the lawyer by using a parable.

Ambush and assault were frequent occurrences on the Jericho road from Jerusalem down to the Dead Sea region. Yet again an unfortunate traveller had been assaulted, robbed and left for dead (v. 30). Other travellers who passed that way saw the injured man, but passed by on the other side. Two of them were Jews and co-religionists of the lawyer, a priest and a Levite, no less. A third traveller was a Samaritan, despised by the Jews and of another religion, *saw the man, took pity on him, bandaged his wounds, cleansing them with oil and wine, put him on his donkey and took him to an inn and took care of him. When the Samaritan had to continue his journey he gave the inn-keeper some more money to provide for the man's needs, promising to return and pay for any extra expense involved.*

Luke 10:36 - 37
*"Which of these three do you think was a neighbour to the man who fell into the hands of robbers?" **37** The expert in the law replied, "The one who had mercy on him." Jesus told him, "Go and do likewise."*

Jesus did not teach a universal brotherhood of man. He taught and demonstrated a universal neighbourhood of man. All people are my neighbours. As Brother Andrew (Founder of Open Doors) said, 'I Shall Love All Moslems.'

THANK YOU, HEAVENLY FATHER:

For the two lessons this narrative teaches: *'I cannot save myself by my own efforts'*, and *'whose neighbour am I?'*
For Christian churches and charities at home and abroad who are ministering to the poor, the broken and dying in Christ's name.

IN JESUS NAME, AMEN

53. Luke 10:38 - 42
At the Home of Martha and Mary

Luke 10:38 - 40
As Jesus and his disciples were on their way, he came to a village where a woman named Martha opened her home to him.
³⁹ She had a sister called Mary, who sat at the Lord's feet listening to what he said. ⁴⁰ But Martha was distracted by all the preparations that had to be made. She came to him and asked, "Lord, don't you care that my sister has left me to do the work by myself? Tell her to help me!"

This home in Bethany, just south of Jerusalem, was one of many where Jesus was welcomed and refreshed during his itinerant ministry. This narrative reads as if this was his first time to call at this home because Luke introduces Martha as if she were a new acquaintance – *'a woman named Martha opened her home to him.'* If this is correct then we are learning how this family met Jesus.

The two sisters, Martha and Mary, were opposites temperamentally. Martha is an action woman. Mary is a calmer, meditative type of person. Right from his first meeting, Jesus noticed this contrast in the sisters: *'Mary sat at the Lord's feet listening to what he said.'* Luke refers to Jesus as *'Lord'* – a favourite designation of his.

Both sisters wanted to stop what they were doing and listen to Jesus. Mary did this without delay, but for poor Martha the tyranny of the urgent meant that she could not stop immediately. *'Martha was distracted by all the preparations that had to be made.'*

Every housewife knows the feeling. Perhaps there was a pot of food close to boiling point, or some other such thing requiring her attention. Jesus would have understood this. Martha, possibly a little peeved, complained to the Lord, *"Lord, don't you care that my sister has left me to do the work by myself? Tell her to help me!"*

Luke 10:41 - 42
"Martha, Martha," the Lord answered, "you are worried and upset about many things, ⁴² but only one thing is needed. Mary has chosen what is better and it will not be taken away from her."

In contrast to common rabbinic practice Jesus encouraged women to listen to his teaching and even to become part of his ministry (recall 8:3). Jesus responded to Martha with tenderness. In repeating her name as he did: 'Martha, Martha', his words were endearing. He described her as *'worried and upset about many things'* or literally *'she was drawn in different directions.'*

He wanted her to know that he understood her dilemma and loved her no less for the difficult choice she had to make. She had to attend to *'the preparations that had to be made'*.

But neither did he hesitate to make an important point to both sisters: *'but only one thing is needed. Mary has chosen what is better and it will not be taken away from her."*

Practical service has its place and is truly acceptable to the Lord, but if we are never quiet, if our spirits are always on the stretch, then we will 'burn out', as we say. If we become like an archer's bow that is always taut, and never relaxed, we shall lose our power. An archer always relaxes the bow-string when the bow is not in use. Serving Jesus Christ is not a frenzy of religious activity undertaken in our own strength. *'Martha, are you listening?'*

Mary, on the other hand, was commended in the presence of Martha for having *'chosen what is better.'* The implication is that nothing is better than to *'sit at Jesus' feet listening to what he is saying'*. So Mary is not to be upset over Martha's complaint about her temporary inactivity.

To listen to Jesus as Mary did is the best thing one can do, even better than serving. However, this must not be pressed into advocating a life of contemplation over a life of serving, or of celibacy over marriage.

There is a double emphasis here: listening and serving. One does not cancel the other. Every believer in Jesus needs to learn that devotion and duty are both important in their relationship with him. May the Lord preserve us from becoming so busy working for Christ that we have no time to sit at his feet.

This is the time to make the seeking of the kingdom of God the main business of our lives. We cannot afford to be casual about it for Christ requires our total commitment. The time we spend at the feet of Jesus and what we learn there can never be taken from us. We will possess it forever.

THANK YOU, HEAVENLY FATHER:

For this narrative of a home in Bethany where Jesus was always welcome and his words were treasured;
For the sisters, in whom we recognise ourselves, and from whom we learn so much that is helpful in our relationship with Jesus;
For the fact that '*to everything there is a season and a time for every purpose under heaven*' (Ecclesiasates 3:10).

IN JESUS' NAME, AMEN

54. Luke 11:1 - 13
Jesus' Teaching on Prayer

Luke 11:1 - 4
One day Jesus was praying in a certain place. When he finished, one of his disciples said to him, "Lord, teach us to pray, just as John taught his disciples."

² He said to them, "When you pray, say: "'Father, hallowed be your name, your kingdom come. ³ Give us each day our daily bread. ⁴ Forgive us our sins, for we also forgive everyone who sins against us. And lead us not into temptation.'"

Here we see discipleship *'working'*. The way they observed Jesus praying prompted a request from his disciples that he would teach them to pray. A second reason was that they knew that John the Baptist did this for his disciples. A third reason was that they saw a difference between his praying and theirs. No-one is born 'a good prayer' - we have to learn to pray.

How should we pray? Jesus answered without hesitation: '*When you pray, say*': and he gave them a model prayer.

In Luke this is a short version; there is a long(er) version in Matthew 6:9 – 13. Jesus did not put any restriction on their adopting this prayer verbatim, but most commentators see it a model for the disciples' prayers. The first impression was that Jesus addressed God in a way that no Jew had addressed Him before: that is as 'Father'. The Jewish leaders would pounce on Jesus for calling God his 'Father', but Jesus' point here is that he transfers this privilege to his disciples. They too are to address God as 'Father'. Then some directions follow.

Prayer is addressed to God directly: 'Father'. Jesus could say 'My Father' when addressing God. The primary request is that God's name is hallowed, to be held in reverence by all who know it.

Next in priority is the growth of God's kingdom on earth. If the disciples prayed for Jesus and his ministry and prayed for God's blessing on their own ministry they were praying that God's kingdom would grow.

Then a request for the supply of our daily needs is fitting. The term *'our daily bread'* is not restricted to food. It includes the basic necessities of life, but not luxuries. There must be a place for personal confession of sin: but notice that it is conditional. We must forgive those who sin against us if we are to have our sins forgiven.

A petition for safe guidance and for protection from temptation is a very practical conclusion: *'and lead us not into temptation.'* In this short model prayer Jesus had given his disciples some very helpful guidance.

Luke 11:5-10

Then he said to them, "Suppose one of you has a friend, and he goes to him at midnight and says, 'Friend, lend me three loaves of bread, ⁶because a friend of mine on a journey has come to me, and I have nothing to set before him.' ⁷ "Then the one inside answers, 'Don't bother me. The door is already locked, and my children are with me in bed. I can't get up and give you anything.' ⁸ I tell you, though he will not get up and give him the bread because he is his friend, yet because of the man's boldness he will get up and give him as much as he needs."

⁹ "So I say to you: Ask and it will be given to you; seek and you will find; knock and the door will be opened to you. ¹⁰ For everyone who asks receives; he who seeks finds; and to him who knocks, the door will be opened."

Jesus turns now to a question that is always associated with prayer: 'How does God answer our prayers?' (v. 5ff).

Jesus asks the disciples to imagine how they might appeal to a neighbour for help. It is *'an unearthly hour'* of the night when most folk are in bed. Nevertheless a friend has just arrived at your home and you have no food to set before him. You have an idea. You will ask your neighbour. You are not really surprised at his response *'We are all in bed.'* Not for friendship' sake, but because you asked your neighbour and kept on asking at such an awkward hour, he rose from his bed and gave you as much as you needed. What does this say about praying to God? The answer is in vv. 9 & 10. 'Ask. . .

Seek. . .Knock. . . For everyone who asks receives; he who seeks finds; and to him who knocks, the door will be opened.'

Luke 11:10 – 13
"Which of you fathers, if your son asks for a fish, will give him a snake instead? ¹² Or if he asks for an egg, will give him a scorpion? ¹³ If you then, though you are evil, know how to give good gifts to your children, how much more will your Father in heaven give the Holy Spirit to those who ask him!"

Next Jesus turns to those who are fathers. How do they meet the requests of their children? They never give them a harmful gift (vv. 11-12). In fact, the children know they will only receive good things from their fathers. Earthly fathers are not perfect, but they know to give their children good things. The application is obvious: *how much more will your Father in heaven give the Holy Spirit to those who ask him!"* (v. 13).

THANK YOU, HEAVENLY FATHER:

For the patience of Jesus as he taught his disciples some of the most fundamental lessons about their relationship with You;
For the homespun illustrations that Jesus employed to shed light on his teaching: so heart warming.
For Your generosity as the Father of such a large family in heaven and on earth;

IN JESUS' NAME, AMEN

55. Luke 11:14 - 28
Jesus' and Beelzebub

Luke 11:14 - 16
Jesus was driving out a demon that was mute. When the demon left, the man who had been mute spoke, and the crowd was amazed. [15] *But some of them said, "By Beelzebub, the prince of demons, he is driving out demons."* [16] *Others tested him by asking for a sign from heaven.*

Jesus was driving out a demon that had made a man unable to speak. The watching crowd was amazed. We may presume that the man and his next-of-kin were delighted at his deliverance. However there were some who thought nothing of casting aspersions on this action of Jesus.

They implied that the demon came out of the man so easily that Jesus must be in league with Beelzebub, the prince of demons—an utterly slanderous pronouncement. They did not know how wrong they were, nor who had inspired their malicious thoughts. Other people demanded that Jesus perform a miracle from heaven to prove that he was working with God.

Luke 11:17 – 20
Jesus knew their thoughts and said to them: "Any kingdom divided against itself will be ruined, and a house divided against itself will fall. [18]*If Satan is divided against himself, how can his kingdom stand? I say this because you claim that I drive out demons by Beelzebub.* [19] *Now if I drive out demons by Beelzebub, by whom do your followers drive them out? So then, they will be your judges.* [20] *But if I drive out demons by the finger of God, then the kingdom of God has come to you."*

Jesus knew what they were thinking, and he challenged and corrected them straight away. *'I am not an agent of Beelzebub,'* Jesus affirmed, *'haven't you seen me cast out a demon?'* I'm stronger than Satan, he was saying. *A divided kingdom cannot stand. A divided household (or family) will fall. If Satan is as divided as you say, his kingdom will not stand.* These were simple truths with a tremendous application.

The name Beelzebub belonged to a heathen god referred to in 2 Kings 1:3. It had various meanings *'Lord of the flies'* or *'Lord of the Court'* or *'Lord of the Place'*. How it came to a name used for Satan is not known.

Turning to the Pharisee and their disciples, Jesus asked, *'When you and your followers practice exorcism and cast out demons by whose power do they do it?'* He knew that he wouldn't get an answer to his question. They would not say either that they did it by God's help or the devil's. He would leave them to judge that. Then he dropped a bombshell among them: *'If I drive out demons by the finger of God, then the kingdom of God has come to you.'* Yes, the kingdom of God had come and Jesus ministry was evidence of its presence.

Luke 11:21 – 23
When a strong man, fully armed, guards his own house, his possessions are safe. [22] *But when someone stronger attacks and overpowers him, he takes away the armour in which the man trusted and divides up the spoils* [23] *"He who is not with me is against me, and he who does not gather with me, scatters."*

If Satan is casting out demons then he is committing suicide. Someone stronger than the prince of this world has appeared. I am stronger than Satan. I have taken the spoil from him by setting a man free to speak. In time I will rob him of everything he has. Are you with me or for me? Are you gathering people like the man I freed? Or are you expelling them because you do not care for people like him?

Luke 11:24 – 26
"When an evil spirit comes out of a man, it goes through arid places seeking rest and does not find it. Then it says, 'I will return to the house I left.' [25] *When it arrives, it finds the house swept clean and put in order.* [26] *Then it goes and takes seven other spirits more wicked than itself, and they go in and live there. And the final condition of that man is worse than the first."*

It is said that nature abhors a vacuum. When Jesus casts out demons from an individual he does not leave an unfurnished house behind waiting for the first squatter to come along and claim it. If Christ is not in occupation of a life then the devil will return with greater force and reduce that life to ruins. So the final condition of that man is worse than the first. That is food for thought. Reformation without Christ in residence in the heart is a dangerous condition.

Luke 11:27 – 28

As Jesus was saying these things, a woman in the crowd called out, "Blessed is the mother who gave you birth and nursed you." 28 He replied, "Blessed rather are those who hear the word of God and obey it."

A woman in the crowd spoke a benediction to Jesus (v. 27). Jesus returned her kind thought and enlarged it. The woman was right and Jesus appreciated what she said about his mother. However, there is an even greater blessing than being the mother of Jesus: *"Blessed rather are those who hear the word of God and obey it."*

THANK YOU, HEAVENLY FATHER:

For the power of Jesus' words and miracles;
For the healing of this man, so that dumbness was gone immediately and he could speak;
For the fulness of the Holy Spirit in lives in which Satan once had possession;

IN JESUS' NAME, AMEN

56. Luke 11:29 – 32
The Sign of Jonah

Luke 11:29 - 32
As the crowds increased, Jesus said, *"This is a wicked generation. It asks for a miraculous sign, but none will be given it except the sign of Jonah. ³⁰ For as Jonah was a sign to the Ninevites, so also will the Son of Man be to this generation.*

³¹ The Queen of the South will rise at the judgment with the men of this generation and condemn them; for she came from the ends of the earth to listen to Solomon's wisdom, and now one greater than Solomon is here.

³² The men of Nineveh will stand up at the judgment with this generation and condemn it; for they repented at the preaching of Jonah, and now one greater than Jonah is here."

In v. 16 people wanted a sign from Jesus, but here he rebukes them for making such a request. How much more did some of them want? They had seen him heal a demon-possessed man. They had watched him throughout his ministry and had seen one sign after another testifying to his identity, and demonstrating a power that only God could manifest. Yet they weren't satisfied.

What was the sign that Jesus was pointing to by mentioning the sign of Jonah? It wasn't Jonah's ordeal in the belly of the great fish. It was the sign of Jonah's preaching and particularly the message he preached, the certainty of judgment.

God had sent Jonah as a sign to the Ninevites. God had sent his Son to this generation.

If we remember when Jonah preached to the Ninevites it will help us understand why Jesus referred to the prophet. Jonah preached to them after his ordeal in the belly of the great fish. The fish literally vomited the prophet out on dry land and it was then that he preached to them. (Before, he had been unwilling.)

He seemed to appear out of nowhere, a gaunt, bleached, wrinkled figure, looking like someone returned from the dead, preaching a message of judgement. *'Yet forty days and Nineveh will be overthrown.'* The Ninevites believed the message of Jonah, both king and commoner, and God spared them from judgment.

The ministry of Jesus was very like that of Jonah. There was a difference however: Jesus' sign would be his resurrection.

Enter the Queen of Sheba. Why did Jesus mention her at this point? Her visit to meet King Solomon was legendary. She had travelled across the world to listen to Solomon's wisdom, but the Pharisees, who were supposed to be majoring in the quest for truth, wouldn't cross the street to hear the Son of God.

Jesus gave his hearers a solemn warning if they continued in unbelief.

"The Queen of the South will rise at the judgment with the men of this generation and condemn them; for she came from the ends of the earth to listen to Solomon's wisdom, and now one greater than Solomon is here"(v. 31).

Who will rise at the judgment? The Queen of Sheba will be there. The people of Nineveh will be there. The people who were listening to Jesus that day, whom he called *'this generation'*, would be there. What was Jesus' point?

"The men of Nineveh will stand up at the judgment with this generation and condemn it; for they repented at the preaching of Jonah, and now one greater than Jonah is here" (v. 32).

The people had asked for a sign from heaven (v. 16). In due time Jesus and his Father would give them a convincing sign, in which the Lord would be completely victorious over them and over all sin, to their final dismay.

He would be raised from the dead and be raised to the right hand of God until on a day already determined by his Father he will come to judge the world with justice (Acts 17:31).

The people to whom Jesus spoke so directly had yet to repent at his preaching, despite the fact that he was *'greater than Jonah.'*

THANK YOU, HEAVENLY FATHER:

For Your patience with an unbelieving world and with those who, having heard the gospel, are still in rebellion against You (2 Peter 3:9);

For the preaching of Jesus, in terms that were crystal-clear, so that the most stubborn hearers were without excuse for their unbelief;

For the privilege of having known the Scriptures from childhood (like Timothy (2 Timothy 3:14-15). The old stories, learned and loved, were used by the Holy Spirit to bring us to Jesus;

For evangelists and pastors who are involved in world evangelisation, so that the nations of the world are not denied the Word of God in their own languages and come to faith in Jesus;

57. Luke 11:33 - 36
The Lamp of the Body

Luke 11:33 - 36
"No-one lights a lamp and puts it in a place where it will be hidden, or under a bowl. Instead he puts it on its stand, so that those who come in may see the light.

³⁴ Your eye is the lamp of your body. When your eyes are good, your whole body also is full of light. But when they are bad, your body also is full of darkness. ³⁵ See to it, then, that the light within you is not darkness.

³⁶ Therefore, if your whole body is full of light, and no part of it dark, it will be completely lighted, as when the light of a lamp shines on you."

'There are none so blind as those who will not see', is an old proverb. It seems applicable here.

Sources tell us that this proverb has been traced back to 1546, and resembles the biblical verse Jeremiah 5:21 *('Hear now this, O foolish people, and without understanding; which have eyes, and see not; which have ears, and hear not')*. The full saying is: *'There are none so blind as those who will not see. The most deluded people are those who choose to ignore what they already know'*.

The context in this section of Luke 11 is still the request for a sign from heaven (v. 16).

Jesus could speak of himself as the light of the world, and say it truthfully. No one could ever accuse him of hiding his light. In v. 33 *'the lamp'* is a metaphor for Jesus.

Luke seems to be making the point that if one's spiritual sight is not damaged there is no need for a spectacular sign from heaven. The light of Jesus himself, which shines for all to see, makes any other sign pale by comparison.

'Your eye is the lamp of your body' (v. 34a).

In this verse *'the lamp'* is a metaphor for one's reaction to Jesus. This is a very powerful illustration.

'When your eyes are good, your whole body also is full of light' (v.34b)

If our eyes are looking to Jesus then he becomes the light of life to us and our whole body is full of light.

'But when they are bad, your body also is full of darkness' (v. 34c).

How a person reacts to Jesus and his ministry determines one's ultimate spiritual condition. If we are blind to the light of Jesus, then whatever *'light'* we may claim to have, our body is full of darkness.

'See to it, then, that the light within you is not darkness' (vv. 34 – 35).

We are responsible for what we do with the light of Jesus Christ; *see then that the light within you is not darkness (v. 35)*. Make sure that what directs your thoughts, your life, is in fact the true light and not darkness.

Just as Jesus caught the attention of his hearers with this brief and very direct discourse, he now brings it to a conclusion on a very practical note.

'Therefore, if your whole body is full of light, and no part of it dark, it will be completely lighted, as when the light of a lamp shines on you." (v.36)

In the final analysis unbelief is not an intellectual problem; it is a moral problem. Men loved darkness because their deeds were evil. Alas, many of Jesus' hearers continued to stumble on in the darkness.

THANK YOU, HEAVENLY FATHER:

For the moment that the Holy Spirit shined into our hearts, dispelling the darkness that had reigned there for so long, so that for the first time we could 'see Jesus';
For the insights into men's hearts that Jesus gave in this message: we are thankful for his insights and applications of what people do with the light of the Gospel;

For the picture of Jesus himself that the discourse reveals; we are resolved to walk in His light for as long as we shall live.

In Jesus' Name, Amen

58. Luke 11:37 - 53
Six Woes

Luke 11:37 - 41
When Jesus had finished speaking, a Pharisee invited him to eat with him; so he went in and reclined at the table. ^{38} *But the Pharisee, noticing that Jesus did not first wash before the meal, was surprised.*

^{39} *Then the Lord said to him, "Now then, you Pharisees clean the outside of the cup and dish, but inside you are full of greed and wickedness.* ^{40} *You foolish people! Did not the one who made the outside make the inside also?* ^{41} *But give what is inside the dish to the poor, and everything will be clean for you."*

We might assume that when the Pharisee gave Jesus an invitation to eat with him that he had a cosy tete-a-tete in mind. There would be nothing cosy about it, but there would be a lot of straight talking.

First of all Jesus did not wash his hands ceremoniously before reclining at the table. The host noticed this omission and was surprised. Jesus took the initiative and responded to the man's thoughts and began to pronounce six woes against everyone in the room.

He denounced the Pharisees for their fastidiousness in washing the outside of the body, and their negligence of cleanliness on the inside: *'inside you are full of greed and wickedness' (v. 39)*. As if God, who made their bodies, had not also given them hearts and souls.

With regard to greed, Jesus knew of the Pharisees' love of money. This is why he challenged them to give to the poor (v. 41). That alone would be evidence of some improvement on the inside. God is more concerned about the state of a man's heart than with the appearance of his hands.

Luke 11:42
"Woe to you Pharisees, because you give God a tenth of your mint, rue and all other kinds of garden herbs, but you neglect justice and the love of God. You should have practised the latter without leaving the former undone."

Ostentatiously and meticulously they tithed the very herbs in their gardens, but they forgot or ignored the weightier matters of virtue, kindness and true humility.

Luke 11:43
"Woe to you Pharisees, because you love the most important seats in the synagogues and greetings in the market-places."

They insisted on having seats of importance at any function, whether in the synagogue or in the market-place, forgetting that they were obnoxious in the sight of God.

Luke 11:44
"Woe to you, because you are like unmarked graves, which men walk over without knowing it."

A traveller might walk on an old grave unwittingly. Even so, he would be regarded as unclean. They were like old unmarked graves, full of decay and putrefaction. Their hearts were filthy.

Luke 11:45
One of the experts in the law answered him, "Teacher, when you say these things, you insult us also."

It was a startling change for the lawyers (those in the Pharisaic community who were most responsible for Pharisaic teaching) to hear themselves being criticised. Usually it was the other way round. They could dish out criticism to others, but they couldn't take it when they were on the receiving end.

Luke 11:46
Jesus replied, "And you experts in the law, woe to you, because you load people down with burdens they can hardly carry, and you yourselves will not lift one finger to help them."

Jesus condemns these men for creating innumerable laws and traditions, thus making serving God impossible for the average Jew.

In Acts 15:10 the apostles described these additional laws as *'a yoke that neither we nor our fathers have been able to bear.'*

Luke 11:47 - 49
"Woe to you, because you build tombs for the prophets, and it was your forefathers who killed them. ⁴⁸ So you testify that you approve of what your forefathers did; they killed the prophets, and you build their tombs. ⁴⁹ Because of this, God in his wisdom said, 'I will send them prophets and apostles, some of whom they will kill and others they will persecute."

These 'holy men' would hypocritically build tombs to honour the prophets while not honouring their message. It was their fore-fathers who had killed the prophets whom the present generation professed to honour!

Neither had they recognised the modern-day prophets such as John the Baptist and Jesus. The Baptist had been murdered and Jesus would be crucified. This generation of Jewish leaders was behaving like their fathers before them.

Luke 11:50 - 53
"Therefore this generation will be held responsible for the blood of all the prophets that has been shed since the beginning of the world, ⁵¹ from the blood of Abel to the blood of Zechariah, who was killed between the altar and the sanctuary. Yes, I tell you, this generation will be held responsible for it all."

God in his wisdom would hold them responsible for all such crimes from the beginning of creation until the final judgment. Abel, the firstborn of Adam and Eve, was murdered by his brother Cain. The record is in Genesis 4:1-16. Zechariah (v. 51) was a high priest whose death is recorded in 2 Chron. 24:20-22. Both were righteous men.

Luke 11:52

"Woe to you experts in the law, because you have taken away the key to knowledge. You yourselves have not entered, and you have hindered those who were entering."

These leading expositors of the law are condemned for interpreting the Scriptures falsely and adding their many traditions that deprived the people of the key to knowledge. Their treatment of John the Baptist and Jesus showed they had not entered the kingdom of God themselves, and were obstructing those who would.

Luke 11:53

When Jesus left there, the Pharisees and the teachers of the law began to oppose him fiercely and to besiege him with questions,

The battle lines are now clearly drawn. From now on the Jewish leaders would oppose Jesus fiercely. A new level of antagonism to Jesus began at this point.

THANK YOU, HEAVENLY FATHER:

For stopping Saul of Tarsus when he was *'still breathing out murderous threats against the Lord's people'* (Acts 9:1) and saving him by Your grace;

For the ability of the Holy Spirit to overcome all negative influences in the way of sinners, so that they willingly surrender themselves to Jesus Christ as their Lord and Saviour;

For the great numbers of your people who are faithful intercessors on behalf of religious leaders and others in secular authority that they might be saved;

IN JESUS' NAME, AMEN

59. Luke 12:1- 12
Warnings and Encouragments

Luke 12:1
Meanwhile, when a crowd of many thousands had gathered, so that they were trampling on one another, Jesus began to speak first to his disciples, saying: "Be on your guard against the yeast of the Pharisees, which is hypocrisy."

News must have travelled fast because in what appears to be a short time *'a crowd of many thousands had gathered, so that they were trampling on one another.'* Never mind the crowd for a moment, Jesus had something on his mind to tell his disciples: *"Be on your guard against the yeast of the Pharisees, which is hypocrisy.'* Yeast, or leaven, was an agent that our mothers and grandmothers used to add to their baking bowls. When the dough had been prepared it was set aside to 'prove'. The yeast aerated the dough. After 30 – 40 minutes, when the dough had grown until nearly twice its original size, it was put in the oven to bake. The end product made good eating.

Jesus used the metaphor of yeast or leaven on more than one occasion, sometimes in a positive way to illustrate the growth of his kingdom, and sometimes in a negative way as here, warning the disciples to watch out for a destructive kind of leaven like the hypocrisy of the Pharisees.

It is never safe to be two-faced. Like yeast, the Pharisees' influence was pervasive. Verses 2 & 3 include a number of proverbial sayings which like good proverbs, are self-explanatory.

Luke 12:2 - 3
"There is nothing concealed that will not be disclosed, or hidden that will not be made known. ³ What you have said in the dark will be heard in the daylight, and what you have whispered in the ear in the inner rooms will be proclaimed from the roofs."

The purpose of this section of Luke's gospel, although spoken in the hearing of the public, was to comfort the disciples so that they did not succumb to fear or to worry.

Luke 12:4 - 6

"I tell you, my friends, do not be afraid of those who kill the body and after that can do no more. [5] But I will show you whom you should fear: Fear him who, after the killing of the body, has power to throw you into hell. Yes, I tell you, fear him. [6] Are not five sparrows sold for two pennies? Yet not one of them is forgotten by God. [7] Indeed, the very hairs of your head are all numbered. Don't be afraid; you are worth more than many sparrows.

In the face of increased opposition from the Pharisees and their ilk, Jesus knew that they were capable persecuting him and his disciples to death: *'Don't fear those who kill the body, fear God.'* This is a fear born of awe, reverence and humility in the presence of God's majesty.

Think of how God cares for the sparrows. Not one of them is forgotten by God. This doesn't mean he is an ornithologist. The very hairs of your head are numbered. This doesn't mean that he is a statistician.

Luke 12:8-9, 11-12

"I tell you, whoever acknowledges me before men, the Son of Man will also acknowledge him before the angels of God [9] But he who disowns me before men will be disowned before the angels of God."

[11] "When you are brought before synagogues, rulers and authorities, do not worry about how you will defend yourselves or what you will say, [12] for the Holy Spirit will teach you at that time what you should say."

Jesus could anticipate his disciples and those who would believe on him being hauled before religious and civil courts on trial for their lives. However great the pressure, they were not to be ashamed of belonging to him. Such courage will be rewarded in eternity. In the moment of greatest public exposure the Holy Spirit would teach them what to say.

Luke 12:10

"And everyone who speaks a word against the Son of Man will be forgiven, but anyone who blasphemes against the Holy Spirit will not be forgiven."

This is probably the most fearful warning ever to come from the lips of Jesus. It warns against the sin that cannot and will not be forgiven. When the Pharisees were accusing Jesus of performing his miracles by the power of Satan they were on dangerous ground. Blasphemy against the Holy Spirit is verbal; it is a sin in word.

When a person has become enlightened by the Holy Spirit to the true identity of Jesus and then calls Jesus the devil - that seems to be the unforgivable sin.

THANK YOU, HEAVENLY FATHER:

For the pastoral care of Jesus for his disciples;
For sustaining the Suffering Church of Jesus Christ around the world
    where totalitarian governments and dictators persecute it;

IN JESUS' NAME, AMEN

60. Luke 12:13-21
The Parable of the Rich Fool

Luke 12:13 - 21

Someone in the crowd said to him, "Teacher, tell my brother to divide the inheritance with me." ¹⁴ Jesus replied, "Man, who appointed me a judge or an arbiter between you?"

¹⁵ Then he said to them, "Watch out! Be on your guard against all kinds of greed; a man's life does not consist in the abundance of his possessions."

¹⁶ And he told them this parable: "The ground of a certain rich man produced a good crop. ¹⁷ He thought to himself, 'What shall I do? I have no place to store my crops.'

¹⁸ "Then he said, 'This is what I'll do. I will tear down my barns and build bigger ones, and there I will store all my grain and my goods. ¹⁹ And I'll say to myself, "You have plenty of good things laid up for many years. Take life easy; eat, drink and be merry." '

²⁰ "But God said to him, 'You fool! This very night your life will be demanded from you. Then who will get what you have prepared for yourself?'

²¹ "This is how it will be with anyone who stores up things for himself but is not rich towards God."

If you were a pastor you would soon discover that you don't know what the next knock on your front door or the next ring of the telephone will bring. It could be good news or bad news. It could send your spirits into the heavens or into your boots. Here, Jesus' ministry was like that.

Someone in the crowd had a bright idea: he would ask Jesus to settle a family dispute: *"Teacher, tell my brother to divide the inheritance with me."* To which Jesus replied: *"Man, who appointed me a judge or an arbiter between you?"*

Jesus rejected the role of referee between these two brothers. He hadn't come to settle family disputes. In fact, his coming would at times divide families. In his superior wisdom he used the moment to teach a very important lesson to the people around him: *"Watch out! Be on your guard against all kinds of greed; a man's life does not consist in the abundance of his possessions."* It was a warning against covetousness. Jesus rejected the request because it was prompted by greed. The meaning and purpose of life is not found in the accumulation of wealth and possessions. (1 Timothy 6:6-10)

Jesus then taught the parable of the Rich Fool. Observe a few facts:

The man was already rich when the story begins v. 16. God had given him a good harvest, more than he had room enough to store in his barns.

The rich man made plans to become richer v. 18. *'This is what I'll do. I will tear down my barns and build bigger ones, and there I will store all my grain and my goods.'*

The rich man thought he had a lease of his life v. 19. *'And I'll say to myself, "You have plenty of good things laid up for many years. Take life easy; eat, drink and be merry."* The man was a hedonist.

<u>The rich man's plans were cancelled when he received a summons from heaven v. 20</u>. *"But God said to him, 'You fool! This very night your life will be demanded from you. Then who will get what you have prepared for yourself?'* All that he had was on loan to him, and could be called in at any time.

I think we see the issue. This greedy man made plans. God intervened. That night the rich man entered eternity utterly bankrupt, a spiritual pauper. God called him away from this life. What value then was all that he had planned and worked for? *'Then who will get what you have prepared for yourself?'*

Riches were the currency of life on earth, but they were not legal tender in the life to come. If a person possessed all the wealth in all the bank vaults on earth, the combined value would not purchase salvation from hell and a place in heaven.

Jesus conclusion of the parable leaves us all silent, perhaps speechless *v. 21"This is how it will be with anyone who stores up things for himself but is not rich towards God."* He had neglected his soul. He lost that too.

THANK YOU, HEAVENLY FATHER:

For the fact that Your people are richer than millionaires, just because You care;
For the fact that *no eye has seen, no ear has heard, no mind has conceived what You have prepared for them that love You* (1 Cor. 2:9-10);
For Your ability to *make all grace abound to us, so that in all things at all times, having all that we need, we will abound in every good work* (2 Cor. 9:8);
For the fact that You honour them that honour You;

IN JESUS' NAME, AMEN

61. Luke 12:22 - 34
Do Not Worry

It is no surprise that this section of Jesus' teaching occurs where it does. We have only to bear in mind the parable of the Rich Fool earlier in this chapter (vv. 13 – 21). Knowing his story, we have been well-warned about covetousness. In three short sections, Jesus is knocking away all the crutches that believers lean on, when they should be leaning on him.

Luke 12:22 – 26
Then Jesus said to his disciples: "Therefore I tell you, do not worry about your life, what you will eat; or about your body, what you will wear. ²³ Life is more than food, and the body more than clothes.

²⁴ Consider the ravens: They do not sow or reap, they have no storeroom or barn; yet God feeds them. And how much more valuable you are than birds! ²⁵ Who of you by worrying can add a single hour to his life? ²⁶ Since you cannot do this very little thing, why do you worry about the rest?"

Jesus is knocking away the crutch of worry. Can you think of anything more foolish or futile than worry? Did you know that worrying consumes a lot of energy? Sometimes we can worry ourselves until we are exhausted and our physical strength is at an all time low. Worry will not add an inch to our height or a single additional hour to our life. Jesus could speak with a sense of humour: *Since you cannot do this very little thing, why do you worry about the rest?*

Luke 12:27 – 31
"Consider how the lilies grow. They do not labour or spin. Yet I tell you, not even Solomon in all his splendour was dressed like one of these.

²⁸ If that is how God clothes the grass of the field, which is here today, and tomorrow is thrown into the fire, how much more will he clothe you, O you of little faith!

²⁹ And do not set your heart on what you will eat or drink; do not worry about it. ³⁰ For the pagan world runs after all such things, and your Father knows that you need them. ³¹ But seek his kingdom, and these things will be given to you as well."

Jesus is knocking away the crutch of our own efforts to obtain what we want (i.e. in case he may not permit us to have it!)

What is that we pour our energy into every day? What difference in priorities is there between unbelievers we meet or work alongside? Is the work we do for our employer done for the glory of Jesus? What we want for ourselves and what God sees we need may be poles apart. How will we honour the Lord in the way we spend our wages? If we make the extension of his kingdom our priority he gives a guarantee that the things we need will be given to us as well.

Luke 12:32 – 34
"Do not be afraid, little flock, for your Father has been pleased to give you the kingdom.
³³ Sell your possessions and give to the poor. Provide purses for yourselves that will not wear out, a treasure in heaven that will not be exhausted, where no thief comes near and no moth destroys. ³⁴ For where your treasure is, there your heart will be also."

Jesus is knocking away the crutch of wealth (be it much or little), so that we will lean on him.

Later, Paul would write to the Christians at Colosse: *'Since, then, you have been raised with Christ, set your hearts on things above, where Christ is seated at the right hand of God. ² Set your minds on things above, not on earthly things' (Col 3:1 – 2).*

That quotation is a very neat summary of Jesus' teaching here. We have to bear in mind that the apostles (including Paul) were specially chosen by Christ to be the foundation members and leaders in his church. When the apostles, in their pastoral letters, apply the doctrines of the gospel to everyday life, they are in fact teaching with the authority of Christ.

THANK YOU, HEAVENLY FATHER:

For Your patience with us when we insist on taking things into own hands as if we didn't have a Heavenly Father;
For your forgiveness when you reveal our carnal behaviour to us and we sincerely repent of it;
For Your provision of our needs all our lives through, and in the future all the way to heaven;
For doing exceeding more abundantly more for us than we could ever ask or think;

IN JESUS' NAME, AMEN

62. Luke 12:35 – 48
Watchful Servants

This is a complete change of focus: watchfulness with respect to Jesus' Second Coming in Glory. Three instances of watchfulness follow: the watching servants (vv. 36-38), the watchful householder (vv. 39-40, and the servant in authority (vv. 42-48).

Lk 12:35 - 38 The Watching Servant

"Be dressed ready for service and keep your lamps burning, [36] like men waiting for their master to return from a wedding banquet, so that when he comes and knocks they can immediately open the door for him. [37] It will be good for those servants whose master finds them watching when he comes. I tell you the truth, he will dress himself to serve, will have them recline at the table and will come and wait on them. [38] It will be good for those servants whose master finds them ready, even if he comes in the second or third watch of the night.

Here is a command to be ready and to have a lamp lit in preparation for the Master's return. The command in v. 35 appears elsewhere: Ephesians 6:14; 1 Peter 1:13. It literally means *'stand, with your waist belted'*. In other words ready for whatever action is required. It means *'being on duty'* in contrast to *'being off duty'*. Instead of waiting until the last moment, be prepared to act. If the Master's knock is not promptly answered he will know immediately if his servants are watchful. He will honour these who were watchful, to the extent of donning a servant's apron and waiting on his servants. His coming may not be at a convenient hour of the day – it could be in the middle of the night – but he wants to find us watching!

Lk 12:39 – 40 The Watchful Householder

"But understand this: If the owner of the house had known at what hour the thief was coming, he would not have let his house be broken into. [40] You also must be ready, because the Son of Man will come at an hour when you do not expect him."

This is a warning to be ready because the Son of Man will come at an unannounced time. A thief doesn't send a stamped, addressed postcard to tell the time he will enter your home. That is not how a thief operates.

How wise the Lord was by not setting a day and hour for his coming again. Better to have his people in a state of watchfulness and readiness instead of slothfulness and neglect. So he may come at a time when we do not expect him. In fact that is how his coming will seem. Let us not miss the warning: *'You must be ready, because the Son of Man will come at an hour when you do not expect him.'*

[41] Peter asked, *"Lord, are you telling this parable to us, or to everyone?"*

Peter, please listen well! You and your colleagues were the target of the previous parable, and even more so of the final one.

Lk 12:42 – 48 The Servant in Authority

The Lord answered, "Who then is the faithful and wise manager, whom the master puts in charge of his servants to give them their food allowance at the proper time? [43] *It will be good for that servant whom the master finds doing so when he returns.* [44] *I tell you the truth, he will put him in charge of all his possessions.*

[45] *But suppose the servant says to himself, 'My master is taking a long time in coming,' and he then begins to beat the menservants and maidservants and to eat and drink and get drunk.* [46] *The master of that servant will come on a day when he does not expect him and at an hour he is not aware of. He will cut him to pieces and assign him a place with the unbelievers.* [47] *That servant who knows his master's will and does not get ready or does not do what his master wants will be beaten with many blows.*

[48] *But the one who does not know and does things deserving punishment will be beaten with few blows.*

From everyone who has been given much, much will be demanded; and from the one who has been entrusted with much, much more will be asked."

This section is about the role of those to whom the Master has entrusted his household. Those who faithfully discharge their duties will be blessed (vv. 43-44). The apostles were like managers in Christ's kingdom and church. Faithful managers are described in vv. 42 – 44. Careless managers are described in vv. 45ff. Managers know their Master's will (v. 47) and are responsible for the preparedness of the house. Note the mention of a day and an hour in v. 46. 'Managers' i.e. apostles, pastors, elders, teachers will give account of their stewardship.

THANK YOU, HEAVENLY FATHER:

For the ministry of Jesus with regard to his coming again; our hearts respond *'Even so, come Lord Jesus';*
For the part we have been given *'in gathering in the lost ones, for whom our Lord did die'* through prayer, gospel witness and godly living;
For the ministry of Your Holy Spirit: may he grant your people a revival of readiness for Jesus' return;

IN JESUS' NAME, AMEN

63. Luke 12:49 - 53
Not Peace but Division

Lk 12:49 – 53
*"I have come to bring fire on the earth, and how I wish it were already kindled! *⁵⁰* But I have a baptism to undergo, and how distressed I am until it is completed! *⁵¹* Do you think I came to bring peace on earth?*

*No, I tell you, but division. *⁵²* From now on there will be five in one family divided against each other, three against two and two against three. *⁵³* They will be divided, father against son and son against father, mother against daughter and daughter against mother, mother-in-law against daughter-in-law and daughter-in-law against mother-in-law."*

In the previous section Jesus' coming was at the Parousia. Here his coming is with reference to his ministry. Jesus was making it clear that there were certain events in his ministry that were still in the future, and he had an intense longing for their completion. He was not deterred by what lay ahead. He would still dedicate himself to doing the will of his Father.

One of the effects of his ministry would be *'to bring fire to the earth'*. He then said *'how I wish it were already kindled!* (v. 49). Next he said, *'I have a baptism to undergo, and how distressed I am until it is completed! Do you think that I came to bring peace on earth?'*

The fire mentioned in v. 49, is not the final judgment. The context in which Jesus said these things suggests that the fire could refer to how the coming of God's kingdom divides people into two camps. Does this sound strange? It shouldn't.

If we refer back to Luke 2:34 – 35 we will read of Simeon telling Mary *'this child is set for 'the falling and rising of many in Israel, and to be a sign that will be spoken against, so that the thoughts of many hearts will be revealed'*.

There were those people who were drawn to Jesus and brought into a union with him that the world has never known. Yet he was also an instrument of division. Jesus was thinking of his suffering and death when he used the illustration of baptism (v. 50). Jesus would be submerged in sorrow – covered – overwhelmed. A fearful baptism lay ahead of him: a baptism of suffering, of wounds, of crucifixion, of blood and of death. No previous experience of his earthly life compared with it. Psalm 42:7 prophesied *'All your waves and breakers have swept over me'*. That would be Jesus' experience.

His effect on people would turn the even tenor of their lives to strife and anguish on his account. He prophesied the effect on a family circle where the members were divided about him.

"From now on there will be five in one family divided against each other, three against two and two against three. **53** *They will be divided, father against son and son against father, mother against daughter and daughter against mother, mother-in-law against daughter-in-law and daughter-in-law against mother-in-law."*

Can we imagine it? Perhaps we experienced it when we first shared with our family what Jesus had done in our life. We were the objects of scorn and ridicule. We were threatened with being turned out of our home if we persisted with this *'Jesus-nonsense'*. Perhaps the only way to be *'at peace'* with them was to move out before we were put out.

In the world of Islam a family member who believes in Jesus may be disowned, beaten or worse for their profession of faith.

If the cost of following Jesus means that we are ostracised by our nearest and dearest, that is the price we must pay. We will continue to love them, pray for them and show them every possible kindness (whether they will receive it or not). The Holy Spirit will be our indwelling comforter and our strength for living.

If we knew of a new believer who was expelled by his family because he had become a Christian, would we be willing to provide help for him, either in the short or the long term? Would we actively help them find a place of their own to live and eventually to call 'home'?

THANK YOU, HEAVENLY FATHER:

For Christian parents and relatives, who did everything possible to point us to their Lord and Saviour;
For the joy with which they received our news when we told them '*I have become a Christian!*'
For Jesus Christ, Your one and only Son, who loved us and gave himself for us;

IN JESUS' NAME, AMEN

64. Luke 12:54 – 59
Interpreting the Times

Luke 12:54 – 56
He said to the crowd: "When you see a cloud rising in the west, immediately you say, 'It's going to rain,' and it does. ⁵⁵ And when the south wind blows, you say, 'It's going to be hot,' and it is. ⁵⁶ Hypocrites! You know how to interpret the appearance of the earth and the sky. How is it that you don't know how to interpret this present time?"

Jesus ministered to people who were close to the land, or perhaps not many generations removed from it. Probably the majority of his listeners were observant rural people. Nowadays fewer and fewer people are dependent on agriculture. I think that children who don't have the privilege of growing up in the country miss a lot of nature's lessons. Country people are not very old until they learn to read the signs of the weather and the clouds. This is the wisdom that Jesus is referring to in vv. 54 – 55.

The cloud rising in the west (coming in off the Mediterranean Sea) denoted rain. When the wind was from the desert in the south it brought warm weather. Jesus mentioned the signs of the weather in order to point to something much more important, the signs of the times (v. 56). His comment was true then, and it is still true. *'You know how to interpret the appearance of the earth and the sky. How is it that you don't know how to interpret this present time?'*

The phrase he used was *'they were unable to analyse the present time'*.

To be able to do that would require them to take note of what God was doing in that day and in their presence. They had seen amazing things e.g. *'the blind receive their sight, the lame walk. . . the dead are raised, and the good news is preached to the poor'*.

Even Jesus' opponents knew that his exorcisms meant something and needed to be explained (11:15). If they had been open to the truth as it was expressed in the words and works of Jesus, they would have been able to interpret the present and recognise that God's kingdom had in fact arrived. They had missed all of the signs that the Old Testament prophets had talked about. Every pious Jew should have been able to see that Jesus was the fulfilment of the Old Testament prophets. They could read the weather, but the things that mattered, ultimately and eternally, they were not able to grasp.

Understanding the previous section was fairly easy. We know and can read the signs of the weather.

Now we are puzzled, wondering why Jesus switched to avoiding incarceration in prison.

Luke 12:57 – 59

"Why don't you judge for yourselves what is right? 58 As you are going with your adversary to the magistrate, try hard to be reconciled to him on the way, or he may drag you off to the judge, and the judge turn you over to the officer, and the officer throw you into prison. 59 I tell you, you will not get out until you have paid the last penny."

Right away we can understand that Jesus was urging people to make wise judgments: *"Why don't you judge for yourselves what is right?"(v. 57)*. The word picture is of two people who are in dispute over some issue and they are taking the case to law (v. 58). That should be the last resort in any matter.

Your accuser is adamant that you are in the wrong. You do not see the matter in that light. Wisdom ought to tell you that it would be best to reach a settlement before you get to court, because if the case went to the judge the end would never be in doubt and you would end up in prison. *'You will not get out until you have paid the last penny.'*

In the same way it is never wise to leave repentance until the last moment of your life. You might be totally incapable of repentance at that point. *'Now is the accepted time and now is the day of salvation'* (2 Corinthians 6:2 KJV).

N.B. Beware of constructing *a 'doctrine of a second chance'* or a *'doctrine of purgatory'* on the words *'you will not get out until you have paid the last penny.'* Once judgment is passed in the divine court, there will be no reprieve and no getting out.

THANK YOU, HEAVENLY FATHER:

For Your forgiveness: when we confess our sins You are faithful and just and will forgive us our sins and purify us from all unrighteousness;
For the assurance that *'there is now no condemnation to them that are in Christ Jesus'* (Romans 8:1).

IN JESUS' NAME, AMEN

65. Luke 13:1 - 9
Repent or Perish

Lk 13:1 - 9
Now there were some present at that time who told Jesus about the Galileans whose blood Pilate had mixed with their sacrifices. ² *Jesus answered, "Do you think that these Galileans were worse sinners than all the other Galileans because they suffered this way?* ³ *I tell you, no! But unless you repent, you too will all perish.* ⁴ *Or those eighteen who died when the tower in Siloam fell on them—do you think they were more guilty than all the others living in Jerusalem?* ⁵ *I tell you, no! But unless you repent, you too will all perish."*

⁶ *Then he told this parable: "A man had a fig-tree, planted in his vineyard, and he went to look for fruit on it, but did not find any.* ⁷ *So he said to the man who took care of the vineyard, 'For three years now I've been coming to look for fruit on this fig-tree and haven't found any. Cut it down! Why should it use up the soil?'*

⁸ *"'Sir,' the man replied, 'leave it alone for one more year, and I'll dig round it and fertilise it.* ⁹ *If it bears fruit next year, fine! If not, then cut it down.'"*

Some people came to Jesus bringing news of an atrocity committed by Pilate who had ordered the murders of some Galileans who were offering sacrifices in the Temple. It gave Jesus the opportunity to ask a leading question: *"Do you think that these Galileans were worse sinners than all the other Galileans because they suffered this way?* He answered his question: *'I tell you, no!'* (v. 3). That was the moment to make his point: *'But unless you repent, you too will all perish.'*

Then Jesus added another story of tragedy: *'Or those eighteen who died when the tower in Siloam fell on them—do you think they were more guilty than all the others living in Jerusalem?'* He answered his question: *'I tell you, no! But unless you repent, you too will all perish.'* Jesus did not mean that his listeners would die in similar ways, but that if death were to overtake them as suddenly, and they had not repented of their sins before God, they would most surely perish.

I've used the word tragedy to include both instances (vv. 1 & 4). How do we react to tragedy? In today's world we have become used to hearing of so many terrible crimes against the person, and also of natural disasters involving floods and collapsing buildings, that we are barely moved by feelings of compassion for the victims.

However, in these instances Jesus turned tragedy to opportunity! One man's tragedy is my opportunity. What kind of opportunity would that be? It is my opportunity to repent of my sins and get right with God.

That concluded part one of what Jesus was saying on this occasion. His teaching about tragedy was followed with a parable about a fig tree (vv. 6-9).

The owner of a vineyard made a visit to examine the crop. When he came to the fig tree he was disappointed to find no fruit on it (v. 6). Naturally he spoke to the husbandman (gardener) and told him that the tree had been barren for three years, therefore it was to be cut down. It was only wasting space (v. 7).

The gardener wasn't a mere hired hand. He too had a personal interest in the owner's property. He made an earnest plea that the tree should be spared for another year. Let me dig around it and fertilise it. *'If it bears fruit next year, fine! If not, then cut it down'* (v. 8). The lesson that Jesus is teaching in this instance is similar to the previous one. Instead of cutting us down for our sins and spiritual barrenness God has spared our lives, not to allow us to go on wasting them, but that we may repent of our sins, and begin to bear spiritual fruit for his glory. As Peter explained in his second letter:

2 Peter 3:8 - 9 *'But do not forget this one thing, dear friends: With the Lord a day is like a thousand years, and a thousand years are like a day. The Lord is not slow in keeping his promise, as some understand slowness. He is patient with you, not wanting anyone to perish, but everyone to come to repentance.'*

THANK YOU, HEAVENLY FATHER:

For Your patience us with us while we were yet sinners, giving us multiplied opportunities to turn from our sin and turn to the Saviour;
For sparing our lives until this day, through dangers seen and unseen, so that we could be wise and consider our latter end;
For speaking to us in so many ways, for urging us to *'flee from the wrath to come'*;
For Your servants, faithful pastors and friends, who spoke to us about what Jesus meant to them and encouraged us to follow him too;
For the moment when Jesus drew us to himself with cords of love and gave us eternal life;

IN JESUS' NAME, AMEN

66. Luke 13:10 - 17
A Crippled Woman healed on the Sabbath day.

Lk 13:10 – 17
On a Sabbath Jesus was teaching in one of the synagogues, ¹¹ and a woman was there who had been crippled by a spirit for eighteen years. She was bent over and could not straighten up at all. ¹² When Jesus saw her, he called her forward and said to her, "Woman, you are set free from your infirmity." ¹³ Then he put his hands on her, and immediately she straightened up and praised God.

¹⁴ Indignant because Jesus had healed on the Sabbath, the synagogue ruler said to the people, "There are six days for work. So come and be healed on those days, not on the Sabbath."

¹⁵ The Lord answered him, "You hypocrites! Doesn't each of you on the Sabbath untie his ox or donkey from the stall and lead it out to give it water? ¹⁶ Then should not this woman, a daughter of Abraham, whom Satan has kept bound for eighteen long years, be set free on the Sabbath day from what bound her?"

¹⁷ When he said this, all his opponents were humiliated, but the people were delighted with all the wonderful things he was doing.

This is the last incident that Luke will record of Jesus teaching in a synagogue. In the congregation on that Sabbath there was a woman who had been in the grip of an evil spirit for all of eighteen years. Her condition was pitiful, *'she was bent over and could not straighten up at all.'*

Jesus had only to set eyes on her and his help was immediately forthcoming: *'When Jesus saw her, he called her forward and said to her, "Woman, you are set free from your infirmity." Then he put his hands on her, and immediately she straightened up and praised God.'*

The ruler of the synagogue was an example of legalism. He was raging because Jesus had healed this woman, and in addition, had done it on the Sabbath day! He turned to his own people and said: *"There are six days for work. So come and be healed on those days, not on the Sabbath."*

Jesus didn't let this outrage pass. He addressed everyone present: *"You hypocrites! Doesn't each of you on the Sabbath untie his ox or donkey from the stall and lead it out to give it water? Then should not this woman, a daughter of Abraham, whom Satan has kept bound for eighteen long years, be set free on the Sabbath day from what bound her?"*

If the Law of Moses provided for animals to be watered on the Sabbath day, then a daughter of Abraham whom Satan has kept bound for eighteen long years is entitled to the refreshment of healing and be set free. Jesus traced her illness to Satan. Notice that he called the woman *'a daughter of Abraham'* including her as one of the covenant people.

The confrontation concluded with Jesus' opponents humiliated and the people rejoicing at his marvellous deeds (v. 17).

There is more than one emphasis in this event, among them the hostility that official Judaism displayed toward Jesus. Here they were indignant that he claimed to do God's work on the Sabbath day. When official Judaism chose to disregard God's mercy toward people as desperate as a woman crippled for eighteen years, that religion was doomed, judgment would be forthcoming.

Jesus' love for the outcasts and oppressed also reverberates throughout the story. Luke is delighted that divine salvation is coming to the powerless.

On the issue of showing kindness and mercy on the Sabbath day, the legalists could never win against the words of Jesus.

THANK YOU, HEAVENLY FATHER:

For the fact that when the Lord's hand touched the woman's bent body, suddenly she was straight and thanked God – we join her in praising You for this wonderful miracle of healing;
For the fact that though the woman came to the synagogue sorrowing, she went home rejoicing because she met Jesus there;
For the fact that *'Jesus is stronger than Satan and sin and Satan to Jesus must bow'*;
For the gentleness of Jesus' touch, his gracious words and wonder-working power revealed in this miracle;

For the sound of the woman's voice, lifted in praise and thanksgiving to You for her deliverance by Jesus;

IN JESUS' NAME, AMEN

67. Luke 13:18 - 21
The Parables of the Mustard Seed and the Yeast

Luke 13:18 – 21
Then Jesus asked, "What is the kingdom of God like? What shall I compare it to? [19] It is like a mustard seed, which a man took and planted in his garden. It grew and became a tree, and the birds of the air perched in its branches."
[20] Again he asked, "What shall I compare the kingdom of God to? [21] It is like yeast that a woman took and mixed into a large amount of flour until it worked all through the dough."

We don't have to search long to discover the subject of these two brief parables. Jesus announced the subject and in doing so set his hearers thinking about possible answers. The subject is the kingdom of God.

It is not clear why he took up this subject. It may be because he had already given so much evidence of the kingdom having already come. He wants people to think of where the kingdom goes from here.

In the first parable there is a contrast between the size of one tiny mustard seed and the tree that will grow from it.

If you hold a single mustard seed in your hand it looks insignificant. At that stage the seed is not much larger than a speck of dust. It is the smallest of all seeds.

In the growing process it looks like a plant,. . . a shrub,. . . a large shrub. . . and then it becomes a tree large enough for the birds of the air to perch in its branches and between 10 and 12 feet in height. It is common to see a cloud of birds around such trees, for they love the little black mustard seeds.

In the second parable there is a contrast between the dough before and after yeast has been added to the flour.

Jesus didn't supply an application of the parable because everyone would know exactly what he meant, for every household made its own bread. If the woman who is baking forgets to add yeast to the bread mixture then the bread will not rise during the baking process. It will be flat and leaden in texture. Let's say that this woman is experienced enough that she doesn't make the mistake that a new bride might make. She adds the yeast to the bread mixture, and sets it aside for 30 – 40 minutes to *'prove'*. In that time the yeast makes the dough rise, until it is almost twice its original size. When it is put in the oven the cooking process begins and during the process the bread rises so then when it is taken from the oven the loaf has a very light texture and is good eating.

The difference between the mustard seed and the yeast is plain for all to see (or perhaps not!).

The mustard tree's growing process is plain to see, until it is fully grown.

The yeast within the dough works secretly.

Frequently Jesus used yeast as a symbol of evil, but not always. Here the illustration is a positive one, not only demonstrating that the use of yeast is essential to producing good bread but that is works secretly.

You may well come across a host of wonderful suggestions about the meaning of these parables with some sounding far-fetched. Best to dismiss them all, for the simple reason that the listeners who were the first to hear them would catch Jesus' emphases and be edified accordingly. Suffice to say that both are growth parables

If we put together the kingdom evidence that Luke has been recording in his *'Life of Christ'* then there has already been remarkable growth. Only the King knows what is really happening, because out of sight from human eyes, the work and influence of the kingdom is ongoing.

Thank You, Heavenly Father:

For the work of Your kingdom in the world today in both its operations, some visible and some unseen by human eyes, but always growing;

For allowing us to see the progress of Your kingdom from time to time as we read the newspapers and watch television news programmes. We cannot always interpret what you are doing, but we know that political change takes place only with Your permission and within Your purposes;

For the petitions that Jesus included in the model prayer that he gave his disciples: *'Your kingdom come, Your will be done on earth as it is in heaven'*

IN JESUS' NAME, AMEN

68. Luke 13:22 - 30
The Narrow Door

Luke 13:22 – 30
Then Jesus went through the towns and villages, teaching as he made his way to Jerusalem.
²³ Someone asked him, "Lord, are only a few people going to be saved?"
He said to them, ²⁴ "Make every effort to enter through the narrow door, because many, I tell you, will try to enter and will not be able to. ²⁵ Once the owner of the house gets up and closes the door, you will stand outside knocking and pleading, 'Sir, open the door for us.'
"But he will answer, 'I don't know you or where you come from.'
²⁶ "Then you will say, 'We ate and drank with you, and you taught in our streets.'
²⁷ "But he will reply, 'I don't know you or where you come from. Away from me, all you evildoers!'
²⁸ "There will be weeping there, and gnashing of teeth, when you see Abraham, Isaac and Jacob and all the prophets in the kingdom of God, but you yourselves thrown out. ²⁹ People will come from east and west and north and south, and will take their places at the feast in the kingdom of God. ³⁰ Indeed there are those who are last who will be first, and first who will be last."

Luke is back on course and is continuing to record Jesus' journey to Jerusalem. It took him through many towns and villages. Somewhere on the journey someone asked Jesus a question: *"Lord, are only a few people going to be saved?"*

Jesus said nothing about statistics in his reply, but took the opportunity to exhort the questioner to enter through the narrow door that leads to the kingdom without delay.

He emphasised that only a little time remained until the owner of the house will get up and close the door, and many will be left outside knocking and pleading *'Sir, open the door for us.'* But the owner will answer *'I don't know you or where you come from. Away from me, all you evildoers!'*

Jesus had still more to say: *"There will be weeping there, and gnashing of teeth, when you see Abraham, Isaac and Jacob and all the prophets in the kingdom of God, but you yourselves thrown out."*

More than that: *'People will come from east and west and north and south, and will take their places at the feast in the kingdom of God.'*

There was an intended shock in vv. 28 & 29: *'There will be weeping there, and gnashing of teeth, when you see Abraham, Isaac and Jacob and all the prophets in the kingdom of God, but you yourselves thrown out.'*

Not only will Abraham, Isaac and Jacob be there but others also, from all points of the compass, will be in the kingdom along with them. Jesus was speaking about the many Gentile believers who belonged to the kingdom of God.

Jesus ended with these words: *"Indeed there are those who are last who will be first, and first who will be last."* This was a well-known proverb that the hearers would recognise.

Jesus was making it plain that many who expected to enter God's kingdom ('first') will be excluded ('last'), while outsiders who had expected to be excluded ('last') will be included ('first'). Many of Israel's outcasts will be included and many of Israel's elite will be excluded. To be included in God's kingdom means taking one's place at the Messianic banquet that Jesus longed for so much (Luke 22:15 – 16). What an occasion that will be!

The utter humiliation and disappointment of those who are excluded is evident by their *'weeping and gnashing of teeth'*. Matthew also used this expression in his gospel to describe the horrors of eternal punishment. Their sense of loss is well-nigh inexpressible.

THANK YOU, HEAVENLY FATHER:

For sending Your Son into the world to save sinners;
For Jesus' voluntary sacrifice of himself, to put away our sin, a sacrifice the never will need to be repeated;

For the assurance that nothing in all creation shall be able to separate us from the love of God that is in Christ Jesus our Lord (Rom 8:38-39);

IN JESUS' NAME, AMEN

69. Luke 13:31 - 35
Jesus' Sorrow for Jerusalem

Luke 13:31 – 35
At that time some Pharisees came to Jesus and said to him, "Leave this place and go somewhere else. Herod wants to kill you."
³² He replied, "Go tell that fox, 'I will drive out demons and heal people today and tomorrow, and on the third day I will reach my goal.' ³³ In any case, I must keep going today and tomorrow and the next day—for surely no prophet can die outside Jerusalem!
³⁴ "O Jerusalem, Jerusalem, you who kill the prophets and stone those sent to you, how often I have longed to gather your children together, as a hen gathers her chicks under her wings, but you were not willing! ³⁵ Look, your house is left to you desolate. I tell you, you will not see me again until you say, 'Blessed is he who comes in the name of the Lord.'"

For whatever reason some Pharisees wanted Jesus off their territory. They disguised their request in what seemed to be concern for his safety! *'Herod wants to kill you'*, they said (v. 31).

In Jesus' reply he gave Herod a one-word character reference: he called him *'a fox'*. Most people know that foxes are renowned for their cunning.

Jesus was not in the least concerned whether Herod knew his plans and whereabouts. He gave the Pharisees a message for Herod: *'Go tell that fox, 'I will drive out demons and heal people today and tomorrow, and on the third day I will reach my goal' (v. 32)*. In other words, I have no plans to stop what I am doing.

Then for the Pharisees' enlightenment Jesus added: *'In any case, I must keep going today and tomorrow and the next day—for surely no prophet can die outside Jerusalem!'* Jesus' reference to the third day was not a veiled prediction of his resurrection, but was a colloquial Semitic expression for having completed something.

Jesus is really saying that Herod has neither power to interrupt his ministry nor to kill him. When the time comes for Jesus to die, it will be in Jerusalem (v. 33).

Jerusalem, Israel's capital and holy city had a large place in Jesus' heart. In this lament (vv. 34-35) he pours out his heart's desire for its salvation, but alas, the city's window of opportunity was closing and its days were numbered

³⁴ "O Jerusalem, Jerusalem, you who kill the prophets and stone those sent to you, how often I have longed to gather your children together, as a hen gathers her chicks under her wings, but you were not willing!"

Jesus thought of the city's spiritual privileges: *'O Jerusalem, Jerusalem, you who kill the prophets and stone those sent to you.'* No one knew the city's spiritual history like he did.

The contrast in the lament is between Jesus' desire: *'How often I have longed to gather your children together, as a hen gathers her chicks under her wings'* and the city's stubborn rejection of him: *'But you were not willing!'*

The city's future lay heavily on his mind: *'Look, your house is left to you desolate. I tell you, you will not see me again until you say, 'Blessed is he who comes in the name of the Lord.'*

The crowds in Jerusalem would welcome Jesus' triumphal entry into the city on what has become known as Palm Sunday *(19:28-44)*. The city would be completely destroyed by the Roman armies in AD 68-70 and be left desolate.

Therefore it seems that Jesus was not thinking of entering Jerusalem before his death, but was looking down the years to his coming again when he will return to the world in clouds of glory.

Alas, those who then would be saying, *'Blessed is he who comes in the name of the Lord'* would be saying it too late.

Psalm 118:28 *'Blessed is he who comes in the name of the Lord.'*

Rev 1:7 *Look, he is coming with the clouds, and every eye will see him, even those who pierced him; and all the peoples of the earth will mourn because of him.*

THANK YOU, HEAVENLY FATHER:

For Your complete knowledge of all things in heaven above and on the earth beneath;
For Your pleasure in Jesus Your Son as he walked in harmony with your will while on earth;
For the love of Jesus for sinners: its dimensions are beyond human comprehension;
For the certainty of the Second Coming of Jesus, in power and glory when every eye shall see him, even those who pierced him;

IN JESUS' NAME, AMEN

70. Luke 14:1 - 14
Jesus at a Pharisee's House

Luke 14:1 – 6 (ANIV)
One Sabbath, when Jesus went to eat in the house of a prominent Pharisee, he was being carefully watched. ² There in front of him was a man suffering from dropsy. ³ Jesus asked the Pharisees and experts in the law, "Is it lawful to heal on the Sabbath or not?" ⁴ But they remained silent. So taking hold of the man, he healed him and sent him away.

⁵ Then he asked them, "If one of you has a son or an ox that falls into a well on the Sabbath day, will you not immediately pull him out?" ⁶ And they had nothing to say.

It appears that there were two groups of people at this feast in a Pharisee's house: there were lawyers and there were other guests. It is difficult to see how there was much cordiality at the feast because it says that Jesus '*was being carefully watched*'. The word means to *observe carefully*, and it has been used in the sense of *watching in espionage*.

There has been quite a bit of discussion about the presence of the sick man in v. 2. He had dropsy, a disease in which watery fluid collects in the body. Some are adamant that the Pharisees had deliberately arranged the scene. Others say that the man was responsible for his own actions, and therefore for his being there. Jesus could read everyone around him like a book, and was well aware that his healing of this man on a Sabbath would bring everything out into the open.

Jesus decided to 'break the ice'. He asked the Pharisees and experts in the law, *"Is it lawful to heal on the Sabbath or not?"* probably expecting an outburst of opposition in response. Nobody spoke. Very well then, Jesus said nothing either. He reached out and took hold of the man, healed him instantly, and the man walked away.

Jesus justified his action by giving examples of less lofty Sabbath deeds that even his opponents would deem legitimate, such as rescuing a child (a son) or an ox that fell into a well on the Sabbath day.

His question to them was: *'will you not immediately pull him out?'* Still nobody spoke a word – *because they had nothing to say! (v. 6).*

Luke 14:7 – 11
When he noticed how the guests picked the places of honour at the table, he told them this parable:⁸ "When someone invites you to a wedding feast, do not take the place of honour, for a person more distinguished than you may have been invited. ⁹ If so, the host who invited both of you will come and say to you, 'Give this man your seat.' Then, humiliated, you will have to take the least important place. ¹⁰ But when you are invited, take the lowest place, so that when your host comes, he will say to you, 'Friend, move up to a better place.' Then you will be honoured in the presence of all your fellow guests. ¹¹ For everyone who exalts himself will be humbled, and he who humbles himself will be exalted."

Jesus next addressed the guests who had been invited to the meal. He noticed how they had rushed to occupy the most prominent seats and positions of honour. Jesus asked: *'What if a guest more important than you has been invited?'* When that guest comes along the host will ask you to vacate the seat you had taken because it had been reserved for the newcomer. Imagine how embarrassed you will feel as you move down the table to a place of less importance. Christ's ethic is that you occupy a lower place first. From there the host may invite you to a better place. Then you will be seen to be a guest of honour in the presence of everyone else. Exalting yourself can be followed by a comedown! Whereas modesty and humility can be followed by promotion (v. 11).

Luke 14:12 – 14
Then Jesus said to his host, "When you give a luncheon or dinner, do not invite your friends, your brothers or relatives, or your rich neighbours; if you do, they may invite you back and so you will be repaid. ¹³ But when you give a banquet, invite the poor, the crippled, the lame, the blind, ¹⁴ and you will be blessed. Although they cannot repay you, you will be repaid at the resurrection of the righteous."

Finally Jesus addressed the host. Hospitality of the flattering, tit-for-tat kind was too much in vogue. They knew very well what Jesus was describing. In return your guests will invite you to their home and so your original hospitality will be repaid. Then Jesus issued a challenge: *'But when you give a banquet, invite the poor, the crippled, the lame, the blind, **14** and you will be blessed. Although they cannot repay you, you will be repaid at the resurrection of the righteous.'* You do not need them to *'repay'* you because they don't have the means to do so. There will be a blessing for this kind of hospitality in the future at the resurrection (v. 14).

THANK YOU, HEAVENLY FATHER:

For the lessons of true humility and true hospitality taught by Jesus in the home of the Pharisee;
For Christ's promise that even a cup of cold water given in his name will not lose its reward (Matthew 10:42);

IN JESUS' NAME, AMEN

71. Luke 14:15 - 24
The Parable of the Great Banquet

Luke 14:15 – 24
When one of those at the table with him heard this, he said to Jesus, "Blessed is the man who will eat at the feast in the kingdom of God."

[16] Jesus replied: "A certain man was preparing a great banquet and invited many guests. [17] At the time of the banquet he sent his servant to tell those who had been invited, 'Come, for everything is now ready.'

[18] "But they all alike began to make excuses. The first said, 'I have just bought a field, and I must go and see it. Please excuse me.'

[19] "Another said, 'I have just bought five yoke of oxen, and I'm on my way to try them out. Please excuse me.'

[20] "Still another said, 'I have just got married, so I can't come.'

[21] "The servant came back and reported this to his master. Then the owner of the house became angry and ordered his servant, 'Go out quickly into the streets and alleys of the town and bring in the poor, the crippled, the blind and the lame.'

[22] "'Sir,' the servant said, 'what you ordered has been done, but there is still room.'

[23] "Then the master told his servant, 'Go out to the roads and country lanes and make them come in, so that my house will be full. [24] I tell you, not one of those men who were invited will get a taste of my banquet.'"

We are still at table in the Pharisee's house: vv. 1-14 were part one of the story. It would seem that at least one of the guests had found his tongue and made a positive comment to Jesus: *"Blessed is the man who will eat at the feast in the kingdom of God."* In reply Jesus spoke a parable to which all the other guests could listen in.

So at least one man had been alert to all that had happened in the Pharisee's house in part one. His remark about the blessedness of sharing in the Messianic banquet picks up the motif of the banquet and the resurrection at the last day (v. 7-14). There is also a prominent link between *'invite the poor, the crippled, the lame, the blind'* of v. 13 and v. 21 with the master's endeavour to have every seat taken at his banquet and so he ordered his servant to *'bring in the poor, the crippled, the blind and the lame.'*

We need to follow the flow of the parable and, if we are observant, we shall not miss a single point of importance.

A great banquet was given. vv. 15-16

(THINK: Messianic banquet/God's kingdom had now come).

When everything was ready a servant was sent out to call those who were invited to *'Come, for all things are ready.'*

The invited guests refused to come. vv. 17, 18, 19 & 20

(THINK: The Pharisees and the religious elite of Israel had rejected the Messiah and his teachings).

The outcasts of society were brought in as guests to the banquet. vv. 21 & 22

(THINK: The least in Israel entered God's kingdom instead of the religious elite).

Even more distant outcasts were brought in as guests. vv. 23

(THINK: The Gentiles entered God's kingdom instead of Israel). The Master wanted his house to be full.

The exclusion of the original invited guests is emphasized in verse 24: *'I tell you, not one of those men who were invited will get a taste of my banquet.'*

We do not know if any of the Pharisees or other guests saw themselves in the parable. In telling the parable Jesus had been holding up a mirror to them, in which they could see themselves.

The excluded guests did not want to come anyway: recall their *'excuses'* in vv. 18-20, but there was great significance in the reality part.

When Jesus portrayed their refusals he was representing people who foolishly declined God's gracious offer of salvation. Those who do not become part of the present kingdom will not share in its future consummation.

THANK YOU, HEAVENLY FATHER:

For the privilege of having heard the voice of Jesus calling us to repentance and to faith in him, and for the fact that he not only called us once but many times;
For all believers around the world who are faithfully witnessing and evangelising by every means that You are pleased to bless to the salvation of many;
For the petitions that Jesus gave us in the his model prayer; we pray them here and now: *'Your kingdom come, Your will be done on earth as it is in heaven';*
For the confidence that burns in our hearts when we pray: *for Yours is the kingdom, the power and the glory, for ever. Amen.*

IN JESUS' NAME, AMEN

72. Luke 14:25 - 35
The Cost of Being a Disciple

Luke 14:25 – 35
Large crowds were travelling with Jesus, and turning to them he said:²⁶ "If anyone comes to me and does not hate his father and mother, his wife and children, his brothers and sisters—yes, even his own life—he cannot be my disciple. ²⁷ And anyone who does not carry his cross and follow me cannot be my disciple."

²⁸ "Suppose one of you wants to build a tower. Will he not first sit down and estimate the cost to see if he has enough money to complete it? ²⁹ For if he lays the foundation and is not able to finish it, everyone who sees it will ridicule him, ³⁰ saying, 'This fellow began to build and was not able to finish.'"

³¹ "Or suppose a king is about to go to war against another king. Will he not first sit down and consider whether he is able with ten thousand men to oppose the one coming against him with twenty thousand? ³² If he is not able, he will send a delegation while the other is still a long way off and will ask for terms of peace. ³³ In the same way, any of you who does not give up everything he has cannot be my disciple."

³⁴ "Salt is good, but if it loses its saltiness, how can it be made salty again? ³⁵ It is fit neither for the soil nor for the manure heap; it is thrown out."

"He who has ears to hear, let him hear."

The fact that large crowds were following Jesus did not mean that they had all become disciples. This is why we find him spelling out the cost of discipleship at various places in his ministry.

"If anyone comes to me and does not hate his father and mother, his wife and children, his brothers and sisters—yes, even his own life—he cannot be my disciple. ²⁷ And anyone who does not carry his cross and follow me cannot be my disciple."

Jesus is answering a question that a Roman jailer in Philippi would ask some years later: *'What must I do to be saved?' (Acts 16:31)*

The first condition is that one must love and obey Jesus more than anyone else, even our own families. Jesus is not demanding blind, raging hatred of one's family. Being Jesus' disciple means primary allegiance to him. No one and nothing can usurp his supreme position. This command is absolute, and cannot be tossed aside because we don't particularly like it.

The second condition is illustrated by a call to suffering, to martyrdom if necessary. Jesus spoke of this as *'taking up our cross and following him'*. Again we cannot toss this condition aside.

Response to these two conditions is also expressed in the Christian confession *'Jesus Christ is Lord.'* Later when Rome persecuted Christians they were required to confess that *'Caesar is Lord'*. Christians refused and, confessing that *'Jesus Christ is Lord'*, went to their deaths. Jesus' conditions of discipleship still have not changed.

In vv. 26-27 disciples must be able to follow.
Jesus provides two further illustrations of 'counting the cost'.

In vv. 28-30 builders must be able to finish. Scattered around the world are unfinished projects usually called 'follies'. They represent someone's bright idea, for example to build a tower, but without the resources to finish. For as long as any trace of a folly remains people will say, *'This fellow began to build and was not able to finish.'*

In vv. 31-32 kings must be able to fight. Any king going to war must count the cost. Will his ten thousand men be able to defeat his adversary who has twenty thousand men? If he has any doubts of success then he would be well advised to negotiate a peace treaty, and so avoid a terrible loss of life in both armies. That is not cowardice, it is common sense.

In v. 33 Jesus repeats the cost of discipleship. *'In the same way, any of you who does not give up everything he has cannot be my disciple'*. An old-fashioned term for this was *'full surrender'*. There is nothing old-fashioned about it. It still applies.

When salt is mentioned we think of food and table salt. Salt from the Dead Sea, if carelessly processed, would become insipid or poor tasting. If that happened it became an environmental hazard, for it would ruin soil or even a manure heap. Bad salt is worth nothing and is only for throwing out. Jesus' hearers understood and did not miss his meaning.

"He who has ears to hear, let him hear." Being a Christian means following Jesus. No less.

Thank You, Heavenly Father:

For the clarity of Jesus' teaching on discipleship, then and now;
For the privilege of giving Jesus *'what we cannot keep to gain what we cannot lose';* (Jim Saint, martyred missionary to the Auca Indians)
For *'the surpassing greatness of knowing Jesus Christ my Lord, for whose sake I have lost all things'.* (Apostle Paul in Phil 3:8)

In Jesus' Name, Amen

73. Luke 15:1 - 33
The Parables of the Lost Sheep, the Lost Coin, and the Gracious Father

Luke 15:1 – 7

Now the tax collectors and "sinners" were all gathering round to hear him.² But the Pharisees and the teachers of the law muttered, "This man welcomes sinners, and eats with them."

As always the common people heard Jesus gladly. But the critics were present and expressing their disgust at the company that Jesus kept. Their complaint has become a well-known gospel text: *"This man welcomes sinners, and eats with them."* That is good news.

Jesus responded to the critics and told three parables which are connected by a common theme:

THE JOY OF THE LOST BEING FOUND.

Then Jesus told them this parable:⁴ "Suppose one of you has a hundred sheep and loses one of them. Does he not leave the ninety-nine in the open country and go after the lost sheep until he finds it? ⁵ And when he finds it, he joyfully puts it on his shoulders ⁶ and goes home. Then he calls his friends and neighbours together and says, 'Rejoice with me; I have found my lost sheep.' ⁷ I tell you that in the same way there will be more rejoicing in heaven over one sinner who repents than over ninety-nine righteous persons who do not need to repent."

Shepherds in the Middle East are not like Australian sheep-farmers of today. They didn't own thousands of acres of ranch land, nor did they number their flocks in thousands. A shepherd in Jesus' time knew each of his sheep by name. In that 'below the bread line' economy a shepherd placed great value on his sheep and went to great lengths to provide for their welfare. So at the end of day the Shepherd would literally become *'the door of the sheep'* as he sat in the opening to the sheepfold and 'rod-ing' the sheep as they passed him one by one. Psalm 23, properly understood, says a lot about shepherds and their methods. To lose one sheep out of one hundred was a significant loss.

For the shepherd the lost sheep had commercial value. He made a thorough search for it placing himself in danger of life and limb going over hill and dale. When he found it and carried it home on his shoulders. Then he called his friends and neighbours to rejoice with him. The sheep that was lost had been found.

'I tell you that in the same way there will be more rejoicing in heaven over one sinner who repents than over ninety-nine righteous persons who do not need to repent' (v. 7).

Luke 15:8 - 10
"Or suppose a woman has ten silver coins and loses one. Does she not light a lamp, sweep the house and search carefully until she finds it? ⁹ And when she finds it, she calls her friends and neighbours together and says, 'Rejoice with me; I have found my lost coin.' ¹⁰ In the same way, I tell you, there is rejoicing in the presence of the angels of God over one sinner who repents."

The scene changes to a woman doing her housework. She was in the habit of wearing ten coins on a cord around her head. It had probably been a wedding present. But one day she discovers to her horror that one coin is missing and so everything else is put 'on hold' until she finds the lost coin. We can see her looking everywhere, sweeping and searching in v. 8. What was all the fuss about? It's not difficult to understand her.

For the woman the lost coin had sentimental value. The story had a happy ending: the coin was found, she shared her joy with her neighbours and they came and rejoiced with her.

10 "In the same way, I tell you, there is rejoicing in the presence of the angels of God over one sinner who repents."

Luke 15:11 – 32

Jesus continued: "There was a man who had two sons. ¹² The younger one said to his father, 'Father, give me my share of the estate.' So he divided his property between them.

¹³ "Not long after that, the younger son got together all he had, set off for a distant country and there squandered his wealth in wild living. ¹⁴ After he had spent everything, there was a severe famine in that whole country, and he began to be in need. ¹⁵ So he went and hired himself out to a citizen of that country, who sent him to his fields to feed pigs. ¹⁶ He longed to fill his stomach with the pods that the pigs were eating, but no-one gave him anything.

¹⁷ "When he came to his senses, he said, 'How many of my father's hired men have food to spare, and here I am starving to death! ¹⁸ I will set out and go back to my father and say to him: Father, I have sinned against heaven and against you. ¹⁹ I am no longer worthy to be called your son; make me like one of your hired men.' ²⁰ So he got up and went to his father. "*But while he was still a long way off, his father saw him and was filled with compassion for him; he ran to his son, threw his arms around him and kissed him.*

²¹ "The son said to him, 'Father, I have sinned against heaven and against you. I am no longer worthy to be called your son.'

²² "But the father said to his servants, 'Quick! Bring the best robe and put it on him. Put a ring on his finger and sandals on his feet. ²³ Bring the fattened calf and kill it. Let's have a feast and celebrate. ²⁴ For this son of mine was dead and is alive again; he was lost and is found.' So they began to celebrate.

²⁵ "Meanwhile, the older son was in the field. When he came near the house, he heard music and dancing. ²⁶ So he called one of the servants and asked him what was going on. ²⁷ 'Your brother has come,' he replied, 'and your father has killed the fattened calf because he has him back safe and sound.'

²⁸ "The older brother became angry and refused to go in. So his father went out and pleaded with him. ²⁹ But he answered his father, 'Look! All these years I've been slaving for you and never disobeyed your orders. Yet you never gave me even a young goat so I could celebrate with my friends. ³⁰ But when this son of yours who has

squandered your property with prostitutes comes home, you kill the fattened calf for him!'
³¹ "'My son,' the father said, 'you are always with me, and everything I have is yours. ³² But we had to celebrate and be glad, because this brother of yours was dead and is alive again; he was lost and is found.'"

Shall we call this the Parable of *'the Lost Son'*, or *'the Gracious Father'*, or *'the Lost Son who stayed at Home'*? The emphasis of the three parables shines through more brightly than before: the joy of the lost being found.

The details of the parable are mostly local colour, but the human aspects of the story are real enough and pull at our heart-strings. The younger son leaving home without a forwarding address, ending up penniless and in want is a scenario that has been repeated in every generation. In time he realised that his circumstances were due entirely his own foolishness, and he resolved to return home. There the watching father looked down the road every day as he waited and hoped to see his boy coming up the road

For the father his lost son had human value. When father and son ran into each other's arms, the boy trying to express his repentance and the father pouring out words of forgiveness, it was a sight to behold! The father's joy knew no bounds.

The father said to his servants, 'Quick! Bring the best robe and put it on him. Put a ring on his finger and sandals on his feet. ²³ Bring the fattened calf and kill it. Let's have a feast and celebrate. ²⁴ For this son of mine was dead and is alive again; he was lost and is found.' So they began to celebrate.'

But there was an elder son (vv. 11-12 & vv 25-32). If we reflect for a moment we ask ourselves: 'Who does he represent?' Well, as so often happened in Jesus' word-pictures he had been holding up a mirror in which everyone in the crowd could see themselves. The *'tax collectors'* and *'sinners'* could see themselves as *'lost property'*. They knew it and felt it, having been despised by the religious elite for as long as they could remember. This was why they appreciated Jesus' love for them so much. Who does the elder brother represent? Look back to v. 2. and we shall find a clue. What was the complaint of the Pharisees?

"This man welcomes sinners, and eats with them."

Now read vv. 25 to 30 and hear the elder son speaking most disrespectfully to his father. He finds fault after fault with how his father had behaved toward him, forgetting that he owed his father everything that he had. Don't you catch an echo from v. 2? Read the father's final pleas to his firstborn son:

'My son,' the father said, 'you are always with me, and everything I have is yours. 32 But we had to celebrate and be glad, because this brother of yours was dead and is alive again; he was lost and is found.'

The Pharisees could find fault with Jesus because of the company he kept, the elder son could criticise his father's provision for him most ungraciously and ungratefully, but nothing in the whole wide world could prevent the father rejoicing that what was lost had been found.

The lost of Israel were finding forgiveness, sinners were finding salvation. It was time to rejoice. In heaven God rejoiced. This is what life in the kingdom of God is all about. Will we be the church of the elder brother or the church of the loving Father?

THANK YOU, HEAVENLY FATHER:

For all that Jesus suffered when he came into the world to seek and to save that which was lost;
For the joy we experience when lost ones, for whom Jesus had been seeking and we have been praying for so long, are found;

IN JESUS' NAME, AMEN

74. Luke 16:1 - 15
The Parable of the Shrewd Manager

Luke 16:1 –8a
Jesus told his disciples: "There was a rich man whose manager was accused of wasting his possessions. ² So he called him in and asked him, 'What is this I hear about you? Give an account of your management, because you cannot be manager any longer.'

³ "The manager said to himself, 'What shall I do now? My master is taking away my job. I'm not strong enough to dig, and I'm ashamed to beg—⁴ I know what I'll do so that, when I lose my job here, people will welcome me into their houses.

⁵ "So he called in each one of his master's debtors. He asked the first, 'How much do you owe my master?' ⁶ "'Eight hundred gallons of olive oil,' he replied. "The manager told him, 'Take your bill, sit down quickly, and make it four hundred.'

⁷ "Then he asked the second, 'And how much do you owe?' 'A thousand bushels of wheat,' he replied." He told him, 'Take your bill and make it eight hundred.'

⁸ "The master commended the dishonest manager because he had acted shrewdly."

This narrative bristles with questions. It is so unlike Jesus' usual stories and the lessons he taught from them. Let's identify the characters.

Part 1: There is trouble ahead!
v. 1 a rich man (who owned an estate and was an absentee landlord).

v. 1 The rich man's manager, or land-steward, was accused of wasting / squandering his master's possessions. Presumably the employer had made the accusation. Before dismissing the manager he demanded to see the ledgers, so that he could find out where and how money had been siphoned away. The manager knows he is in trouble.

Part 2: The Manager has an idea vv. 3-7
He is thinking of yet another way to line his pockets before being dismissed. He called in

tenants of the estate who, for whatever reasons, had unpaid debts. He thought: *'when I'm out a job here I'll still have friends in the community'* (vv. 3-4)

The first debtor had his debt of 800 gallons of olive oil reduced to 400.

Another debtor had his debt of 1000 bushels of wheat reduced to 800.

Part 3: The Master commended the dishonest manager because he acted shrewdly, even after being found guilty and been dismissed. The manager's ingenious way of thinking ahead to extract still more money from the estate astonished the master. So much that he actually commended the dishonest manager for his craftiness and initiative even after his wrongdoing was discovered and he was in disgrace.

The above three points seem to sum up the narrative. Here comes the really difficult part.

How are we to understand the use that Jesus made of the behaviour of the dishonest manager?

Luke 16:8b - 13

"For the people of this world are more shrewd in dealing with their own kind than are the people of the light. ⁹ I tell you, use worldly wealth to gain friends for yourselves, so that when it is gone, you will be welcomed into eternal dwellings."

¹⁰ "Whoever can be trusted with very little can also be trusted with much, and whoever is dishonest with very little will also be dishonest with much. ¹¹ So if you have not been trustworthy in handling worldly wealth, who will trust you with true riches? ¹² And if you have not been trustworthy with someone else's property, who will give you property of your own?"

¹³ "No servant can serve two masters. Either he will hate the one and love the other, or he will be devoted to the one and despise the other. You cannot serve both God and Money."

¹⁴ The Pharisees, who loved money, heard all this and were sneering at Jesus. ¹⁵ He said to them, "You are the ones who justify yourselves in the eyes of men, but God knows your hearts. What is highly valued among men is detestable in God's sight."

Jesus makes a number of observations about the business world.

The dishonest manager used money (even if it wasn't his own) to make friends with a view to calling on them if the need ever arose. *⁴ I know what I'll do so that, when I lose my job here, people will welcome me into their houses.* This was his way of laying-by for a rainy day.

The people of this world could teach believers a thing or two about the use of worldly wealth – but without stooping to wrong-doing. This means *'Would that true believers were as clever in spiritual matters as are these crooks in plying their trade.'* (v. 8)

The diligence of worldly men about the things of time, should put to shame the carelessness of professing Christians about the things of eternity. (v. 9)

Jesus is here making it clear that he is not approving or excusing dishonesty and unfaithfulness by pointing to the matter of character i.e. loyalty and dependability (vv. 10 – 13). These are things that an employer expects from his employees. Whoever we are, believers or pagans, if we are not faithful in little we will not be faithful in much.

Again, whoever we are, whether believers or pagans, we cannot do the impossible i.e. at one and the same time serve two masters (v. 13) It is impossible to serve God and Money.

Luke 16:14 - 16

The Pharisees, who loved money, heard all this and were sneering at Jesus. ¹⁵ He said to them, "You are the ones who justify yourselves in the eyes of men, but God knows your hearts. What is highly valued among men is detestable in God's sight.

The Pharisees were smiling derisively at Jesus. Can't you see a *'we know better than you; you don't know what you are talking about'* look on their faces? Jesus, ostensibly talking to his disciples, knew that the Pharisees had heard his every word, and he knew that he had injured their pride.

In his closing sentences Jesus unmasked them completely. Their righteousness was only a façade. He had painted them in their true colours.

THANK YOU, HEAVENLY FATHER:

For the searchlight of Your written Word, penetrating our innermost
 being and testing our motives;
For the many useful spiritual lessons we can learn from the people
 and things in the world around us; open our eyes to see;
For Your many promises that You will provide our needs, without us
 stooping to methods that dishonour You;
For the greatest gift of all, Your indescribable gift of Jesus Your Son;

IN JESUS' NAME, AMEN

75. Luke 16:16 - 18
Additional Teachings

We wonder why Luke put these three statements together because we cannot see any connection between what preceded them and what follows them.

Luke 16:16
"The Law and the Prophets were proclaimed until John. Since that time, the good news of the kingdom of God is being preached, and everyone is forcing his way into it."

Jesus' first statement seems to be a thinly disguised rebuke, but to whom? He is referring to the great preaching ministries of the Old Testament until John the Baptist appeared preaching the coming of the kingdom of God. God had given him a fruitful ministry which resulted in many people being prepared for the coming of Jesus who also preached the kingdom of God. People were pressing into it, but the Pharisees, who were supposed to be the leaders of righteousness, stood outside the gates and resisted it. Their religion and self-righteousness prevented them entering.

Luke 16:17
"It is easier for heaven and earth to disappear than for the least stroke of a pen to drop out of the Law."

Jesus used hyperbole to demonstrate how strongly he felt that the Old Testament scriptures would be fulfilled. He was not saying that parts of letters, letters, or even individual words would be fulfilled. We can illustrate what Jesus meant by his reference to *'the least stroke of a pen'*. In the Hebrew language some letters are distinguished only by a small mark (somewhat like the difference between the uppercase letters Q and O in English.) – but smaller than that. The publicans and sinners in their penitence were more responsive to the Scriptures than the Pharisees with their pride.

Luke 16:18

"Anyone who divorces his wife and marries another woman commits adultery, and the man who marries a divorced woman commits adultery."

Why raise the subject of divorce and remarriage? Unless divorce and the allied problems of remarriage were among the things that Jesus had denounced in vv. 15 and 17. The Pharisees and Scribes were in confusion about the laws of divorce and remarriage. In fact, Judaism was divided on these subjects. The result of the confusion was that women were very insecure and could be divorced by their husbands on a mere whim.

Aware of the outlook of some of the rabbis the Lord spoke of divorce and endorsed certain principles which they had ignored.

Matthew 5:31-32.
"It has been said, 'Anyone who divorces his wife must give her a certificate of divorce.' ³² But I tell you that anyone who divorces his wife, except for marital unfaithfulness, causes her to become an adulteress, and anyone who marries the divorced woman commits adultery."

THANK YOU, HEAVENLY FATHER:

For this era of grace when the door to the kingdom of God is still open,
    and sinners may enter through faith alone in Jesus Christ;
For the gift of Holy Scripture, divinely inspired and miraculously
    preserved so that we read it, obey it and circulate it;
For Your servants to whom you have given language skills so that
    the work of Bible translation continues daily;
For the many languages of earth in which Your word is available;
For creating mankind to live in families and for loving mothers
    and fathers;
For the gift of marriage and procreation, love and companionship;

IN JESUS' NAME, AMEN

76. Luke 16:19 - 31
The Rich Man and Lazarus

Luke 16:19 – 31
"There was a rich man who was dressed in purple and fine linen and lived in luxury every day. [20] *At his gate was laid a beggar named Lazarus, covered with sores* [21] *and longing to eat what fell from the rich man's table. Even the dogs came and licked his sores.*

[22] *"The time came when the beggar died and the angels carried him to Abraham's side. The rich man also died and was buried.* [23] *In hell, where he was in torment, he looked up and saw Abraham far away, with Lazarus by his side.* [24] *So he called to him, 'Father Abraham, have pity on me and send Lazarus to dip the tip of his finger in water and cool my tongue, because I am in agony in this fire.'*

[25] *"But Abraham replied, 'Son, remember that in your lifetime you received your good things, while Lazarus received bad things, but now he is comforted here and you are in agony.* [26] *And besides all this, between us and you a great chasm has been fixed, so that those who want to go from here to you cannot, nor can anyone cross over from there to us.'*

[27] *"He answered, 'Then I beg you, father, send Lazarus to my father's house,* [28] *for I have five brothers. Let him warn them, so that they will not also come to this place of torment.'*

[29] *"Abraham replied, 'They have Moses and the Prophets; let them listen to them.'*

[30] *"'No, father Abraham,' he said, 'but if someone from the dead goes to them, they will repent.'*

[31] *"He said to him, 'If they do not listen to Moses and the Prophets, they will not be convinced even if someone rises from the dead.'"*

The important thing to remember as we think about this section of Luke's gospel is that this is a parable. The characters are given names, but the narrative is cast as a parable with the general introduction *'There was a rich man. . . .'* It is also about the life to come. Someone entitled it *'Place of Comfort; Place of Torment'*. That is an accurate title.

This is one of the clearest biblical passages indicating a clear separation between the righteous dead and the unbelieving dead. However we must be careful not to build doctrine on parables. Parables contain a large amount of local colour. Their emphases can come at the beginning, or the middle or the end. Generally speaking a parable has one emphasis which it makes clearly. That is what we need to look for.

There was a vast difference between the Rich Man and Lazarus in their lifetimes (v 20 & 21).
The rich man was dressed in purple and fine linen and lived in luxury every day. At his gate was laid a beggar named Lazarus, covered with sores and longing to eat what fell from the rich man's table. Even the dogs came and licked his sores.

The rich man lived in luxury every day. Poor Lazarus was laid at his gate in the hope that some charity might be shown to him but charity was scarce. He longed to eat what fell from the rich man's table. He was a beggar. He was also a sick man. The dogs of the street licked his sores. There is said to be healing in the lick from a dog's tongue, but Lazarus was very sick. The rich man's dogs were better fed.

There was a vast difference between the Rich Man and Lazarus in their deaths (vv 22 & 23).
"The time came when the beggar died and the angels carried him to Abraham's side. The rich man also died and was buried. [23] In hell, where he was in torment, he looked up and saw Abraham far away, with Lazarus by his side."

Jesus did not say whether Lazarus had the dignity of a funeral and a burial. Jesus included the detail that when the Rich Man died, he was buried.

There was a vast difference between the Rich Man and Lazarus in their eternal destinies.

The angels had carried Lazarus to Abraham's side (v. 22).The phrase *'at Abraham's side'* is a Jewish expression which meant being in *'GanEden'* (Paradise) and at the Messianic banquet. Lazarus clearly enjoyed close fellowship with Abraham in the afterlife.

The rich man was *'In hell'* and *'in torment' (v. 23)*. Eternity for Lazarus meant heavenly rest and comfort. For the rich man it meant hell and torment.

Jesus used the word *'hell'* (*hades*) to refer to the rich man's eternal state. *'Hades'* was *the place of the dead* or *the place where the unrighteous dead go*. The parable represents the rich man as being able to see Lazarus in heaven, but does any other scripture teach this? I think not. Jesus included this detail to make the parable work. It is a certainty that heaven and hell are far apart, separated by a great unbridgeable chasm which is uncrossable. In hell the rich man prayed! First, he prayed that Lazarus be sent *'to dip the tip of his finger in water and cool my tongue, because I am tormented in this fire' (v. 24)*. Abraham answered that his request could not be granted (vv. 25-26)

The rich man had a second prayer request: *'Then I beg you, father, send Lazarus to my father's house, for I have five brothers. Let him warn them, so that they will not also come to this place of torment' (vv 27-28)*.

He prayed for his five brothers asking that Lazarus be sent to warn them about hell. Abraham answered that what he asked was impossible (vv. 25 & 26), and for a very good reason.

"Abraham replied, 'They have Moses and the Prophets; let them listen to them.' [30] *"'No, father Abraham,' he said, 'but if someone from the dead goes to them, they will repent.'* [31] *"He said to him, 'If they do not listen to Moses and the Prophets, they will not be convinced even if someone rises from the dead.'"*

Why did Lazarus go to *'Abraham's bosom'* (heaven)? Because at a time known only to God, he had *'pressed into the kingdom'*.

The rich man's fate was not due to his being rich, but because he had never repented.

Was there a reverent silence when Jesus finished speaking? A lot of people had learned a lot of biblical truth from his teaching.

THANK YOU, HEAVENLY FATHER:

For revealing the way of salvation to us through Your Word and through Your Son Jesus;
For what Jesus revealed in telling the story of the Rich Man and Lazarus so that his listeners, and we today, may *'press into the kingdom'* and avoid hell, as a matter of urgency;
For every faithful pastor, evangelist, Sunday school teacher and witness who today will speak to other people about Jesus;
For all those godly men and women who influenced us to follow Jesus;
For the many assurances of salvation that we find in the scriptures;

IN JESUS' NAME, AMEN

77. Luke 17:1 - 10
Sin, Faith, Duty

The NIV section heading is convenient, but it tends to hide the value of each section. Sin, faith, duty are acceptable headings. Each part of this section is capable of standing alone and each has a clear lesson to teach us

Luke 17:1 – 3
Jesus said to his disciples: "Things that cause people to sin are bound to come, but woe to that person through whom they come. ² It would be better for him to be thrown into the sea with a millstone tied round his neck than for him to cause one of these little ones to sin. ³So watch yourselves.

We are responsible for what we do and say before others. The key words are in v. 3 **'So watch yourselves.'** Jesus drew the attention of the disciples to a common human fault: how people cause one another to stumble. Jesus used the word *'skandala'* meaning things that cause people to sin. (Guess which English word comes from *'skandala'*.)

He is referring to anything that might cause believers (the *'little ones'* of v. 2) to lose or lessen their allegiance to Jesus. Jesus views this as a serious matter: *better for us to be drowned than to cause another person to stumble!* It is easy to blame other people for being stumbling-blocks. We need to *'watch ourselves'*. We must behave and speak responsibly before others.

Luke 17:3b – 6
"If your brother sins, rebuke him, and if he repents, forgive him. ⁴ If he sins against you seven times in a day, and seven times comes back to you and says, 'I repent,' forgive him." ⁵The apostles said to the Lord, "Increase our faith!"

⁶ He replied, "If you have faith as small as a mustard seed, you can say to this mulberry tree, 'Be uprooted and planted in the sea,' and it will obey you."

To restore a relationship quickly should be the desire of every believer. How often should believers forgive each other? How often should I forgive my brother? This is the issue raised in this section. It is obvious that Jesus' words in v. 4 mean that our forgiveness should be unlimited. Small wonder that the disciples responded with what may have been an impromptu prayer: *'Increase our faith!'* which means *'Give us a greater faith than we already have.'*

Jesus' answer in v. 6 was the answer to the disciples' prayer. Literally, *'If you have faith, you could'*. The point at issue is not the frequency or infrequency of my forgiveness, but the restoration of my brother. Let's keep the main thing the main thing!

Luke 17:7 - 10

"Suppose one of you had a servant ploughing or looking after the sheep. Would he say to the servant when he comes in from the field, 'Come along now and sit down to eat'? ⁸ Would he not rather say, 'Prepare my supper, get yourself ready and wait on me while I eat and drink; after that you may eat and drink'? ⁹ Would he thank the servant because he did what he was told to do? ¹⁰ So you also, when you have done everything you were told to do, should say, 'We are unworthy servants; we have only done our duty.'"

Faithfulness in doing our duty does not require a compliment. This servant was the farmer's only slave. He not only ploughed the fields and looked after the sheep, but prepared his master's food as well. It was his lot, it was his job, and he accepted it without murmuring.

It was unthinkable that when the servant came in from the farmyard at night that the master would put on an apron, tell the servant to sit down and proceed to prepare supper for him! We can imagine those listening to Jesus being highly amused at the very idea of it (v. 7). No, the servant would prepare the master's supper and then the master would eat first (v. 8). That was *'the pecking order'* (no pun intended) in the master's kitchen. Here is the line that teaches the lesson: *Would he thank the servant because he did what he was told to do? (v. 9)*

So you also, when you have done everything you were told to do, should say, 'We are unworthy servants; we have only done our duty.'

There is no need to seek compliments for doing our duty for Jesus or for anyone else. If compliments come, well and good! Think rather, of the eternal reward.

THANK YOU, HEAVENLY FATHER:

For the desire the Holy Spirit has placed in our hearts that we should be Christlike in our words and actions;
For the discipline of grace that the Holy Spirit can apply to our lives so that we can forgive others who sin against us, even as we ourselves have been forgiven;
For the privilege of being Your servants and for the joy of being in Your service.

IN JESUS NAME, AMEN

78. Luke 17:11 - 19
Ten Healed of Leprosy

Luke 17:11 – 19
Now on his way to Jerusalem, Jesus travelled along the border between Samaria and Galilee. [12] As he was going into a village, ten men who had leprosy met him. They stood at a distance [13] and called out in a loud voice, "Jesus, Master, have pity on us!"

[14] When he saw them, he said, "Go, show yourselves to the priests." And as they went, they were cleansed.

[15] One of them, when he saw he was healed, came back, praising God in a loud voice. [16] He threw himself at Jesus' feet and thanked him — and he was a Samaritan.

[17] Jesus asked, "Were not all ten cleansed? Where are the other nine? [18] Was no-one found to return and give praise to God except this foreigner?" [19] Then he said to him, "Rise and go; your faith has made you well."

The border between Samaria and Galilee was a sensitive area at the best of times because relationships between Jews and Samaritans had been strained for centuries. The situation confronting Jesus was not at all political; he was met by no less than ten lepers. They stood at a distance as lepers were required by law to do at all times. That did not deter their purpose. They called in a loud voice: *"Jesus, Master, have pity on us!"* (v. 13)

Jesus' response was immediate. He said, *"Go, show yourselves to the priests."* And as they went, they were cleansed (v. 14). The point is two-fold: first, they would have to obey Jesus' direction; second, to re-enter society they had to be declared clean by a priest (Leviticus 14:1-32).

The precise moment when the healings took place is a secondary matter: *'as they went they were healed.'* Their obedience to Jesus shows a measure of faith on the part of all ten lepers. *'Cleansed'* refers to healing from leprosy.

One of them, when he saw he was healed, came back, praising God in a loud voice. [16] He threw himself at Jesus' feet and thanked him — and he was a Samaritan.

The one leper who returned did three things:**(1)** he was praising God; in a loud voice; **(2)** he threw himself at Jesus' feet; and **(3)** he thanked him. As Luke tells the story he used a clause that is emphatic – *'and he was a Samaritan.'* We catch echoes of the story of the Good Samaritan.

In later years when the young churches were reading the Gospel by Luke they would be excited to read about Jesus' ministry to individual Samaritans. In the Acts the young churches took the gospel to the nations surrounding Israel.

Jesus asked, "Were not all ten cleansed? Where are the other nine? [18] Was no-one found to return and give praise to God except this foreigner?" [19] Then he said to him, "Rise and go; your faith has made you well."

Jesus asked three rhetorical questions:**(1)** Were not all ten cleansed? **(2)** Where are the other nine? **(3)** Was no-one found to return and give praise to God except this foreigner?"

Then he had a special word of assurance for leper number 10: *"Rise and go; your faith has made you well."* Literally; Your faith has saved you.'

THANK YOU, HEAVENLY FATHER:

For the barriers that Jesus crossed in order to minister to people in need: racial, cultural, religious and political;
For the simple faith to which Jesus responded in order to transform people's lives;
For this demonstration of Jesus' uniqueness;
For Jesus' exercise of the divine prerogative of forgiving sins;

IN JESUS' NAME, AMEN

79. Luke 17:20 - 37
The Coming of the Kingdom of God

Luke 17:20 – 37
Once, having been asked by the Pharisees when the kingdom of God would come, Jesus replied, "The kingdom of God does not come with your careful observation, ²¹ nor will people say, 'Here it is,' or 'There it is,' because the kingdom of God is within you."

²² Then he said to his disciples, "The time is coming when you will long to see one of the days of the Son of Man, but you will not see it. ²³ Men will tell you, 'There he is!' or 'Here he is!' Do not go running off after them. ²⁴ For the Son of Man in his day will be like the lightning, which flashes and lights up the sky from one end to the other. ²⁵ But first he must suffer many things and be rejected by this generation.

²⁶ "Just as it was in the days of Noah, so also will it be in the days of the Son of Man. ²⁷People were eating, drinking, marrying and being given in marriage up to the day Noah entered the ark. Then the flood came and destroyed them all.

²⁸ "It was the same in the days of Lot. People were eating and drinking, buying and selling, planting and building. ²⁹ But the day Lot left Sodom, fire and sulphur rained down from heaven and destroyed them all.

³⁰ "It will be just like this on the day the Son of Man is revealed. ³¹ On that day no-one who is on the roof of his house, with his goods inside, should go down to get them. Likewise, no-one in the field should go back for anything. ³² Remember Lot's wife! ³³ Whoever tries to keep his life will lose it, and whoever loses his life will preserve it. ³⁴ I tell you, on that night two people will be in one bed; one will be taken and the other left. ³⁵ Two women will be grinding grain together; one will be taken and the other left."

[36 This verse is omitted from the best Gk. MSS and is not included here.]

³⁷ "Where, Lord?" they asked. He replied, "Where there is a dead body, there the vultures will gather."

Isn't it amazing that the Pharisees were never too busy that they couldn't turn up wherever Jesus was preaching and teaching? Here they are again, this time asking him when the kingdom of God would come. To this day there are people whose thinking about the kingdom is confused. This section will clarify our thoughts to a great extent. Just remember that the kingdom of God is both 'now' and 'not yet'. The kingdom is both 'outward' and 'inward.'

vv 20-21 The *'now'* of the kingdom. Jesus replied, *"The kingdom of God does not come with your careful observation, [21] nor will people say, 'Here it is,' or 'There it is,' because the kingdom of God is within you*

'Within you' can mean *'in your midst'* or *'in your hearts'* or *'in your reach.'* Since Jesus the King was present, God's reign had already begun. So the translation *'in your midst'* or *'in the midst of you'* is preferred.

vv 22-37 The *'not yet'* of the kingdom
"The time is coming when you will long to see one of the days of the Son of Man, but you will not see it. [25] But first he must suffer many things and be rejected by this generation. Jesus was even then on a journey to Jerusalem where he would offer himself to God on the cross as one sacrifice for sin forever. His death and burial, his resurrection and ascension to heaven would follow. The consummation of the kingdom when the Son of Man will come again is *'not yet'* (vv. 23-37).

All that Jesus said on the subject is listed below.

Don't go running to a particular place because you have heard rumours that I have come (v. 23);
There will be a visibility about the coming of the Son of Man, illuminating everywhere from one end of the sky to the other(v. 24);
But first he must suffer many things and be rejected by this generation (v. 24);
In Noah's day people, although warned, perished in the flood of great waters. The Son of Man will come as suddenly (vv. 26-27);

In Lot's day the people of Sodom and Gomorrah perished suddenly. The Son of Man will come as suddenly (vv. 28-29);

The coming of the Son of Man will catch people just as unprepared (v. 30). Householders (v. 31a), farmhands (v, 31b), people at home asleep in the night (v. 34), housewives grinding meal at the mill (v. 35). All will be taken by surprise when the Son of Man comes again. Lot's wife is an Old Testament example of a woman who hesitated and perished (v. 32-33; Genesis 19:26).

Some people wanted more information: *'Where, Lord?'* they asked. Jesus replied: *'Where there is a dead body, there the vultures will gather.'* Just as vultures know where carcasses are, so the world will know when and where the Son of Man returns (v. 37).

WE THANK YOU, HEAVENLY FATHER:

For the fact that the date of Jesus' Coming Again is known only to You;
For the fact that the entire universe is safe in Your hands;
For the hope that we shall see Jesus and be like him when he returns;

IN JESUS' NAME, AMEN

80. Luke 18:1 - 8
The Parable of the Persistent Widow

Luke 18:1 - 8
Then Jesus told his disciples a parable to show them that they should always pray and not give up.
² He said: "In a certain town there was a judge who neither feared God nor cared about men. ³ And there was a widow in that town who kept coming to him with the plea, 'Grant me justice against my adversary.'
⁴ "For some time he refused. But finally he said to himself, 'Even though I don't fear God or care about men, ⁵ yet because this widow keeps bothering me, I will see that she gets justice, so that she won't eventually wear me out with her coming!'"
⁶ And the Lord said, "Listen to what the unjust judge says. ⁷ And will not God bring about justice for his chosen ones, who cry out to him day and night? Will he keep putting them off? ⁸ I tell you, he will see that they get justice, and quickly. However, when the Son of Man comes, will he find faith on the earth?"

The opening sentence of this section is like a postscript pinned to the end of Luke 17:37. If the disciples were ever discouraged by the thought that the coming of Jesus was a long way into the future, then the remedy would be *'always pray and not give up.'*

In the light of the context perhaps a frequent prayer could *be 'Your kingdom come, Your will be done on earth as it is in heaven.'* Jesus is recommending continual prayer, not continuous, nonstop prayer.

In any case, as the following parable teaches, it is especially important for persistent prayer to characterise the Christian life. This will ensure that a community of faith will exist when the Son of Man comes (v. 8).

The parable supplies an illustration of persistent prayer. It is about an unjust judge, indifferent to God or the circumstance of other people, including a widow in importunate circumstances. She was so desperate and the judge was so indifferent that she resorted to pestering him with her plea *'Grant me justice against my adversary' (v. 3).*

For some time he refused, until he decided that the only way to get peace from this woman was to see that she got justice (v. 5).

'Even though I don't fear God or care about men, [5] yet because this widow keeps bothering me, I will see that she gets justice, so that she won't eventually wear me out with her coming!'"
And the Lord said, "Listen to what the unjust judge says.'

He was not teaching us think of our Heavenly Father as an unjust, uncaring, unprincipled judge somewhere in the heavens. That is not the God we know or to whom we come.

'And will not God bring about justice for his chosen ones, who cry out to him day and night? Will he keep putting them off? [8] I tell you, he will see that they get justice, and quickly.'

If the unjust judge yielded to the continuous cries of the widow, who was a stranger, and granted her the justice she sought from him, *how much more will God,* who is just and a loving heavenly Father, answer the prayers of his people who cry out to him day and night. He will not keep putting them off. God's chosen ones are those who have responded to him in repentance and faith and are the recipients of his love and grace.

'However, when the Son of Man comes, will he find faith on the earth?"

We believe that he will find a people without number, who are watching and waiting for him, day and night.

THANK YOU, HEAVENLY FATHER:

For the encouragement in prayer that this parable gives us;
For Your eye that is always on us and Your ear that is always open to us;
For the obvious principles of prayer, so simple that even infant lips can pray;

For the fact that You are able to do exceeding abundantly above all that we can ask or think;
For the fact that You are our refuge and strength, and a very present help in time of trouble.

IN JESUS' NAME, AMEN

81. Luke 18:9 - 14
The Parable of the Pharisee and the Tax Collector

Luke 18:9 - 14
To some who were confident of their own righteousness and looked down on everybody else, Jesus told this parable: ¹⁰ *"Two men went up to the temple to pray, one a Pharisee and the other a tax collector.*

¹¹ *The Pharisee stood up and prayed about himself: 'God, I thank you that I am not like other men—robbers, evildoers, adulterers—or even like this tax collector.* ¹² *I fast twice a week and give a tenth of all I get.'*

¹³ *"But the tax collector stood at a distance. He would not even look up to heaven, but beat his breast and said, 'God, have mercy on me, a sinner.'*

¹⁴ *"I tell you that this man, rather than the other, went home justified before God. For everyone who exalts himself will be humbled, and he who humbles himself will be exalted."*

Jesus was a keen observer of people. His word-pictures of various individuals are spell-binding. There is an economy of words in this parable and yet there is an astonishing amount of detail. We would recognise these two men if we met them at the bus stop!

This is another parable about prayer.

Jesus' special purpose in teaching it is disclosed in the opening sentence: *'To some who were confident of their own righteousness and looked down on everybody else, Jesus told this parable.'*

Here is how a self-righteous man prays.

'The Pharisee stood up and prayed about himself:' Isn't this astonishing? The subject of his prayer was *'about himself'*. No sense of entering the divine presence in prayer, no sense of unworthiness, no sense of sin, no need to ask forgiveness!

Depending on our point of view, this man's prayer either gets worse or better as he continues.: *'God, I thank you that I am not like other men—robbers, evildoers, adulterers—or even like this tax collector. ¹² I fast twice a week and give a tenth of all I get.'*

He mentioned the name of God once, and used the personal pronoun 'I' four times. He believed that he practised righteousness meticulously. A man wrapped up in himself makes a very small parcel.

Here is how a sinner prays.

"But the tax collector stood at a distance. He would not even look up to heaven, but beat his breast and said, 'God, have mercy on me, a sinner.' The tax collector prayed about himself – but he had not come to impress God about his self-righteousness. No, he had come to confess before God the shame he felt about his spiritual condition. So ashamed was he that he could only beat his breast, and not so much as looking up to heaven, pray from the depths of his soul with as much honesty as he was capable of: *'God, have mercy on me, a sinner.'*

Here is how God answers a sinner's prayer.

"I tell you that this man, rather than the other, went home justified before God. For everyone who exalts himself will be humbled, and he who humbles himself will be exalted."

It was the tax collector, and not the Pharisee, who went home *'justified'*. The tax collector used the word *'mercy'* and in doing so was asking God to cover his sins and remove his wrath. He went home, not only a forgiven man, but also in a new condition before God, and in a new relationship with God.

THANK YOU, HEAVENLY FATHER:

For allowing us to see ourselves as we really are in Your sight;
For accepting us just as we are, when we come as sinners to Jesus;
For the sacrifice that Jesus offered on Calvary's cross, to save us from sin and death, when we were without strength to save ourselves;

For the gift of Your righteousness, in place of the filthy rags of our self-righteousness;
For the gift of Your Holy Spirit, who indwells us and tells us that we are children of God through faith in Christ Jesus;
For the fact that absolutely nothing in the entire universe can ever separate us from Your love in Jesus Christ our Lord;

IN JESUS' NAME, AMEN

82. Luke 18:15 - 17
The Little Children and Jesus

Luke 18:15 - 17
People were also bringing babies to Jesus to have him touch them. When the disciples saw this, they rebuked them. [16] But Jesus called the children to him and said, "Let the little children come to me, and do not hinder them, for the kingdom of God belongs to such as these [17] I tell you the truth, anyone who will not receive the kingdom of God like a little child will never enter it."

Jesus loved children and welcomed them to his side. He was once a child, but there is a silence about his childhood years. Stories about young people such as baby Moses, the boy Samuel, Mrs. Naaman's servant, and the boy who gave Jesus his lunch of sardines and a few scones are well known. It seems very strange that the Bible says comparatively little about young children.

The reason for a scarcity of material on children is that the Bible, in both parts, emphasises the responsibility of parents for the spiritual upbringing of their children. Timothy may well have been in his early or mid-teens when he became a believer, mainly due to being taught the scriptures by his mother and grandmother. There were no Sunday schools in those days.

People were also bringing babies to Jesus to have him touch them. When the disciples saw this, they rebuked them (v. 15).

The parents had their reasons for bringing their babies to Jesus so that he could touch them. Were they being superstitious? Jesus had never taught what the touch of his hand would mean in the life of children so young. The disciples were at a loss about what to do, because they didn't understand either! So, imagining that they were deflecting pressure off Jesus, the disciples rebuked the mothers.

But Jesus called the children to him and said, "Let the little children come to me, and do not hinder them, for the kingdom of God belongs to such as these" (v. 16).

Babies are incapable of a conscious faith. Jesus' words of welcome to the mothers and babies confirmed his love for them. We might ask if the action of the mothers was in itself an acted prayer, seeking a blessing on their children? Mothers want the best for their children. This event permits us to teach these two facts:**(1)** Jesus' love for children; and **(2)** the mothers' desire for a blessing for their children.

Jesus' took everyone's thoughts much further than the delightful scene before them. He took the opportunity to teach older children and adults a lesson about entering the kingdom of God.

"The kingdom of God belongs to such as these. I tell you the truth, anyone who will not receive the kingdom of God like a little child will never enter it" (vv. 16-17).

Children, however young, have only to learn. Older children and adults frequently have a lot to unlearn. Children are accepting of many things. Adults allow silly things such as pride and position to get in their way, in this case, of receiving the kingdom of God. So the child in its mother's arms or in the arms of Jesus, is utterly relaxed and trusting. This is how we need to believe in Jesus.

Jesus was not saying that all children, simply because they are children, have received God's kingdom. Neither was he attributing to children an innate goodness. Rather he was underlining a quality possessed by little children that is essential for entering God's kingdom: unquestioning acceptance and a simple faith free from doubt.

We must not describe Jesus' blessing the children *as 'a baptism without water'*. That is not warranted by this passage of scripture. It is doubtful if Luke had any thought of baptism in mind, because for him baptism was connected with repentance and faith.

THANK YOU, HEAVENLY FATHER:

For Jesus' love for children and the lessons he taught about them;
For believing parents everywhere, who are diligent in training their
> children to know and love God;
For so many of us who, like young Timothy, first heard the gospel
> story and was taught to memorise the scriptures at home;
For entrusting us with children of our own: we commit them to Your
> fatherly care;

IN JESUS' NAME, AMEN

83. Luke 18:18 - 30
The Rich Ruler

Luke 18:18 - 30
A certain ruler asked him, "Good teacher, what must I do to inherit eternal life?"
[19] "Why do you call me good?" Jesus answered. "No-one is good—except God alone. [20]You know the commandments: 'Do not commit adultery, do not murder, do not steal, do not give false testimony, honour your father and mother.'"
[21] "All these I have kept since I was a boy," he said.
[22] When Jesus heard this, he said to him, "You still lack one thing. Sell everything you have and give to the poor, and you will have treasure in heaven. Then come, follow me."
[23] When he heard this, he became very sad, because he was a man of great wealth [24] Jesus looked at him and said, "How hard it is for the rich to enter the kingdom of God! [25] Indeed, it is easier for a camel to go through the eye of a needle than for a rich man to enter the kingdom of God."
[26] Those who heard this asked, "Who then can be saved?"
[27] Jesus replied, "What is impossible with men is possible with God."
[28] Peter said to him, "We have left all we had to follow you!"
[29] "I tell you the truth," Jesus said to them, "no-one who has left home or wife or brothers or parents or children for the sake of the kingdom of God [30] will fail to receive many times as much in this age and, in the age to come, eternal life."

Had this man been a bystander, overhearing all that had passed between the disciples, and the mothers and children? If so, he missed or had quickly forgotten the emphasis Jesus made in his comment: *'I tell you the truth, anyone who will not receive the kingdom of God like a little child will never enter it" (v. 17).*

The ruler's question indicates that he did not get the Lord's message about simple, childlike faith (v. 18). His question was: *"Good teacher, what must I do to inherit eternal life?"* Jesus tested the young man's use of words: *"Why do you call me good?"* Jesus answered: "No-one is good—except God alone' (v. 19). Then Jesus tested the young man's 'goodness': *You know the commandments: 'Do not commit adultery, do not murder, do not steal, and do not give false testimony, honour your father and mother '(v. 20)*

The man thought he would pass this test with flying colours: *"All these I have kept since I was a boy" (v. 20).* But Jesus approached him from another direction: *"You still lack one thing. Sell everything you have and give to the poor, and you will have treasure in heaven. Then come, follow me" (v. 22)*

Jesus had put his finger on a problem that many rich people have: those who profess to be believers may end up trying to serve two masters (16:13).

Selling his possessions and giving them to the poor was not necessary for salvation. This was Jesus' way of spelling out that one must choose between God and money. *When he heard this, he became very sad, because he was a man of great wealth (v. 23).*

Jesus had seen into the depths of the man's heart: *"How hard it is for the rich to enter the kingdom of God! 25 Indeed, it is easier for a camel to go through the eye of a needle than for a rich man to enter the kingdom of God."* So the man who had presented as a candidate for the kingdom of God failed to enter.

Those who heard this asked, *"Who then can be saved?"* Jesus replied, *"What is impossible with men is possible with God" (vv. 26-27).* For Luke salvation came from God, and God can break the hold that riches have on a person.

Peter said to him, *"We have left all we had to follow you!"* *"I tell you the truth,"* Jesus said to them, *"no-one who has left home or wife or brothers or parents or children for the sake of the kingdom of God will fail to receive many times as much in this age and, in the age to come, eternal life." (vv. 28-30.)*

Peter and other apostles had lasting memories of *'leaving all they had'* to follow Jesus. Jesus complimented them saying that no one who had left family *'for the sake of the kingdom of God'* would go without. That person would receive *'many times as much at this time and in the age to come, eternal life'* (v. 30).

THANK YOU, HEAVENLY FATHER:

For the surpassing greatness of knowing Christ Jesus as Lord (Phil.3:8);
For opening our eyes to see that all that glitters on earth is not gold; that true riches are spiritual and eternal;
For the blessings You have showered upon us since we began following Jesus;
For Your grace enabling us to press on toward the goal to win the prize for which God has called us heavenward in Christ Jesus;

In Jesus' Name, Amen

84. Luke 18:31 - 34
Jesus Predicts His Death

Luke 18:31 - 34
Jesus took the Twelve aside and told them, "We are going up to Jerusalem, and everything that is written by the prophets about the Son of Man will be fulfilled. ³² He will be turned over to the Gentiles. They will mock him, insult him, spit on him, flog him and kill him. ³³On the third day he will rise again."

³⁴ The disciples did not understand any of this. Its meaning was hidden from them, and they did not know what he was talking about.

Jesus came into the world at his incarnation to fulfil a mission given him by his Father. Paul the apostle expressed it like this: *'Christ Jesus came into the world to save sinners.'*

For some time now we have been travelling with Jesus on the road to Jerusalem and Calvary, where he would be crucified, ever since Luke 9:21-22. Jesus kept nothing back from his disciples that they needed to know.

From that point forward we can trace Jesus' increasing awareness of his death; Luke 9:21-22, 43-45 & 51, 18:31-34; entering Jerusalem 19:28; instituting the Lord's Supper 22:14-22; until he was crucified at Calvary 23:33.

We must not gloss over the section in Luke 18:31-34 as if we knew all there is to know about the suffering and death of our Lord Jesus Christ.

Jesus took the Twelve aside and told them, *"We are going up to Jerusalem, and everything that is written by the prophets about the Son of Man will be fulfilled (v. 31).* This was for the disciples' ears only. His emphasis on this occasion was on the fulfilment of *'everything that is written by the prophets about the Son of Man.'* At the heart of the sentence is the affirmation that *'God will bring them about.'*

This emphasis also allows us to see that Jesus drew great consolation from the Old Testament scriptures. He knew them well, but that was not how he read his Bible. He comforted (strengthened) himself by reading the prophecies that were specific to him and meditating on them.

"He will be turned over to the Gentiles. They will mock him, insult him, spit on him, flog him and kill him. On the third day he will rise again" (vv. 32-33).

The prophecies that Jesus cherished spoke to him in astonishing detail about what he would suffer at the hands of sinners. Peter remembered the Lord's words much later when preaching in Jerusalem after the ascension: *'Indeed Herod and Pontius Pilate met together with the Gentiles and the people of Israel in this city to conspire against your holy servant Jesus, whom you anointed. They did what your power and will had decided beforehand should happen' (Acts 4:27-28).*

At the time when Jesus was disclosing these things to the disciples they *'did not understand any of this.'*

It seems to have been a divine 'blinding' because Luke explains: *'Its meaning was hidden from them, and they did not know what he was talking about.'* God had chosen to veil the truth from them.

Only after the resurrection would the necessity of Jesus' death be made clear, when on the evening of Resurrection Day Jesus expounded the scriptures to his disciples in the Upper Room at Jerusalem (Luke 24:25-35 and 44-49).

Luke 24:44 - 49

He said to them, "This is what I told you while I was still with you: Everything must be fulfilled that is written about me in the Law of Moses, the Prophets and the Psalms."

⁴⁵ Then he opened their minds so they could understand the Scriptures. ⁴⁶ He told them, "This is what is written: The Christ will suffer and rise from the dead on the third day, ⁴⁷ and repentance and forgiveness of sins will be preached in his name to all nations, beginning at Jerusalem.

⁴⁸ You are witnesses of these things. ⁴⁹ I am going to send you what my Father has promised; but stay in the city until you have been clothed with power from on high."

THANK YOU, HEAVENLY FATHER:

For Your trustworthy word from which Jesus gleaned such assurance and comfort when anticipating his death at Calvary;
For the Holy Spirit who will open our understanding as we read the scriptures so that we may be guided and sustained throughout each day;
For the disciples, though only men at best, whom You would fill with the Holy Spirit empowering them to be witnesses to Jesus;

IN JESUS' NAME, AMEN

85. Luke 18:35 - 43
A Blind Beggar receives his Sight

Luke 18:35 - 43
As Jesus approached Jericho, a blind man was sitting by the roadside begging. ³⁶ When he heard the crowd going by, he asked what was happening. ³⁷ They told him, "Jesus of Nazareth is passing by."

³⁸ He called out, "Jesus, Son of David, have mercy on me!"

³⁹ Those who led the way rebuked him and told him to be quiet, but he shouted all the more, "Son of David, have mercy on me!"

⁴⁰ Jesus stopped and ordered the man to be brought to him. When he came near, Jesus asked him, ⁴¹ "What do you want me to do for you?"

"Lord, I want to see," he replied.

⁴² Jesus said to him, "Receive your sight; your faith has healed you." ⁴³ Immediately he received his sight and followed Jesus, praising God. When all the people saw it, they also praised God.

Scripture and song are astonishingly powerful influences in a person's life. Some of the sections in this Gospel prompted so many memories of Sunday school teachers, faithful pastors, gospel songs and hymns that were instrumental in bringing me to faith in Jesus Christ as a boy of eleven years of age. Writing these notes has been a heart-warming experience.

As Jesus approached Jericho, a blind man was sitting by the roadside begging (v. 35).

The picture is so vivid that we can see him sitting there utterly dependent on public charity. He is aware that a crowd of people is approaching and asked the reason. They told him, *"Jesus of Nazareth is passing by."*

It's amazing what a blind man can learn sitting by the roadside! He had heard about Jesus and had resolved that if the opportunity ever arose to meet him, he would not let it pass. He was right to make himself heard.

He called out, *"Jesus, Son of David, have mercy on me!"* Those who led the way rebuked him and told him to be quiet, but he shouted all the mor*e, "Son of David, have mercy on me!"* The public were embarrassed by the blind man's cries. So much for human charity!

Jesus stopped and ordered the man to be brought to him. When he came near, Jesus asked him, "What do you want me to do for you?"(vv. 40-41)

"Lord, I want to see," he replied. Jesus said to him, *"Receive your sight; your faith has healed you" (v. 42)*. Jesus, as the Son of God, was well aware of the blind man's circumstances, but it was necessary to hear him speak for himself. The blind man had no hesitation: *'Lord, I want to see.'* The word *'healed'* is literally *'saved'* you.' One word from Jesus brought instant sight,

Immediately he received his sight and followed Jesus, praising God. When all the people saw it, they also praised God. (v. 43)

Who is this who can do such things? It is Jesus, the Son of David, the Lord!

We don't know any more about the blind man's circumstances: had his blindness been congenital, was he poverty-stricken, had he any friends or relatives. For his part he was clear about what he wanted to do: follow Jesus.

Unlike some other situations there is no record of Jesus bidding him to stay at home and be a witness among those who knew him best. He couldn't remain silent and began praising God. The crowd began praising God as well.

We would be very hardhearted in deed if we are not moved to praise God along with them.

THANK YOU, HEAVENLY FATHER:

For the healing power of Jesus;
For the straightforward faith of the man who was blind and which Jesus honoured with the gift of sight;
For those who are ministering in Jesus' name to the needy people of the world through gospel and humanitarian initiatives;
For those who are longing to know Jesus, if someone would tell them how;

IN JESUS' NAME, AMEN

86. Luke 19:1- 10
Zacchaeus the Tax Collector

Luke 19:1 - 10
Jesus entered Jericho and was passing through. ² A man was there by the name of Zacchaeus; he was a chief tax collector and was wealthy. ³ He wanted to see who Jesus was, but being a short man he could not, because of the crowd. ⁴ So he ran ahead and climbed a sycamore-fig tree to see him, since Jesus was coming that way.

⁵ When Jesus reached the spot, he looked up and said to him, "Zacchaeus, come down immediately. I must stay at your house today." ⁶ So he came down at once and welcomed him gladly. ⁷ All the people saw this and began to mutter, "He has gone to be the guest of a 'sinner'."

⁸ But Zacchaeus stood up and said to the Lord, "Look, Lord! Here and now I give half of my possessions to the poor, and if I have cheated anybody out of anything, I will pay back four times the amount."

⁹ Jesus said to him, "Today salvation has come to this house, because this man, too, is a son of Abraham. ¹⁰ For the Son of Man came to seek and to save what was lost."

Jesus had not planned to stop in Jericho, he was just passing through. Luke tells us of a small man there who was very curious about Jesus and was determined to see him. He had been coping with the problems of dwarfism from childhood and had become quite resourceful in achieving what he wanted to do. He had even accumulated great wealth. That may have been because he was a tax collector. He wanted to see *'who Jesus was.'* He had a bright idea. He might even be able to see, without being seen.

A man was there by the name of Zacchaeus; he was a chief tax collector and was wealthy. ³He wanted to see who Jesus was, but being a short man he could not, because of the crowd. ⁴ So he ran ahead and climbed a sycamore-fig tree to see him, since Jesus was coming that way. (vv. 2-4)

Well done, Zacchaeus! So far, so good.

When Jesus reached the spot, he looked up and said to him, "Zacchaeus, come down immediately. I must stay at your house today." ⁶ So he came down at once and welcomed him gladly.

It's a wonder that Zacchaeus didn't fall out of the tree. How did Jesus know his name? How did he know that Zacchaeus wanted to see him? Luke doesn't tell us. For Jesus, meeting Zacchaeus was a divine necessity: *'Come down immediately, I must stay at your house today.'*

Zacchaeus was beside himself with joy. He came down at once and received him joyfully. This is another occasion on which Jesus ignored social taboos by violating a tradition of the Pharisees. The people noticed it immediately: *All the people saw this and began to mutter, "He has gone to be the guest of a 'sinner' (v. 7).*

Let's focus on v. 8. There are several very important things we should note:**(1)** it is a bold and moving confession of sin; **(2)** it is an act of repentance; **(3)** and a confession of faith by Zacchaeus. **(4)** He recognises Jesus as the Christ and calls him 'Lord'; **(5)** he vows to give away half his goods; and **(6)** he is going to make restitution to all the people he cheated, promising to give back four times as much. Phew! that's breath-taking!

A radical change has taken place in the heart and value-system of Zacchaeus. He has found Christ—no—Christ has found Zacchaeus and all he once called gain he now counted loss. Jesus pronounced a benediction on him:

"Today salvation has come to this house, because this man, too, is a son of Abraham. For the Son of Man came to seek and to save what was lost" (vv. 9-10).

Jesus defined his mission in terms of seeking and saving those who are lost. Jesus also recognised Zacchaeus as 'a son of Abraham'. Not only was he a natural son of Abraham the father of the Jewish people, he was also *'a son of Abraham through faith in Jesus Christ.'*

Merely by doing a search on the Internet to see if there was any foundation to a rumour that I had heard, I learned that Zacchaeus continued in the service of Christ. According to Clement of Alexandria he was surnamed Matthias by the apostles and took the place of Judas among them. Later apostolic documents identify Zacchaeus the Publican as the first Bishop of Caesarea. I found other sources that confirmed this appointment. Maybe the information is true. [It depends on whether you regard Clement, the internet or Wikipedia as reliable sources.]

THANK YOU, HEAVENLY FATHER:

For the wonderful change that was wrought in Zacchaeus when he welcomed Jesus into his life;
For the many millions of people down the years, who came to faith in Jesus through the message of Luke 19:10.

IN JESUS' NAME, AMEN

87. Luke 19:11- 27
The Parable of the Ten Minas

Luke 19:11 - 27

While they were listening to this, he went on to tell them a parable, because he was near Jerusalem and the people thought that the kingdom of God was going to appear at once. [12]He said: "A man of noble birth went to a distant country to have himself appointed king and then to return. [13] So he called ten of his servants and gave them ten minas. 'Put this money to work,' he said, 'until I come back.'

[14] "But his subjects hated him and sent a delegation after him to say, 'We don't want this man to be our king.'

[15] "He was made king, however, and returned home. Then he sent for the servants to whom he had given the money, in order to find out what they had gained with it.

[16] "The first one came and said, 'Sir, your mina has earned ten more.' [17] "Well done, my good servant!' his master replied. 'Because you have been trustworthy in a very small matter, take charge of ten cities.'

[18] "The second came and said, 'Sir, your mina has earned five more.'

[19] "His master answered, 'You take charge of five cities.'

[20] "Then another servant came and said, 'Sir, here is your mina; I have kept it laid away in a piece of cloth. [21] I was afraid of you, because you are a hard man. You take out what you did not put in and reap what you did not sow.'

[22] "His master replied, 'I will judge you by your own words, you wicked servant! You knew, did you, that I am a hard man, taking out what I did not put in, and reaping what I did not sow? [23] Why then didn't you put my money on deposit, so that when I came back, I could have collected it with interest?'

[24] "Then he said to those standing by, 'Take his mina away from him and give it to the one who has ten minas.'

[25] "'Sir,' they said, 'he already has ten!'

[26] "He replied, 'I tell you that to everyone who has, more will be given, but as for the one who has nothing, even what he has will be

taken away. ²⁷ But those enemies of mine who did not want me to be a king over them—bring them here and kill them in front of me.'

Luke has been keeping a log of Jesus' journey from Galilee to Jerusalem. He notes that at this point on the journey Jesus told a parable. We shall examine it later. His reason for telling the parable was that he was now near Jerusalem and he sensed that the crowd of people listening to him thought that the kingdom of God was going to appear at once. We cannot be sure what had raised their expectations; but Jesus felt that he needed to temper their optimism with caution.

"A man of noble birth went to a distant country to have himself appointed king and then to return. So he called ten of his servants and gave them ten minas. 'Put this money to work,' he said, 'until I come back' (vv 12-13).

It is thought by many commentators that Jesus was referring to a similar happening in local royalty. When Archelaus, son of Herod the Great, was appointed king of Judea, the Jewish leaders sent a delegation to the Roman emperor pleading with him not to make Archelaus king.

The man who went to a distant country to have himself appointed king was Jesus himself. Following his approaching death and burial, resurrection and ascension to heaven he would be invested by God the Father with his crown as King of the kingdom of God.

So Jesus will be absent for some time. The ten servants represented his disciples with whom he left some money which they could put to work until he would come back. A 'mina' was worth about three months' wages. Ten servants received ten minas.

"But his subjects hated him and sent a delegation after him to say, 'We don't want this man to be our king' (v. 14). In the greater scheme of things this detail depicted the Jewish rejection of Jesus.

He was, in fact, made king and returned home (v. 15a). This depicts Jesus' exaltation in heaven, where he was acclaimed King of Kings and Lord of Lords. In due time the king returned.

Then he sent for the servants to whom he had given the money, in order to find out what they had traded with it (v. 15b). Jesus' return (*the parousia*) is the moment for the judgment of the servants to take place.

The first servant had invested his mina and had gained 10 more i.e. 1000%. and was rewarded accordingly being appointed as ruler of 10 cities (vv 16-.17).

The second servant had invested his mina and had gained 5 more i.e. 500% and was rewarded accordingly being appointed as ruler of 5 cities (v. 18-19).

The third servant had wrapped his mina in a cloth and laid it away so that he could return it to his master in the condition he had received it. He thought of his master as a man who was sharp in his dealings and harsh with his servants. The master was not well pleased (vv. 20-23). The servant was wrong. The master had been generous to the first two servants. Judgment was given. His mina was taken from him and given to the first servant.

Others in the master's employ thought this most unfair (vv. 24-25). It was not for them to judge.

As for the master's enemies (v. 27) he would deal with them as they deserved.

But those enemies of mine who did not want me to be a king over them—bring them here and kill them in front of me.'

We need to remember that Luke's gospel would not be in circulation among the young churches of the first century until long after Jesus' ascension to heaven.

When the gospel was read in the churches the apostles and the members would recognise the prominent features of the parable in the historic events following Jesus resurrection and ascension as they watched and waited for his glorious return.

THANK YOU, HEAVENLY FATHER:

For the privilege of serving Jesus our Lord and King while waiting for his return;

For the motivation he gave us as his servants of the prospect of rewards for faithful service;

For the warning in the parable that what we do not use for Jesus we will lose;

For every opportunity in all walks of life to serve our Lord Jesus Christ by serving others;

IN JESUS' NAME, AMEN

88. Luke 19:28 - 44
The Triumphal Entry

Luke 19:28 - 44

After Jesus had said this, he went on ahead, going up to Jerusalem.

29 As he approached Bethphage and Bethany at the hill called the Mount of Olives, he sent two of his disciples, saying to them, 30 "Go to the village ahead of you, and as you enter it, you will find a colt tied there, which no-one has ever ridden. Untie it and bring it here. 31 If anyone asks you, 'Why are you untying it?' tell him, 'The Lord needs it.'"

32 Those who were sent ahead went and found it just as he had told them. 33 As they were untying the colt, its owners asked them, "Why are you untying the colt?"

34 They replied, "The Lord needs it."

35 They brought it to Jesus, threw their cloaks on the colt and put Jesus on it. 36 As he went along, people spread their cloaks on the road.

37 When he came near the place where the road goes down the Mount of Olives, the whole crowd of disciples began joyfully to praise God in loud voices for all the miracles they had seen:

38 "Blessed is the king who comes in the name of the Lord!"

"Peace in heaven and glory in the highest!"

39 Some of the Pharisees in the crowd said to Jesus, "Teacher, rebuke your disciples!" 40 "I tell you," he replied, "if they keep quiet, the stones will cry out."

41 As he approached Jerusalem and saw the city, he wept over it 42 and said, "If you, even you, had only known on this day what would bring you peace—but now it is hidden from your eyes. 43 The days will come upon you when your enemies will build an embankment against you and encircle you and hem you in on every side. 44 They will dash you to the ground, you and the children within your walls. They will not leave one stone on another, because you did not recognise the time of God's coming to you."

Jesus and his disciples are now within sight of Jerusalem, somewhere in the area of Bethphage and Bethany, two villages situated at the foot of the Mount of Olives. He sent two disciples ahead of him with instructions to bring him an unbroken colt they would find tied there. If anyone questioned them they were to reply, *'The Lord needs it.'* As Jesus had said they were questioned by the animal's owners about why they were untying what didn't belong to them. When they replied, *'The Lord needs it.'* consent was given immediately. We may presume that the owners were friends of Jesus whom we are meeting for the first time.

Possibly the scene in vv. 35 to 38 has been in our minds since childhood when we first heard the story of Jesus entering Jerusalem. In our mind's eye we see him riding on the young donkey and people are scattering their cloaks on the road for the animal to walk over them. When the procession reached the place where the road went down the Mount of Olives the all the disciples were praising God in loud voices for all the miracles they had seen.

Their praise was significant because they were singing a refrain from Psalm 118:26 *'Blessed is he who comes in the name of the Lord.'* to which they added another refrain *'Peace in heaven and glory in the highest'*, a song the angels sang at Jesus' nativity (Luke 2:14).

Actually Jesus was fulfilling a prophecy which said: *'Rejoice greatly, O Daughter of Zion! Shout, Daughter of Jerusalem! See, your king comes to you, righteous and having salvation, gentle and riding on a donkey, on a colt, the foal of a donkey'* (Zech 9:9).

Of course the Pharisees were there to criticise everything Jesus said and did. ' *"Teacher, rebuke your disciples!"* they said, to which Jesus replied, *"I tell you, if they keep quiet, the stones will cry out."*

41 As he approached Jerusalem and saw the city, he wept over it

Only here and at the grave of Lazarus do we read of Jesus weeping in public. This time he was weeping for the fate of Jerusalem and the people of Israel. *"If you, even you, had only known on this day what would bring you peace—but now it is hidden from your eyes"* (v. 42). Then in words that must have been heart-wrenching for him to speak, Jesus prophesied the Destruction of Jerusalem in AD 68-70 when the Roman armies would raze the city to the ground. This would be God's judgment on the city which had *'sinned* away' countless spiritual privileges down the centuries, and had rejected the Son of God.

Thank You, Heavenly Father;

For Jesus Christ, Your Son, the Messiah of Israel and the Saviour of the world;
For the sorrow that Jesus expressed in his lament over Jerusalem; the love of Jesus is something wonderful;
For the day that is coming in which *'every knee shall bow and every tongue confess that Jesus Christ is Lord'*;

In Jesus' Name, Amen

89. Luke 19:45 – 48
Jesus at The Temple

Luke 19:45 – 48
Then he entered the temple area and began driving out those who were selling. ⁴⁶ "It is written," he said to them, 'My house will be a house of prayer'; but you have made it 'a den of robbers'."
⁴⁷ Every day he was teaching at the temple. But the chief priests, the teachers of the law and the leaders among the people were trying to kill him. ⁴⁸ Yet they could not find any way to do it, because all the people hung on his words.

This was not the temple that Solomon built, which on opening day had been filled with the glory of God. The first temple had been plundered by the Babylonians. The second temple had been rebuilt on a smaller scale by Zerubabal and the returned exiles. Currently Herod the Great was in the process of building a third temple for the Jewish people. Although unfinished, there must have been sufficient space within the building for the Jews to meet for worship there.

The Temple had been profaned. There was so much commerce going on that it might as well have been a secular building. When Jesus saw what the building was being used for it nauseated him, and with a holy zeal he drove out the market traders and all the other extortioners who were making a fortune out of selling animals for temple worship.

⁴⁶ "It is written," he said to them, 'My house will be a house of prayer'; but you have made it 'a den of robbers'."
⁴⁷ Every day he was teaching at the temple. But the chief priests, the teachers of the law and the leaders among the people were trying to kill him.

Jesus daily ministry at the Temple was not a civil or a criminal offence. Had he been breaking some local bye-law, why had they not arrested him long ago?

Here they are again – the representatives of official Judaism. It is now clear that they were determined to kill him. Israel's false shepherds actively opposed her True Shepherd.

⁴⁸ Yet they could not find any way to do it, because all the people hung on his words.

Luke tells us repeatedly that the common people loved to listen to Jesus' teaching and preaching. They gathered in droves to hear him. His popularity with them prevented official Judaism making any moves against him.

THANK YOU, HEAVENLY FATHER;

For the fact that You are not confined to any building, therefore *'where'er we seek You, You are found and every place is hallowed ground.'*
For Jesus Christ, the Lord of the Temple, and for his zeal for the reputation of Your house;
For the privilege of having spiritually gifted servants of Yours whose ministry of Your word blesses our souls and strengthens us for daily living.

IN JESUS' NAME, AMEN

90. Luke 20:1 - 8
The Authority of Jesus Questioned

Luke 20:1 – 8
One day as he was teaching the people in the temple courts and preaching the gospel, the chief priests and the teachers of the law, together with the elders, came up to him. ² "Tell us by what authority you are doing these things," they said. "Who gave you this authority?" ³He replied, "I will also ask you a question. Tell me, ⁴ John's baptism—was it from heaven, or from men?"

⁵ They discussed it among themselves and said, "If we say, 'From heaven', he will ask, 'Why didn't you believe him?' ⁶ But if we say, 'From men', all the people will stone us, because they are persuaded that John was a prophet."

⁷ So they answered, "We don't know where it was from."

⁸ Jesus said, "Neither will I tell you by what authority I am doing these things."

One day when Jesus was in the temple courts preaching the gospel he was confronted by Official Judaism (the chief priests and teachers of the law, together with the elders) who put a rather pompous question to him: *"Tell us by what authority you are doing these things," they said. "Who gave you this authority?"* (v. 2)

Israel's false shepherds were challenging Israel's true shepherd. Jesus put their integrity to the test by asking them about their attitude to John the Baptist and his ministry, particularly his baptism of repentance: *"I will also ask you a question. Tell me, John's baptism—was it from heaven, or from men?"* (v. 4). They were on the horns of a dilemma.

They could not answer without a delay while they discussed the question: *"If we say, 'From heaven', he will ask, 'Why didn't you believe him?' But if we say, 'From men', all the people will stone us, because they are persuaded that John was a prophet."* (vv. 5-6). They didn't know which way to turn. So they answered, *"We don't know where it was from."* (v. 7).

That being the case Jesus was under no obligation to validate his ministry by answering their disrespectful questions. Any further discussion with them would have been useless. The hostility of official Judaism toward Jesus was now an established fact.

Something very important is beginning to clarify. The people were opposed to official Judaism. It would not be the Jewish people who would put Jesus on the cross, it would be official Judaism.

THANK YOU, HEAVENLY FATHER:

For protecting the life of Your Son until the appointed hour for him to die would come;
For the common people who heard Jesus gladly;
For the wit and wisdom of Jesus when handling the harsh criticisms of the Jewish leaders;
For the multiplied opportunities that Jesus gave all his hearers 'to press into the kingdom of God';

IN JESUS' NAME, AMEN

91. Luke 20:9 - 19
The Parable of the Tenants

Luke 20:9 – 19
He went on to tell the people this parable: "A man planted a vineyard, rented it to some farmers and went away for a long time. ¹⁰ At harvest time he sent a servant to the tenants so they would give him some of the fruit of the vineyard. But the tenants beat him and sent him away empty-handed. ¹¹ He sent another servant, but that one also they beat and treated shamefully and sent away empty-handed. ¹² He sent still a third, and they wounded him and threw him out.

¹³ "Then the owner of the vineyard said, 'What shall I do? I will send my son, whom I love; perhaps they will respect him.' ¹⁴ "But when the tenants saw him, they talked the matter over. 'This is the heir,' they said. 'Let's kill him, and the inheritance will be ours.' ¹⁵ So they threw him out of the vineyard and killed him.

"What then will the owner of the vineyard do to them? ¹⁶ He will come and kill those tenants and give the vineyard to others."

When the people heard this, they said, "May this never be!"

¹⁷ Jesus looked directly at them and asked, "Then what is the meaning of that which is written:" 'The stone the builders rejected has become the capstone '?

¹⁸ Everyone who falls on that stone will be broken to pieces, but he on whom it falls will be crushed."

¹⁹ The teachers of the law and the chief priests looked for a way to arrest him immediately, because they knew he had spoken this parable against them. But they were afraid of the people.

Although this parable of the wicked tenants was addressed to the same audience (as in v.1), Luke understood the parable to be directed against Jesus' opponents, whom he described as *'teachers of the law and chief priests.'* (v. 19)

The vineyard that the man planted symbolised Israel and its people (v. 9). The servants who were sent to obtain fruit from the tenants represented the prophets and other messengers whom God had sent to Israel down the years. They had been treated abominably (vv. 10-12).

The owner had one more hope for obtaining fruit from his vineyard, and so he sent his son whom he loved. The evil tenants took him outside the vineyard (the crucifixion took place outside the city of Jerusalem) and killed him.

Jesus asked a rhetorical question: *"What then will the owner of the vineyard do to them? He will come and kill those tenants and give the vineyard to others." (vv. 15-16)*

Judgment would come on the tenants and the vineyard would be given to others. Jesus was again anticipating the destruction of Jerusalem in AD 70.

Jesus looked directly at them (the Jewish leaders) and asked, *"Then what is the meaning of that which is written:" 'The stone the builders rejected has become the capstone '? Everyone who falls on that stone will be broken to pieces, but he on whom it falls will be crushed" (vv.17-18)*.

Jesus wasn't letting the Jewish leaders off lightly. He quoted them a prophecy from Psalm 118:22 which referred to builders casting aside the most important stone on a building site: the topmost stone or 'capstone' at the junction of two walls. Verse 18 is a quotation from Isaiah 8:14-15 which demonstrates that those who are offended by the gospel and reject the stone will experience a disastrous judgment.

The teachers of the law and the chief priests looked for a way to arrest him immediately, because they knew he had spoken this parable against them. But they were afraid of the people. (v. 19)

The Old Testament prophets were God's servants; Jesus was God's beloved Son. Jesus had portrayed his opponents as murderers of the Son of God.

The people again are supportive of Jesus. There is no doubt that Luke is preparing his readers for Jesus' death.

THANK YOU, HEAVENLY FATHER;

For those who became believers in Jesus during his earthly ministry: their presence and continual support must have meant so much to him;
For those believers who were not afraid of 'official Judaism' and were unashamed to be seen as being on his side;
For all your people, in various countries of the world, who are being persecuted daily for their loyalty to Jesus;
For all who are ministering to the needs of the Suffering Church;
For all of earth's people who have yet to hear the name of Jesus for the first time;

IN JESUS' NAME, AMEN

92. Luke 20:20 - 26
Paying Taxes to Caesar

Luke 20:20 – 26
Keeping a close watch on him, they sent spies, who pretended to be honest. They hoped to catch Jesus in something he said so that they might hand him over to the power and authority of the governor. [21] *So the spies questioned him: "Teacher, we know that you speak and teach what is right, and that you do not show partiality but teach the way of God in accordance with the truth.* [22] *Is it right for us to pay taxes to Caesar or not?"*

[23] *He saw through their duplicity and said to them,* [24] *"Show me a denarius. Whose portrait and inscription are on it?"*

[25] *"Caesar's," they replied.*

He said to them, "Then give to Caesar what is Caesar's, and to God what is God's."

[26] *They were unable to trap him in what he had said there in public. And astonished by his answer, they became silent.*

This time Official Judaism sent spies to try and catch Jesus in something he said so that they could hand him over to the power and authority of the governor. In other words it would have suited their malevolent purposes if they could catch Jesus on a point of political incorrectness.

They had a catch question ready, and they disguised it in saccharine words: *"Teacher, we know that you speak and teach what is right, and that you do not show partiality but teach the way of God in accordance with the truth."* What flattery! They were speaking with forked tongues. This was where 'they verbally kicked him in the stomach.' It was a sore blow.

He saw through their duplicity and said to them, "Show me a denarius. Whose portrait and inscription are on it?"

They didn't need to be educated men to answer Jesus' question honestly: *"Caesar's," they replied.*

He said to them, *"Then give to Caesar what is Caesar's, and to God what is God's."*

If Jesus had replied 'Yes' to their original question, they would have accused him of siding with the Roman authorities.

If Jesus had replied 'No' the Roman authorities would have accused him of stirring up rebellion among the Jews.

Jesus' answer has since become famous: *give to Caesar what is Caesar's, and to God what is God's."*

This is the consistent teaching of the New Testament with regard to believers paying taxes to the State in which they are citizens. In what other ways can a government raise enough money to pay for the most basic public services right through to civil defence? See Romans 12 & 13, especially 13:7.

We are ending this study on a high note: *They were unable to trap him in what he had said there in public. And astonished by his answer, they became silent (v. 26).*

THANK YOU, HEAVENLY FATHER:

For the wisdom of Your Son Jesus Christ in dealing with the criticisms and questions of his foes;

For Jesus' ability to read men's thoughts and minds 'like a book' so that many of his most venomous critics were reduced to silence by his answers;

For this shining demonstration that the wisdom of Jesus of Nazareth is greater than that of Solomon, who was reputed to be the wisest of men;

For Jesus' teaching about duties to God and to Caesar: because these principles still guide us as believers and as citizens to this day;

IN JESUS' NAME, AMEN

93. Luke 20:27 - 39
The Resurrection and Marriage

Luke 20:27 - 39
Some of the Sadducees, who say there is no resurrection, came to Jesus with a question. [28] "Teacher," they said, "Moses wrote for us that if a man's brother dies and leaves a wife but no children, the man must marry the widow and have children for his brother.

[29] Now there were seven brothers. The first one married a woman and died childless. [30] The second [31] and then the third married her, and in the same way the seven died, leaving no children. [32] Finally, the woman died too. [33] Now then, at the resurrection whose wife will she be, since the seven were married to her?"

[34] Jesus replied, "The people of this age marry and are given in marriage [35] But those who are considered worthy of taking part in that age and in the resurrection from the dead will neither marry nor be given in marriage, [36] and they can no longer die; for they are like the angels. They are God's children, since they are children of the resurrection. [37] But in the account of the bush, even Moses showed that the dead rise, for he calls the Lord 'the God of Abraham, and the God of Isaac, and the God of Jacob'. [38] He is not the God of the dead, but of the living, for to him all are alive."

[39] Some of the teachers of the law responded, "Well said, teacher!" [40] And no-one dared to ask him any more questions.

The Sadducees did not believe in the resurrection of the body (v. 27). They knew that Jesus did, so they asked him a question about levirate marriage. It was about an imaginary woman who, in the course of her life was wife to each of seven brothers who had all predeceased her. The Sadducees question was: *'At the resurrection whose wife will she be, since the seven were married to her?" (v. 33)*

Jesus answered their question by clarifying two things that the Sadducees had never considered.

1.) Marriage is for this life only – it is the key to the continuance of the human race. In the life to come we will not die. (vv. 34-36). *Those who are considered worthy of taking part in that age and in* *the resurrection from the dead will neither marry nor be given in marriage, and they can no longer die; for they are like the angels. They are God's children, since they are children of the resurrection.*

2.) Regarding resurrection, this matter was resolved at the Burning Bush in Moses' time: *"But in the account of the bush, even Moses showed that the dead rise, for he calls the Lord 'the God of Abraham, and the God of Isaac, and the God of Jacob'. 38 He is not the God of the dead, but of the living, for to him all are alive."*

If we recap a little we could ask, 'Where are Abraham, Isaac and Jacob now? The answer is that they are very much alive in the presence of God.

Jesus' position on the resurrection was thoroughly biblical and the Sadducees' position was completely erroneous. Some of the teachers of the law were mightily impressed with Jesus' wisdom: *"Well said, teacher!"*

Verse 40 notes that there were no further questions: *'no-one dared to ask him any more questions.'*

THANK YOU, HEAVENLY FATHER:

For the teaching that is conveyed in this confrontation about resurrection of the body and the life to come;

For the knowledge that You are not the God of the dead, but the God of the Living: we thank you for this comfort;

For the teaching that Jesus gave about resurrection and eternal life: calling himself 'the Resurrection and the Life';

For the further teaching of the New Testament letters about the Last Things;

For our limited knowledge of holy things, because we are hungering and thirsting for more;

IN JESUS' NAME, AMEN

94. Luke 20:40 - 47
Whose Son is Christ?

Luke 21:1 – 4
The Widow's Offering

Luke 20:40 - 44
Then Jesus said to them, "How is it that they say the Christ is the Son of David? ⁴² David himself declares in the Book of Psalms:
   "The Lord said to my Lord: "Sit at my right hand ⁴³ until I make your enemies a footstool for your feet."
   ⁴⁴ David calls him 'Lord'. How then can he be his son?"

In this short section Jesus is challenging official Judaism to discuss a Messianic Scripture found in Psalm 110:1. In taking this initiative, rather than responding to one of frequent their criticisms of him, he was turning their minds to a very important biblical doctrine. *"How is it that they say the Christ is the Son of David?" (v. 40)*

It was a firmly held belief of the Jewish people that the Messiah would be a descendant of David. In order to anchor the discussion Jesus quoted Psalm 110:1 where David wrote about this very issue. *"The Lord said to my Lord: "Sit at my right hand until I make your enemies a footstool for your feet" (Vv. 42-43).*

There are two issues here:(**1**) How did the Jewish teachers understand this Psalm? and (**2**) How did they think about him? The second issue was one on which they would not be forthcoming.

We, with the completed New Testament in our possession, can probably answer Jesus' question more readily than the Jewish teachers. The key to answering his question is found in his incarnation. *'The Word became flesh and dwelt among us.' (John 1:14)*

The Messiah (or the Christ) is David's LORD because he is God; he is also David's SON because he was born as a descendant of David; a point which both Matthew and Luke proved in the family genealogies they included in their gospels (Matthew 1:1-17; Luke 3:23-37). We note that the leaders did not respond to Jesus' answer.

Luke 20:45 - 47
'While all the people were listening, Jesus said to his disciples, ⁴⁶"Beware of the teachers of the law. They like to walk around in flowing robes and love to be greeted in the market-places and have the most important seats in the synagogues and the places of honour at banquets. ⁴⁷ They devour widows' houses and for a show make lengthy prayers. Such men will be punished most severely."

Jesus and the leaders had gathered an audience around them during their exchange (v. 45). There was no way that he could move on without a severe denunciation of these men, and a strong warning to any who were foolish enough to listen to them.

In their love of ceremonial dress, their desire for greetings and compliments, their quest for prominent places, these religious leaders proved themselves to be false shepherds indeed. They used religion to rob the needy and kept the money for themselves. Their ostentatious prayers never went as high as the ceiling. Jesus exposed these false shepherds of Israel and demolished any credibility they ever had.

Luke 21:1 - 4
As he looked up, Jesus saw the rich putting their gifts into the temple treasury. ² He also saw a poor widow put in two very small copper coins.
³ "I tell you the truth," he said, "this poor widow has put in more than all the others. ⁴ All these people gave their gifts out of their wealth; but she out of her poverty put in all she had to live on."

Jesus had been nauseated by his many encounters with the Jewish leaders. At the close this encounter we can imagine that his heart was made glad by something that was happening in a quiet spot in the temple. In complete contrast to the greed of the leaders, Jesus saw a poor widow worshipping God. The widow, not wanting to be noticed save by the God who knows the secrets of us all, was making her contribution of two very small copper coins to the temple offerings. Please note Jesus' words of commendation:

"I tell you the truth, this poor widow has put in more than all the others. All these people gave their gifts out of their wealth; but she out of her poverty put in all she had to live on." (Vv. 3-4)

The widow gave God all she had and trusted him to meet her needs.

THANK YOU, HEAVENLY FATHER:

For Your Son Jesus, the Messiah of the Jews and the Saviour of the world;
For Jesus' ministry in word and deed in his role as the True Shepherd of Israel;
For the example of the widow, who out of her poverty gave all that she had;

IN JESUS' NAME, AMEN

95. Luke 21:5 - 38
Signs of the End of the Age

Luke 21:5 - 38
Some of his disciples were remarking about how the temple was adorned with beautiful stones and with gifts dedicated to God. But Jesus said, [6] "As for what you see here, the time will come when not one stone will be left on another; every one of them will be thrown down.'

[7] "Teacher," they asked, "when will these things happen? And what will be the sign that they are about to take place?"

[8] He replied: "Watch out that you are not deceived. For many will come in my name, claiming, 'I am he,' and 'The time is near.' Do not follow them. [9] When you hear of wars and revolutions, do not be frightened. These things must happen first, but the end will not come right away."

[10] Then he said to them: "Nation will rise against nation, and kingdom against kingdom. [11] There will be great earthquakes, famines and pestilences in various places, and fearful events and great signs from heaven.

[12] "But before all this, they will lay hands on you and persecute you. They will deliver you to synagogues and prisons, and you will be brought before kings and governors, and all on account of my name. [13] This will result in your being witnesses to them. [14] But make up your mind not to worry beforehand how you will defend yourselves. [15] For I will give you words and wisdom that none of your adversaries will be able to resist or contradict. [16] You will be betrayed even by parents, brothers, relatives and friends, and they will put some of you to death. [17] All men will hate you because of me. [18] But not a hair of your head will perish. [19] By standing firm you will gain life.

[20] "When you see Jerusalem being surrounded by armies, you will know that its desolation is near. [21] Then let those who are in Judea flee to the mountains, let those in the city get out, and let those in the country not enter the city. [22] For this is the time of punishment in fulfilment of all that has been written. [23] How dreadful it will be in those days for pregnant women and nursing mothers! There will be

great distress in the land and wrath against this people. ²⁴ *They will fall by the sword and will be taken as prisoners to all the nations. Jerusalem will be trampled on by the Gentiles until the times of the Gentiles are fulfilled.*

²⁵ *"There will be signs in the sun, moon and stars. On the earth, nations will be in anguish and perplexity at the roaring and tossing of the sea.* ²⁶ *Men will faint from terror, apprehensive of what is coming on the world, for the heavenly bodies will be shaken.* ²⁷ *At that time they will see the Son of Man coming in a cloud with power and great glory.* ²⁸ *When these things begin to take place, stand up and lift up your heads, because your redemption is drawing near."*

²⁹ *He told them this parable: "Look at the fig-tree and all the trees.* ³⁰ *When they sprout leaves, you can see for yourselves and know that summer is near.* ³¹ *Even so, when you see these things happening, you know that the kingdom of God is near.*

³² *"I tell you the truth, this generation will certainly not pass away until all these things have happened.* **33** *Heaven and earth will pass away, but my words will never pass away.*

³⁴ *"Be careful, or your hearts will be weighed down with dissipation, drunkenness and the anxieties of life, and that day will close on you unexpectedly like a trap.* ³⁵ *For it will come upon all those who live on the face of the whole earth.* ³⁶ *Be always on the watch, and pray that you may be able to escape all that is about to happen, and that you may be able to stand before the Son of Man."*

³⁷ *Each day Jesus was teaching at the temple, and each evening he went out to spend the night on the hill called the Mount of Olives,* ³⁸ *and all the people came early in the morning to hear him at the temple.*

This is a lengthy section of Luke's gospel. We may feel that the content of its takes us out of our depth. Let's read the passage and find out what it has to say.

Jesus is filling-out the general prophecy he had made to his disciples in vv. 5-6. *"As for what you see here, the time will come when not one stone will be left on another; every one of them will be thrown down."*

vv. 5-7 are about the destruction of the Temple. The whole scene breathed permanence. The grandeur of it tended to anesthetize the visitor so that they became impervious to the spiritual poverty, blindness and even corruption that may underlie such institutions. Twice already in this gospel Jesus had anticipated the Temple's destruction. See Luke 13:34-35 and Luke 19:41-44. Jerusalem would be destroyed as the result of Israel's sin and rejection of the Messiah. Official Israel had rejected him throughout his ministry.

vv. 8–11 are about Signs: Local, National and International. Local signs are clarified in vv. 8; National signs are clarified in v.9. Three exhortations are given: do not follow false Messiahs (v.8); do not be frightened when you hear of wars and revolutions (v. 9a). These things must happen first, but the end will not happen right away (9b). International signs are given in vv 10 – 11. Luke was helping his readers understand that the destruction of Jerusalem and the prophetic pronouncements of the end of history were two distinct matters.

vv. 12–19 are about the Coming Persecution of the Disciples. Persecution will come from Government (vv 12-15), which will result in your being witnesses to them. I will give your words and wisdom when you stand before them. Persecution will come from families and friends (vv. 16-19). The whole flavour of vv. 12-19 indicates that whereas martyrdom may be experienced only by a few, many will experience persecution.

vv. 20 – 24 are about the desolation coming on Jerusalem: v. 24 summarises the awfulness of the event. *They will fall by the sword and will be taken as prisoners to all the nations. Jerusalem will be trampled on by the Gentiles until the times of the Gentiles are fulfilled.* The holy city of Jerusalem would be levelled to the ground. It is recorded that someone took an ox and a plough and succeeded in ploughing a furrow across the site of the former city.

vv. 25-33 are about the Coming of the Son of Man. In vv. 25 Jesus mentioned signs astronomic (25a), international (25b) and oceanic (25c).

The main distinction between the destruction of Jerusalem and the coming of the Son of Man in history is in vv. 27-28. *'At that time they will see the Son of Man coming in a cloud with power and great glory. When these things begin to take place, stand up and lift up your heads, because your redemption is drawing near."*
In v. 32 many of the generation that heard Jesus' words but rejected him, would live to see some of the prophecies of this chapter fulfilled.

vv. 34-37 are about the vigilance of believers until Jesus returns. Two helpful watchwords are given here: be careful (v. 34) and be always on the watch (v. 36). In v. 35 the universality of Jesus' return is spelled out: *For it will come upon all those who live on the face of the whole earth.*

Vv 37-38 are a footnote to chapter 21 and an introduction to chapter 22. That Jesus was able to teach every day in the temple indicates that he was innocent of any wrong-doing. His ministry was not done in a corner but was open for everyone to hear.

THANK YOU, HEAVENLY FATHER:

For what Jesus told us about the future; we know that He holds the future and in the meantime guides us with His hand.

IN JESUS' NAME, AMEN

96. Luke 22:1 - 6
Judas Agrees to Betray Jesus

Luke 22:1 - 6
Now the Feast of Unleavened Bread, called the Passover, was approaching ² and the chief priests and the teachers of the law were looking for some way to get rid of Jesus, for they were afraid of the people.
³ Then Satan entered Judas, called Iscariot, one of the Twelve.
⁴ And Judas went to the chief priests and the officers of the temple guard and discussed with them how he might betray Jesus.
⁵ They were delighted and agreed to give him money. ⁶ He consented, and watched for an opportunity to hand Jesus over to them when no crowd was present.

The significance of that week is recorded simply: *'The Feast of Unleavened Bread, called the Passover, was approaching'*.

So far as Official Judaism was concerned *'they were looking for some way to get rid of Jesus, for they were afraid of the people'*.

In God's economy however, the annual Passover celebrations brought the largest crowds of the year to Jerusalem. There could have been over a million Jews of all nationalities crowding into the city. The Passover celebrated the deliverance of the Israelites from Egypt in Moses' time. The forthcoming trial, crucifixion and death, burial and resurrection of Jesus would achieve a greater deliverance of the human race from sin and death and hell and the grave. That deliverance is still ongoing to this day wherever people become followers of Jesus.

Official Judaism had two problems in plotting Jesus' death. One was they were afraid that the common people would turn on them if they attempted to do such a thing (v. 2). Second, they needed to apprehend Jesus when no crowd was present (v. 6.)

Note the explanatory words in v. 1. Luke is helping his friend Theophilus to understand the significance of these Jewish terms. Jesus had always intended to be in Jerusalem for this particular Passover: *'I have eagerly desired to eat this Passover with you before I suffer'* (v. 14-15).

Luke, alone among the gospel writers, mentions the activity of Satan. He wants to show that behind the actions of men the devil was at work: *'Satan entered Judas' (v. 3)*. Recall how in the wilderness the devil had failed to bring about the downfall of Jesus. There he had attempted to drive a wedge of disobedience between God the Father and God the Son but without success: *'When the devil had finished all this tempting he left him until an opportune time'* (4:13). The devil aggressively attacks Jesus again by using one of his disciples to betray him into the hands of official Judaism.

'Judas went to the chief priests and the officers of the temple guard and discussed with them how he might betray Jesus' (v. 2).

Imagine you belonged to the Sanhedrin (the Jewish Council). The meeting has been convened to decide how to arrest and get rid of Jesus, the itinerant preacher from Galilee who keeps giving the members a hard time. Suddenly, there is a knock on the door, and one of the disciples of Jesus walks in. Why has he come? *To discuss with them how he might betray Jesus!* They were delighted and agreed to give him money. I imagine they can hardly believe their ears.

What will this man accept to do the evil deed? The deal was done quickly: Thirty pieces of silver - the going price for a healthy slave in the local market. Judas told them where they could find Jesus. The trap was easily sprung.

THANK YOU, HEAVENLY FATHER:

For sending Jesus into the world so that the world through him might be saved;
For the fact that the enemies of Jesus were powerless to lay a hand on him until his hour had come;
For the grace of Jesus toward Judas, knowing so much about him and what he would do, yet was gracious and patient with him until the very end;
For the greater mystery: why did Jesus Christ love me and give himself for me?

In Jesus' Name, Amen

97. Luke 22:7 - 18
The Last Passover

Luke 22:7 - 17
Then came the day of Unleavened Bread on which the Passover lamb had to be sacrificed. ^{8} *Jesus sent Peter and John, saying, "Go and make preparations for us to eat the Passover."* ^{9} *"Where do you want us to prepare for it?" they asked.*

^{10} *He replied, "As you enter the city, a man carrying a jar of water will meet you. Follow him to the house that he enters,* ^{11} *and say to the owner of the house, 'The Teacher asks: Where is the guest room, where I may eat the Passover with my disciples?'* ^{12} *He will show you a large upper room, all furnished. Make preparations there."*

^{13} *They left and found things just as Jesus had told them. So they prepared the Passover.* ^{14}*When the hour came, Jesus and his apostles reclined at the table.* ^{15}*And he said to them, "I have eagerly desired to eat this Passover with you before I suffer.* ^{16} *For I tell you, I will not eat it again until it finds fulfilment in the kingdom of God."*

^{17} *After taking the cup, he gave thanks and said, "Take this and divide it among you.* ^{18} *For I tell you I will not drink again of the fruit of the vine until the kingdom of God comes."*

The opening sentence of the section tells us what day of the week it was. It was Thursday of what has become known as Passion Week.

Then came the day of Unleavened Bread on which the Passover lamb had to be sacrificed.

This was the custom in Jewish homes wherever Jews lived and worked around the known world. Ideally they liked to observe it in Jerusalem. Jesus sent Peter and John to make preparations to eat the Passover.

The opening six verses of this chapter tell of the preparations that Jesus' enemies were making for his death.

The following seven verses tell of the preparation the disciples were making to celebrate the Passover and (as far as Jesus was concerned) to inaugurate the Lord's Supper.

We need not delay over the preparations save to note that Jesus had a particular room in mind (v. 9); but didn't disclose the location (he would have known of Judas' pact with official Judaism); that a man carrying a pitcher of water (a task not done by men) would lead them to the room; and the two disciples found things just as Jesus had told them.

The Last Passover of Jesus' Earthly Life

When the hour came, Jesus and his apostles reclined at the table. [15] And he said to them, "I have eagerly desired to eat this Passover with you before I suffer. [16] For I tell you, I will not eat it again until it finds fulfilment in the kingdom of God."

Jesus' forthcoming death would inaugurate the New Covenant (Jeremiah 31:31-34 & Hebrews 8:7-13), therefore the significance of the Passover would be eclipsed. *'I will not eat it again until it finds fulfilment in the kingdom of God.'*

In v. 16 Jesus is referring to the Messianic Banquet at the close of history.

[17] After taking the cup, he gave thanks and said, *"Take this and divide it among you. [18] For I tell you I will not drink again of the fruit of the vine until the kingdom of God comes."*

Please note that the cup in v. 17, for which Jesus gave thanks and then gave to the disciples, was the final one of four used in the Passover Meal.

Jesus would not share again in a meal with the disciples until God's Kingdom would be consummated and his redeemed people will participate with him in his Messianic Banquet (v. 18).

Here we draw a line in the chapter, The Passover Meal had ended.

THANK YOU, HEAVENLY FATHER:

For the great deliverance of Israel from Egypt in the time of Moses
    when the firstborn of Hebrew families were preserved
    from the destroying angel by the blood of the Passover

Lamb having been sprinkled on the lintels and doorposts of their houses;

For the comment made by Paul the Apostle, *'For Christ, our Passover lamb, has been sacrificed.'* (1 Cor. 5:7)

For Jesus' celebration of the Passover Meal as a member of the Jewish people with thanksgiving to God, in the full knowledge that he was *'God's Passover Lamb';*

For the gift of remembrance, particularly of the mercies and faithfulness of God;

IN JESUS' NAME, AMEN

98. Luke 22:19 – 23
The First Lord's Supper

Luke 22:19 – 23
And he took bread, gave thanks and broke it, and gave it to them, saying, "This is my body given for you; do this in remembrance of me."
[20] In the same way, after the supper he took the cup, saying, "This cup is the new covenant in my blood, which is poured out for you.
[21] But the hand of him who is going to betray me is with mine on the table. [22] The Son of Man will go as it has been decreed, but woe to that man who betrays him." [23] They began to question among themselves which of them it might be who would do this.

There were many solemn moments in Jesus' life. There was the moment of his death on the cross. Here, it was the moment when he instituted what has become known as 'The Lord's Supper'. It must have been a deeply moving moment for Jesus. Did the disciples realise how privileged they were that Jesus had shared it with them?

The actions of vv. 19 and 20 were not part of the Passover Meal. It had ended in vv. 17 and 18. We presume that Jesus used a piece of bread and a cup of wine from the Passover Meal for the purposes of the Lord's Supper. It is the new significance of the bread and wine that is important.

Some believers like to think that the Lord is particularly present with us when we meet to remember him. We have to say that he is present with us then as he is in all other parts of a service. If our minds are focussing on what we have come to do at the Lord's Table then, of course, we shall be aware of his presence.

The First Lord's Supper

What did Jesus say and do? The answers are in Luke 22:19 – 20.

And he took bread, gave thanks and broke it, and gave it to them, saying, "This is my body given for you; do this in remembrance of me."

The bread in Jesus' hand was still bread, it had not changed in any way. If the bread had somehow become *'the body of Christ'*, it would have been unlawful for Jews to eat human flesh. The change was in its symbolic significance: *"This is my body given for you. Do this in remembrance of me."*

It would be a good private exercise for us at the Lord's Table to ask ourselves; 'For what was Jesus giving thanks?' That might help us in our thanksgiving. It would certainly help our concentration.

In the same way, after the supper he took the cup, saying, "This cup is the new covenant in my blood, which is poured out for you.

The wine was still wine, it had not changed in any way. If the wine had become *'the blood of Christ'*, it would have been unlawful for Jews to have drunk human blood. We understand its symbolism. It represents the blood of Jesus shed for our sins.

Jesus also said a very significant thing: *"This cup is the new covenant in my blood.'* In that moment Judaism died and Christianity was born. What did Jesus mean by a New Covenant? The first reference is in Jeremiah 31:31-34. The New Covenant is expounded in Hebrews 8 – 10. See chapter 8:7-13 and notice in v. 13 why a New Covenant was needed. The New Covenant is in effect today.

How may we obtain maximum benefit from observing the Lord's Supper? As the years pass we might imagine that our remembering the Lord will improve, that concentration will be less of a battle and so on.

There is only one piece of advice that is useful. Our own personal discipline as we come to the Table will go a long way to make our attendance there meaningful and helpful. That discipline can include such things as personal, private prayer for the Holy Spirit's help in the following moments of remembrance; thinking of verses of Scripture that bear on the suffering and death of Jesus; recalling the lines of a familiar hymn on the cross. All of these are a great aid to memory.

Don't forget to examine ourselves. The moments of remembrance are also moments in which to renew our commitment to Jesus as Lord and Saviour.

Don't forget to look ahead also, because Paul told us *'whenever you eat this bread and drink this cup, you proclaim the Lord's death until he comes.'*

Jesus had a particularly difficult thing to say to the disciples in vv. 21-22.

"But the hand of him who is going to betray me is with mine on the table. ²² The Son of Man will go as it has been decreed, but woe to that man who betrays him."

²³ They began to question among themselves which of them it might be who would do this.

THANK YOU, HEAVENLY FATHER:

For Your love that sought us, for Jesus' blood that bought us, for Your grace that brought us to the fold;
For Jesus' voluntary sacrifice of himself on the cross, the one sacrifice for sins forever, that will never need repetition;

IN JESUS' NAME, AMEN

99. Luke 22:24 - 38
Jesus' Pastoral Ministry After the Supper

Luke 22:24 – 30
Also a dispute arose among them as to which of them was considered to be greatest. [25] *Jesus said to them, "The kings of the Gentiles lord it over them; and those who exercise authority over them call themselves Benefactors.* [26] *But you are not to be like that. Instead, the greatest among you should be like the youngest, and the one who rules like the one who serves.* [27] *For who is greater, the one who is at the table or the one who serves? Is it not the one who is at the table?*

But I am among you as one who serves. [28] *You are those who have stood by me in my trials.* [29] *And I confer on you a kingdom, just as my Father conferred one on me,* [30] *so that you may eat and drink at my table in my kingdom and sit on thrones, judging the twelve tribes of Israel.*

As if Jesus' heart were not carrying burden enough with his death getting ever closer, he has to do some essential *'pastoral'* ministry after the Supper ended.

There was a dispute to be quashed: *'A dispute arose among them as to which of them was considered to be greatest' (v. 24).*

Was this an ongoing dispute that had rankled for weeks or months, or were they arguing about seating arrangements? We don't know how important it was or how it flared up when it did, but Jesus saw it as a matter to be nipped in the bud.

Jesus said to them, "The kings of the Gentiles lord it over them; and those who exercise authority over them call themselves Benefactors, but you are not to be like that. Instead, the greatest among you should be like the youngest, and the one who rules like the one who serves. For who is greater, the one who is at the table or the one who serves? Is it not the one who is at the table? (vv 25-26)

But I am among you as one who serves. Jesus' self-forgetful service to them should have been sufficient to quash the dispute once for all.

Did they realise the honour his Father will confer on them? *You are those who have stood by me in my trials. And I confer on you a kingdom, just as my Father conferred one on me, so that you may eat and drink at my table in my kingdom and sit on thrones, judging the twelve tribes of Israel (vv. 28-30)..* Faithful service to Christ will not be forgotten, but will receive eternal honours.

Luke 22:31 – 34

"Simon, Simon, Satan has asked to sift you as wheat. ³² But I have prayed for you, Simon, that your faith may not fail. And when you have turned back, strengthen your brothers."

³³ But he replied, "Lord, I am ready to go with you to prison and to death." ³⁴ Jesus answered, "I tell you, Peter, before the cock crows today, you will deny three times that you know me."

There was a weakness to be exposed. Not only had Jesus been aware of Satan's pressure on his soul, he is warning his disciples (by naming Simon Peter) that they also will experience this malevolent pressure. *'Simon, Satan is going to sift you like wheat!'*

Simon answered self-confidently *'Lord, I am ready to go with you to prison and to death.'* Before the following morning Simon would deny three times that he ever knew Jesus! (v.34)

But Jesus' intercession for Simon would prove greater than Satan's attempt to undo that disciple's allegiance to Jesus.

Simon did not arm himself with prayer and therefore he found himself denying his Lord. He was totally unprepared for Satan's attacks.

Luke 22:35 – 38

Then Jesus asked them, "When I sent you without purse, bag or sandals, did you lack anything?" "Nothing," they answered.

³⁶ He said to them, "But now if you have a purse, take it, and also a bag; and if you don't have a sword, sell your cloak and buy one. ³⁷ It is written: 'And he was numbered with the transgressors'; and

I tell you that this must be fulfilled in me. Yes, what is written about me is reaching its fulfilment." ³⁸ The disciples said, "See, Lord, here are two swords." "That is enough," he replied.

There was provision to be made. These verses are found only in Luke. They are about the support that travelling preachers need. Where will it come from? Jesus asked them, *"When I sent you without purse, bag or sandals, did you lack anything?" "Nothing,"* they answered.

Jesus envisaged a changed situation in which his disciples would face hostility and persecution. Previously he had been the target for such attacks. From now on the disciples would be in the front line. They will experience the world's hostility as he had done. Jesus quotes Isaiah 53:12 *'And he was numbered with the transgressors'; and I tell you that this must be fulfilled in me. Yes, what is written about me is reaching its fulfilment."*

Sometimes the preacher must provide for his own needs. *"But now if you have a purse, take it, and also a bag; and if you don't have a sword, sell your cloak and buy one. (v. 36)* The disciples said, *"See, Lord, here are two swords." "That is enough,"* he replied.

These lines make strange reading. Only Luke includes them. The obligation to be self-supporting by some kind of *'tent-making ministry'* is understood, but the battle in which the disciples will engage is not fought with earthly weapons. The disciple's weapon is *'the sword of the Spirit'* which is the Word of God. Did the disciples miss the Lord's meaning?

So far as Jesus was concerned the conversation was closed: *'That is enough.'*

THANK YOU, HEAVENLY FATHER:

For Jesus, the model pastor: his care for his men, his patience with their immaturity and so on, passes understanding. We love him and are honoured to serve him;
For the ongoing care that You invest in Your servants, supplying their needs so that they can be single-minded in their gospel ministry;

For the fortitude You give Your servants in lands where the church of Jesus Christ is actively persecuted, many are rendered homeless, many are injured and some are martyred. We commend them and their nearest and dearest to Your fatherly care and provision;

IN JESUS' NAME, AMEN

100. Luke 22:39- 46
Jesus Prays on the Mount of Olives

Luke 22:39 –46
Jesus went out as usual to the Mount of Olives, and his disciples followed him. {40} On reaching the place, he said to them, "Pray that you will not fall into temptation." {41} He withdrew about a stone's throw beyond them, knelt down and prayed, {42} "Father, if you are willing, take this cup from me; yet not my will, but yours be done." {43} An angel from heaven appeared to him and strengthened him. {44} And being in anguish, he prayed more earnestly, and his sweat was like drops of blood falling to the ground.

{45} When he rose from prayer and went back to the disciples, he found them asleep, exhausted from sorrow. {46} "Why are you sleeping?" he asked them. "Get up and pray so that you will not fall into temptation."

It is now Thursday evening of Passion Week. Jesus maintained his normal routine, even though he knew all that awaited him during the remainder of the night and the following day: *Jesus went out as usual to the Mount of Olives, and his disciples followed him. (v, 39)*

It had been customary for Jesus to retreat to this location (the Garden of Gethsemane) to pray. Judas knew of Jesus' prayer habit and used this knowledge to betray Jesus to the Jews. It is a beautiful pastoral touch that Jesus directed the disciples to pray for themselves in all that lay ahead for him. He knew every detail, they did not. *He withdrew about a stone's throw beyond them, knelt down and prayed, "Father, if you are willing, take this cup from me; yet not my will, but yours be done." (vv 41-42)*

An angel from heaven appeared to him and strengthened him. And being in anguish, he prayed more earnestly, and his sweat was like drops of blood falling to the ground. (v. 44)

Here is intensity in prayer that most believers know nothing about. Luke is telling us that Jesus' petition regarding the possibility of his Father taking away the cup of sorrow and suffering was so demanding that it drained his physical energy. Luke searched for a word to illustrate the agony that Jesus was experiencing. The word he found was 'sweating'. Jesus was sweating copiously; in much the same way as blood pours or drips from a wound. Jesus did not sweat blood - he perspired at an excessive rate.

An unknown Christian writer once commented: *'Every life has its Gethsemane, and every Gethsemane has its angel.'*

When he rose from prayer and went back to the disciples, he found them asleep, exhausted from sorrow. "Why are you sleeping?" he asked them. "Get up and pray so that you will not fall into temptation." (Vv 45-46)

We understand to some extent why they fell asleep. It had been a long day since sunrise. They were exhausted and this gave way to sleep. So much had happened during the day that had made them sorrowful. Nevertheless, Jesus repeated his instruction: *"Get up and pray so that you will not fall into temptation."* The circumstances called for earnest prayer for him and for them.

THANK YOU, HEAVENLY FATHER:

For this intimate account of Jesus' prayer habits, his prayerful concern for his disciples and, supremely, in his submission to Your will;

For this example of discipleship in action: Jesus' prayer habits were influential in training the disciples to be men of prayer;

For this revelation that a lot of Jesus' suffering for our sins was already a major factor in his life before he was arrested, tried and crucified;

For the great sacrifice You made in not sparing Your own Son, giving him up for us all that we might live through him;

IN JESUS' NAME, AMEN

101. Luke 22:47 - 54
Jesus is Arrested

Luke 22:47 –53
While he was still speaking a crowd came up, and the man who was called Judas, one of the Twelve, was leading them. He approached Jesus to kiss him, 48 but Jesus asked him, "Judas, are you betraying the Son of Man with a kiss?"

49 When Jesus' followers saw what was going to happen, they said, "Lord, should we strike with our swords?" 50 And one of them struck the servant of the high priest, cutting off his right ear.

51 But Jesus answered, "No more of this!" And he touched the man's ear and healed him.

52 Then Jesus said to the chief priests, the officers of the temple guard, and the elders, who had come for him, "Am I leading a rebellion, that you have come with swords and clubs? 53 Every day I was with you in the temple courts, and you did not lay a hand on me. But this is your hour—when darkness reigns."

54 Then seizing him, they led him away and took him into the house of the high priest.

The location is still the Garden of Gethsemane on the Mount of Olives. Those who made up the crowd that invaded the privacy of Jesus and his disciples are listed in v. 52: *the chief priests, the officers of the temple guard, and the elders.* Official Judaism was there in force—plus Judas.

Judas betrayed Jesus to those who had come to arrest him by kissing him. A kiss was the customary greeting between friends. Judas' action on this occasion only served to underscore the horror of what he was doing. *When Jesus' followers saw what was going to happen, they said, "Lord, should we strike with our swords?" And one of them struck the servant of the high priest, cutting off his right ear. (v. 50)*

It was a foolish and futile action. Trial had come upon them and the disciples neither knew how nor were they able to act properly. The disciples were not professional soldiers and were not used to carrying arms. Whoever had taken the initiative to strike a blow for

Jesus was acting rashly (John says that it was Peter: Jn.18:10). *Jesus answered, "No more of this!" And he touched the man's ear and healed him (v. 51).*

Matthew reports that Jesus said: *"Put your sword back in its place,"* Jesus said to him, *"for all who draw the sword will die by the sword. Do you think I cannot call on my Father, and he will at once put at my disposal more than twelve legions of angels? But how then would the Scriptures be fulfilled that say it must happen in this way?"* (Mt 26:52 – 54).

Jesus said to the chief priests, the officers of the temple guard, and the elders, who had come for him, *"Am I leading a rebellion that you have come with swords and clubs? Every day I was with you in the temple courts, and you did not lay a hand on me. But this is your hour—when darkness reigns" (vv 52-53).*

This is the kind of treatment that Jesus had referred to in v. 37, when he quoted Isaiah 53:12 *'He was numbered with the transgressors.'* Jesus roundly rebuked his opponents for their cowardice. They had been afraid to arrest him in the openness of the Temple.

"But this is your hour—when darkness reigns." Jesus recognised the significance of what was taking place. His hour had come. God's redemptive plan was proceeding to its fulfilment.

There was a conflict taking place between Jesus and Judaism. Another conflict at a deeper level was taking place between the devil, the ruler of this age, and Almighty God. This was indeed an hour of darkness.

Then seizing him, they led him away and took him into the house of the high priest (v. 54). This action marked the moment of arrest. To accomplish a lawful arrest the prisoner must be *'seized.'*

THANK YOU, HEAVENLY FATHER:

For the fortitude of Jesus when surrounded by his enemies, who were intent on killing him;
For his confidence in You, his heavenly Father, believing that You were in complete control of his circumstances;
For the divine necessity of all that Jesus was entering into in his arrest and trials, suffering, crucifixion and death;

For the fact that this was not the end of the story (as Jesus told his disciples after the resurrection); the Son of Man must suffer many things and enter into his glory;

IN JESUS' NAME, AMEN

102. Luke 22:54 - 62
Peter Disowns Jesus

Luke 22:54 –62
Then seizing him, they led him away and took him into the house of the high priest. Peter followed at a distance. ⁵⁵ But when they had kindled a fire in the middle of the courtyard and had sat down together, Peter sat down with them. ⁵⁶ A servant girl saw him seated there in the firelight. She looked closely at him and said, "This man was with him." ⁵⁷ But he denied it. "Woman, I don't know him," he said.

⁵⁸ A little later someone else saw him and said, "You also are one of them."

"Man, I am not!" Peter replied.

⁵⁹ About an hour later another asserted, "Certainly this fellow was with him, for he is a Galilean."

⁶⁰ Peter replied, "Man, I don't know what you're talking about!" Just as he was speaking, the cock crowed. ⁶¹ The Lord turned and looked straight at Peter. Then Peter remembered the word the Lord had spoken to him: "Before the cock crows today, you will disown me three times." ⁶² And he went outside and wept bitterly.

The previous section and this section share v. 54. The first part records the formal arrest of Jesus at the Garden of Gethsemane: *Then seizing him, they led him away and took him into the house of the high priest.* The second part records that *'Peter followed at a distance'* as the entire group moved into the city bound for the high priest's house.

Peter's denials are recorded in all four gospels. All point out that on the night of Jesus' betrayal, Peter denied his Lord three times in the courtyard of the high priest, that a maid questioned Peter, and that a cock crowed 'immediately' after the third denial.

Peter found some warmth at a fire that had been kindled in the middle of the courtyard. No sooner had Peter found a place *'at the fire'* when he found himself *'under fire'* and wishing he was somewhere else.

Denial no. 1 is recorded in vv. 56 - 57. A servant girl saw him seated there in the firelight. She looked closely at him and said, *"This man was with him."* But he denied it. *"Woman, I don't know him,"* he said.

Denial no. 2 is recorded in v. 58. A little later someone else saw him and said, *"You also are one of them." "Man, I am not!"* Peter replied.

Denial no. 3 is recorded in 59 – 62. About an hour later another asserted, *"Certainly this fellow was with him, for he is a Galilean."* Peter replied, *"Man, I don't know what you're talking about!"*

Just as Peter was speaking the Lord turned and looked straight at Peter. Then Peter remembered the word the Lord had spoken to him: *"Before the cock crows today, you will disown me three times."* And he went outside and wept bitterly.

It only took a meeting of eyes to convict Peter of his failure, his sin and his weakness. Words were unnecessary. Peter's tears must have been exceedingly bitter.

Possibly Luke expected his readers to see in Peter's tears not just remorse, but repentance – it is possible that Peter's *'turning back'* to the Lord (22:32) was already under way.

Thank You, Heavenly Father:

For this honest, unvarnished report of a disciples' inner battle with standing up for Jesus; we are deeply grateful that failure need not be final;
For believers everywhere, especially when loyalty to Jesus may mean martyrdom;
For Peter's later spiritual recovery (esp. in John 21:15- 23), when Jesus re-commissioned him to be a shepherd of his sheep;
For Peter's privilege as an apostle of Jesus, when he opened the kingdom of God to the Gentiles in the home of Cornelius (Acts 10:44-48);

In Jesus' Name, Amen

103. Luke 22:63 - 65
The Guards Mock Jesus

Luke 22:63 –65
The men who were guarding Jesus began mocking and beating him. *⁶⁴ They blindfolded him and demanded, "Prophesy! Who hit you?"* *⁶⁵ And they said many other insulting things to him.*

These lines simply reek of man's inhumanity to man. It grieves us deeply that the person on the receiving end of their brutality was Jesus Christ, the Son of God, our Lord and Saviour.

Rome in the 1ˢᵗ century of the Christian era had a highly regulated judiciary in the homeland and its colonies. Was there a Convention of any kind governing warfare as it affected combatants and civilian prisoners? We wonder if it had civil laws governing the treatment of prisoners.

Nowadays 195 countries are signatories of the 1949 Geneva Convention (and its subsequent revisions). This means that the abuse of prisoners in custody is prohibited by international law. This does not mean that abuse never takes place.

As this section of Luke's gospel makes clear, Jesus was at the mercy of the soldiers who were in charge of him. Notice the verbs in the space of three brief verses: *guarding, mocking, and beating*; *blindfolding* and *insulting* him. The soldiers appear to have been undisciplined men. That word *'insulting'* means *'blaspheming'* him.

Jesus had prophesied that he would be treated like this. Luke 18:31 -34

Jesus took the twelve aside and told them, "We are going up to Jerusalem, and everything that is written by the prophets about the Son of Man will be fulfilled.
³² He will be turned over to the Gentiles. They will mock him, insult him, spit on him, flog him and kill him. ³³ On the third day he will rise again."
³⁴ The disciples did not understand any of this. Its meaning was hidden from them, and they did not know what he was talking about.

Throughout the remainder of the night Jesus was made to suffer, but his captors were waiting for the dawn. The force of some of the Greek words used by the various evangelists suggests that their blows were not light taps on the face, but solid punches.

There are commentators believe this scene was so horrible that Luke recorded only the barest details. It is not possible to understand all that the Lord Jesus suffered in that night of horror.

What was happening was taking place with the full authority of the civil and spiritual leadership of the Jewish nation. No wonder retribution would fall on the land and in AD 70 sweep hundreds of thousands into Roman exile.

THANK YOU, HEAVENLY FATHER:

For the amount of suffering that Jesus endured before ever going to the cross;
For the unfathomable wisdom of God that had mapped out such a course for the Son of God to follow in his seeking and saving of that which was lost (Luke 19:10);
For the love of Jesus for sinners: he would go to the cross for the salvation of those who had so cruelly abused him;

IN JESUS' NAME, AMEN

104. Luke 22:66 - 71
Jesus Before The Jewish Council

Luke 22:66 71
At daybreak the council of the elders of the people, both the chief priests and teachers of the law, met together, and Jesus was led before them. ⁶⁷ "If you are the Christ," they said, "tell us."

Jesus answered, "If I tell you, you will not believe me, ⁶⁸ and if I asked you, you would not answer. ⁶⁹ But from now on, the Son of Man will be seated at the right hand of the mighty God."

⁷⁰ They all asked, "Are you then the Son of God?"

He replied, "You are right in saying I am."

⁷¹ Then they said, "Why do we need any more testimony? We have heard it from his own lips."

The full Jewish Sanhedrin is listed in the opening sentence of this section: *the council of the elders of the people, both the chief priests and teachers of the law.* They had convened at daybreak – hardly their usual practice. For them, this was a special occasion because the prisoner was none other than Jesus of Nazareth. They got straight to the point at issue: *"If you are the Christ,"* they said, *"tell us" (v. 67).*

Jesus must have been a pitiful sight after what he had endured during the night at the hands of the Roman soldiers. He stood before them and gave them a straight answer.

"If I tell you, you will not believe me, and if I asked you, you would not answer." In other words, Jesus believed that the proceedings of the Sanhedrin were a charade (v. 68).

"But from now on, the Son of Man will be seated at the right hand of the mighty God" (Vv. 68-69).

They all asked, "Are you then the Son of God?"

He replied, "You are right in saying I am."

Jesus had answered honestly and 'Official Israel' found him guilty of a religious offence: he had claimed to be the Son of God.

Believe it or not, to this day Jews debate the extent of Sanhedrin involvement in Jesus' trial and crucifixion. It is a very sensitive issue.

So far as Christians are concerned we believe the Sanhedrin took the initiative in prosecuting Jesus. All that is lacking in v. 66 are the names of the members.

They believed that Jesus had given them all that they needed to get rid of him. They had asked: *'Are you then THE Son of God?'* He answered in the affirmative, thus claiming to be the Messiah. The trial didn't go any further because in their eyes, Jesus had committed a capital offence.

However the Sanhedrin didn't have the power to execute a man. Their next task would be to accuse Jesus of a crime that the Romans would consider worthy of death.

THANK YOU, HEAVENLY FATHER:

For the fact that, in time, several members of the Jewish Council became believers in Jesus (Nicodemus and Joseph of Arimathea) even though they were secret disciples at first;

For Jesus' unshakeable confidence in the purpose of God and his own exaltation to God's right hand – as he told the Jewish Council (v. 69);

IN JESUS' NAME, AMEN

105. Luke 23:1 - 7
Jesus Before Pilate

Luke 23:1 – 7
Then the whole assembly rose and led him off to Pilate. ² And they began to accuse him, saying, "We have found this man subverting our nation. He opposes payment of taxes to Caesar and claims to be Christ, a king."

³ So Pilate asked Jesus, "Are you the king of the Jews?"

"Yes, it is as you say," Jesus replied.

⁴ Then Pilate announced to the chief priests and the crowd, "I find no basis for a charge against this man."

⁵ But they insisted, "He stirs up the people all over Judea by his teaching. He started in Galilee and has come all the way here."

⁶ On hearing this, Pilate asked if the man was a Galilean.

⁷ When he learned that Jesus was under Herod's jurisdiction, he sent him to Herod, who was also in Jerusalem at that time.

The seat of Roman Government in Judea was in Caesarea. However, Pilate was in Jerusalem during the Passover activities. Here is Jesus being *betrayed into the hands of men* (Luke 9:4) and *being handed over to Gentiles* (Luke 18:32).

Then the whole assembly rose and led him off to Pilate (v. 1). Read the next verse carefully and see how the Jews had invented a political charge against Jesus. The religious charge of the Jewish Council is not mentioned, because they knew that Pilate wouldn't be interested in it.

"We have found this man subverting our nation. He opposes payment of taxes to Caesar and claims to be Christ, a king."

A double charge, if you please, Pilate. Then Pilate went to the point at issue so far as Rome was concerned: Pilate asked Jesus, *"Are you the king of the Jews?"*

"Yes, it is as you say," Jesus replied.

Then Pilate announced to the chief priests and the crowd, *"I find no basis for a charge against this man."*

Jesus' accusers were hoping that Pilate would grasp the political issue, but, much to their disappointment, he did not. Had Pilate been nursing a grudge against Jesus, or wanting to make an example of him, a guilty verdict might have been the outcome.

They Jews wanted Pilate to listen to their charge – he was behaving as if he hadn't heard them properly.

'We have found this man subverting our nation. He opposes payment of taxes to Caesar and claims to be Christ, a king." Pilate had no interest in their accusations against Jesus.

"He stirs up the people all over Judea by his teaching. He started in Galilee and has come all the way here." they insisted.

They had gone too far. When Pilate heard mention of Galilee he asked: *'if the man was a Galilean.'*

When he learned that Jesus was under Herod's jurisdiction, *he sent him to Herod, who was also in Jerusalem at that time. (v. 7)*

THANK YOU, HEAVENLY FATHER:

For Jesus' clear testimony before the Sanhedrin and before Pilate that he was the Son of Man and King of the Jews;
For the evidence that it was Jesus who was in control of these 'legal' proceedings, not the Sanhedrin, Pilate or Herod;
For the fact that he *'who had emptied himself'* and *'became obedient unto death'*, was soon to be highly exalted;

IN JESUS' NAME, AMEN

106. Luke 23:6 - 12
Jesus Before Herod

Luke 23:6 – 12
On hearing this, Pilate asked if the man was a Galilean. ⁷ *When he learned that Jesus was under Herod's jurisdiction, he sent him to Herod, who was also in Jerusalem at that time.* ⁸ *When Herod saw Jesus, he was greatly pleased, because for a long time he had been wanting to see him. From what he had heard about him, he hoped to see him perform some miracle.* ⁹ *He plied him with many questions, but Jesus gave him no answer.*

¹⁰ *The chief priests and the teachers of the law were standing there, vehemently accusing him.*

¹¹ *Then Herod and his soldiers ridiculed and mocked him. Dressing him in an elegant robe, they sent him back to Pilate.*

¹² *That day Herod and Pilate became friends—before this they had been enemies.*

The opening sentences (vv. 6 - 7) explain how Jesus ended up in the presence of Herod the King.

Herod's motive in wanting to see Jesus was that a miracle might be performed for his benefit. Jesus didn't *'do'* miracles that way, merely to entertain. Herod *plied Jesus with many questions, but Jesus gave him no answer (v. 9).*

Jesus was equally indifferent to the accusations that the Jewish officials were heaping on him; *'The chief priests and the teachers of the law were standing there, vehemently accusing him'* (v. 10).

The record stands as written: *Then Herod and his soldiers ridiculed and mocked him. Dressing him in an elegant robe, they sent him back to Pilate (v. 11).*

Herod was a man lacking both character and conviction. He joined his soldiers in mocking Jesus and finding an elegant robe somewhere, put it on Jesus and sent him back to Pilate. It was a mockery of Jesus' kingship.

Verse 12 is ironic in that it took their mutual interest in Jesus of Nazareth (not their respect for him) to bring Herod and Pilate together again in friendship rather than enmity as before.

Neither Pilate nor Herod had found Jesus guilty of any crime. Herod had treated Jesus' appearance before him as a joke.

THANK YOU, HEAVENLY FATHER:

For the innocence of Jesus that is shining through these irregular proceedings of Jewish and Roman law;
For the fact that all who falsely accused Jesus the Son of God, in order to have him killed, will one day stand before him, as their judge;

IN JESUS' NAME, AMEN

107. Luke 23:13 - 25
Jesus is Sentenced by Pilate

Luke 23:13 – 25
Pilate called together the chief priests, the rulers and the people, [14] and said to them, "You brought me this man as one who was inciting the people to rebellion. I have examined him in your presence and have found no basis for your charges against him. [15] Neither has Herod, for he sent him back to us; as you can see, he has done nothing to deserve death. [16]Therefore, I will punish him and then release him."

[17][18] With one voice they cried out, "Away with this man! Release Barabbas to us!" [19] (Barabbas had been thrown into prison for an insurrection in the city, and for murder.)

[20] Wanting to release Jesus, Pilate appealed to them again. [21] But they kept shouting, "Crucify him! Crucify him!"

[22] For the third time he spoke to them: "Why? What crime has this man committed? I have found in him no grounds for the death penalty. Therefore I will have him punished and then release him."

[23] But with loud shouts they insistently demanded that he be crucified, and their shouts prevailed. [24] So Pilate decided to grant their demand. [25] He released the man who had been thrown into prison for insurrection and murder, the one they asked for, and surrendered Jesus to their will.

Pilate has Jesus standing before him for a second time. Herod had sent him back. His first action was to call 'Official Judaism' to consider what should be done with the prisoner. Pilate summarised the case so far.

"You brought me this man as one who was inciting the people to rebellion. I have examined him in your presence and have found no basis for your charges against him. [15] Neither has Herod, for he sent him back to us; as you can see, he has done nothing to deserve death. [16] Therefore, I will punish him and then release him."

This was Pilate's first attempt to have Jesus released.

According to Roman law he ought to have commanded Jesus' release at once. If necessary, he could have kept Jesus in custody for his own safety. However, agitation by the Jews caused Pilate to waver and to disregard the law. He offered the Jews a compromise: he would have Jesus punished and then release him. He offered them an inch, they wanted a mile!

With one voice they cried out, "Away with this man! Release Barabbas to us!" (v. 18)

When offered a choice between Jesus and Barabbas, the Jews demanded the release of Barabbas (a man who had been an insurrectionist and a murderer).

This was Pilate's second attempt to have Jesus released (v. 21).

Wanting to release Jesus, Pilate appealed to them again. *But they kept shouting, "Crucify him! Crucify him!" (v. 21).*

Pilate made a third attempt to have Jesus released (v. 22).

"Why? What crime has this man committed? I have found in him no grounds for the death penalty. Therefore I will have him punished and then release him".
But with loud shouts they insistently demanded that he be crucified, and their shouts prevailed (v. 23).

So Pilate decided to grant their demand (v. 24).

He released the man who had been thrown into prison for insurrection and murder, the one they asked for, and surrendered Jesus to their will. (Vv. 24-25)

Jesus had not been found guilty on any charge, yet he was handed over to the will of his enemies. **That is an awful final clause in v. 24: *'he surrendered Jesus to their will.'*** The human being who had most to do with Jesus' crucifixion was Pontius Pilate, the Roman Governor of Jerusalem. So much for the administration of Roman law!

We try to imagine the noise, the abuse from the crowd, the melee that was going on around Jesus – and then we remember 1Peter 2:21-22.

To this you were called, because Christ suffered for you, leaving you an example that you should follow in his steps.

"He committed no sin, and no deceit was found in his mouth." When they hurled their insults at him, he did not retaliate; when he suffered, he made no threats. Instead, he entrusted himself to him who judges justly.

THANK YOU, HEAVENLY FATHER:

For the opportunity of these moments to bow in meditation, thankfulness and love before our Saviour who suffered so much for our salvation:

IN JESUS' NAME, AMEN

108. Luke 23:26 - 43
The Crucifixion

Luke 23:26 – 43
As they led him away, they seized Simon from Cyrene, who was on his way in from the country, and put the cross on him and made him carry it behind Jesus.

²⁷ A large number of people followed him, including women who mourned and wailed for him. ²⁸ Jesus turned and said to them, "Daughters of Jerusalem, do not weep for me; weep for yourselves and for your children. ²⁹ For the time will come when you will say, 'Blessed are the barren women, the wombs that never bore and the breasts that never nursed!' ³⁰Then they will say to the mountains, "Fall on us!" and to the hills "Cover us!" ³¹ For if men do these things when the tree is green, what will happen when it is dry?"

³² Two other men, both criminals, were also led out with him to be executed. ³³ When they came to the place called the Skull, there they crucified him, along with the criminals—one on his right, the other on his left. ³⁴ Jesus said, "Father, forgive them, for they do not know what they are doing." And they divided up his clothes by casting lots.

³⁵ The people stood watching, and the rulers even sneered at him. They said, "He saved others; let him save himself if he is the Christ of God, the Chosen One."

³⁶ The soldiers also came up and mocked him. They offered him wine vinegar ³⁷ and said, "If you are the king of the Jews, save yourself."

³⁸ There was a written notice above him, which read: THIS IS THE KING OF THE JEWS.

³⁹ One of the criminals who hung there hurled insults at him: "Aren't you the Christ? Save yourself and us!"

⁴⁰ But the other criminal rebuked him. "Don't you fear God," he said, "since you are under the same sentence? ⁴¹ We are punished justly, for we are getting what our deeds deserve. But this man has done nothing wrong."

⁴² Then he said, "Jesus, remember me when you come into your kingdom."

> *[43]{.sup} Jesus answered him, "I tell you the truth, today you will be with me in paradise."*

Evidently there was a lot going on in the background. Luke cannot record everything. We notice in v. 26 that a cross has been obtained. We ask from where and from whom? The crowd is making for Mt. Calvary, the traditional place for crucifixions which were always outside the city. On the way Simon of Cyrene (a North African?) is commandeered to carry Jesus' cross. It was usual for Roman soldiers to requisition citizens on the spot for certain duties. This was how Simon became involved in carrying Jesus' cross.

Why did Jesus need help? This was probably because of Jesus' weakened physical condition following the flogging ordered by Pilate. (Matthew 27:26).

In the crowd there were many women who mourned and wailed for him. Probably these were official mourners, but Jesus, despite his own suffering, had a word for them: *"Daughters of Jerusalem do not weep for me; weep for yourselves and for your children. [29] For the time will come when you will say, 'Blessed are the barren women, the wombs that never bore and the breasts that never nursed!' [30] Then "'they will say to the mountains, "Fall on us!" and to the hills "Cover us!" [31] For if men do these things when the tree is green, what will happen when it is dry?"*

He was thinking of the terrible times that lay ahead for Jerusalem when its citizens would be crushed and murdered by the Roman armies in AD70. In contrast to the joy of childbirth, woman with babies in arms and very young children at their heels will wish that their children had never been born. Instead of thanking the women for their concern for him, Jesus urged them to weep for themselves. He was not seeking sympathy, but rather their faith in him and genuine repentance for sin.

Two other men, both criminals, were also led out with him to be executed. [33] When they came to the place called the Skull, there they crucified him, along with the criminals—one on his right, the other on his left.

Luke stresses the fact that Jesus was crucified between two criminals. '*He was numbered with the transgressors*' (Isaiah 53:12). Jesus was fastened to the cross by nails driven through his hands and feet.

Jesus said, "Father, forgive them, for they do not know what they are doing." And they divided up his clothes by casting lots. (v. 34)

In his prayer on the cross Jesus was acknowledging the guilt of those who were involved in his crucifixion. He is not exonerating them. He is asking his Father to be merciful to them and forgive their behaviour which had been done in ignorance. His seamless robe was disposed of by the soldiers casting lots to see who could claim it.

There is no peace for Jesus even when dying: *The people stood watching, and the rulers even sneered at him. They said, "He saved others; let him save himself if he is the Christ of God, the Chosen One." [36] The soldiers also came up and mocked him. They offered him wine vinegar [37] and said, "If you are the king of the Jews, save yourself." [38] There was a written notice above him, which read: THIS IS THE KING OF THE JEWS.*

As far as Rome was concerned Jesus was crucified on a political charge. Meanwhile, what about the two criminals crucified beside Jesus? *One of the criminals who hung there hurled insults at him: "Aren't you the Christ? Save yourself and us!" [40] But the other criminal rebuked him. "Don't you fear God," he said, "since you are under the same sentence? [41] We are punished justly, for we are getting what our deeds deserve. But this man has done nothing wrong."*

One man railed on Jesus with mocking words (v. 39). The other man reasoned that both of them were getting what they deserved for their crimes: '*but this man has done nothing wrong.*'

Then he said, "Jesus, remember me when you come into your kingdom." [43] Jesus answered him, "I tell you the truth, today you will be with me in paradise."

By contrast with those who taunted Jesus, the man trusted Jesus. He was saved and assured immediately. Jesus saves!

THANK YOU, HEAVENLY FATHER:

For the unsolicited testimony of the repentant criminal when he said of Jesus, *'this man has done nothing wrong'; (v. 41)*

For the answer and the assurance that Jesus gave to the repentant criminal, *"I tell you the truth, today you will be with me in paradise." (v. 43)*

For Jesus' answer to the repentant criminal: he indicated where he was going at the moment of death. His soul would enter paradise (his Father's presence) immediately. The forgiven man would be with him.

IN JESUS' NAME, AMEN

109. Luke 23:44-49
Jesus' Death

Luke 23:44 – 49
It was now about the sixth hour, and darkness came over the whole land until the ninth hour, ⁴⁵ for the sun stopped shining. And the curtain of the temple was torn in two.
⁴⁶ Jesus called out with a loud voice, "Father, into your hands I commit my spirit." When he had said this, he breathed his last.
⁴⁷ The centurion, seeing what had happened, praised God and said, "Surely this was a righteous man."
⁴⁸ When all the people who had gathered to witness this sight saw what took place, they beat their breasts and went away.
⁴⁹ But all those who knew him, including the women who had followed him from Galilee, stood at a distance, watching these things.

According to Jewish time it was now about the sixth hour, mid-day on what is called Good Friday. Two miraculous events happened simultaneously: the sun stopped shining (for three hours until 3 o'clock), and the heavy veil in the Temple that obstructed the entrance to the Holy Place was torn from top to bottom. Both events happened by divine intervention.

Luke is calling attention to a tangible darkness, as if God had switched off the lights of glory. The purpose was that no human eye was permitted to see what took place between God the Father and Jesus Christ his Son on the cross.

The curtain in the Temple was not some delicate piece of fabric but was a heavy item with layer upon layer of folded fabric. God obviously had torn the curtain of the temple. Matthew links this to an earthquake that shook the city at this moment and left the inner sanctum the holy of holies, open to all to look into. The veil that symbolized the barrier between God's inner sanctuary and a polluted human race had been torn apart.

⁴⁶ Jesus called out with a loud voice, "Father, into your hands I commit my spirit." When he had said this, he breathed his last.

Other gospels record well-known words of Jesus from the cross:

Mt 27:46 & Mark 15:33 - 34
About the ninth hour Jesus cried out in a loud voice, "Eloi, Eloi, lama sabachthani?"—which means, **"My God, my God, why have you forsaken me?"**

Jn 19:28 & 30
Later, knowing that all was now completed, and so that the Scripture would be fulfilled, Jesus said, "I am thirsty." When he had received the drink, Jesus said, "It is finished." With that, he bowed his head and gave up his spirit.

The whole scene made a deep impression on a Roman centurion who, we may be sure, had witnessed many a crucifixion.

Luke 23:47
The centurion, seeing what had happened, praised God and said, "Surely this was a righteous man."

Meanwhile the dead body of Jesus hung silently on the cross and the people who had gathered to witness the crucifixion, beat their breasts and went away.
That left a special group of people at the cross.

But all those who knew him, including the women who had followed him from Galilee, stood at a distance, watching these thing.(49).

Only God knew their thoughts. They were actually thinking ahead - as we shall discover later.

Thank You, Heavenly Father:

For allowing us to have the biblical account of the atoning death of Your Son Jesus, recorded by those who were committed to him and loved him;

For all that took place between You, God the Father, and Jesus Christ, Your well beloved Son, in the darkness at the cross;

For Jesus, the one mediator between God and men; we remember his words *'I am the way, the truth and the life, no one comes to the Father but by me'*.

For all that took place at Calvary on 'Good Friday' – *but Sunday was coming!*

IN JESUS' NAME, AMEN

110. Luke 23:50 - 56
The Burial of Jesus

Luke 23:50 – 56
Now there was a man named Joseph, a member of the Council, a good and upright man, [51]who had not consented to their decision and action. He came from the Judean town of Arimathea and he was waiting for the kingdom of God.

[52] Going to Pilate, he asked for Jesus' body. [53] Then he took it down, wrapped it in linen cloth and placed it in a tomb cut in the rock, one in which no-one had yet been laid. [54] It was Preparation Day, and the Sabbath was about to begin.

[55] The women who had come with Jesus from Galilee followed Joseph and saw the tomb and how his body was laid in it. [56] Then they went home and prepared spices and perfumes. But they rested on the Sabbath in obedience to the commandment.

Meet Joseph of Arimathea. We are very pleased to meet him because he was a member of the Sanhedrin, the group we have called 'Official Judaism' for the sake of convenience. It saved space omitting the constituent parts of the Council.

We are very pleased to meet Joseph because Luke tells us that this member of the Jewish Council *'had not consented to their decision and action'* concerning Jesus.

We are glad that the death of Jesus stirred Joseph. We learn that he had a deep, personal reason for going to Pilate to ask for the body of Jesus, which was really 'government property.'

He came from the Judean town of Arimathea and he was waiting for the kingdom of God.

Joseph had been a secret believer; now it was time for his secret to be a secret no longer.

Going to Pilate, he asked for Jesus' body. [53] Then he took it down, wrapped it in linen cloth and placed it in a tomb cut in the rock, one *in which no-one had yet been laid. ⁵⁴ It was Preparation Day, and the Sabbath was about to begin.*

Pilate may have been glad to get rid of the body of Jesus so easily and quietly. He gave consent that Joseph should have custody of the body of the deceased. We also learn that Joseph had a very limited amount of time to carry out any plans he had because the Sabbath would begin by early evening.

The other gospels add a little more detail – Luke must have felt the urgency of the matter when writing about this.

We learn from Matthew (27:57-60) that Joseph was a rich man, and had already prepared his own tomb hewn from the rock with a big stone at the entrance. Mark (15:42-47) doesn't enlarge on the main details. John (19:38 – 42) records that Joseph had the assistance of Nicodemus (*who came to Jesus by night - John 3)* who provided seventy five pounds of spices to prepare the body of Jesus for burial. John says Jesus' body was placed in a new tomb in which no one had ever been laid, but doesn't say that it belonged to Joseph.

Watch what a special group of people were doing:

The women who had come with Jesus from Galilee followed Joseph and saw the tomb and how his body was laid in it. ⁵⁶ Then they went home and prepared spices and perfumes.

They marked the spot so that they could find the grave easily on Sunday morning. Alas, the thought of resurrection hadn't occurred to any of them and was far from their minds.

THANK YOU, HEAVENLY FATHER:

For the kind hands and loving hearts that performed the last offices for the body of Jesus;
For the women who went to make preparations to complete Jesus' burial;
For two men, both members of the Jewish Council, who had been secret believers, but saw their opportunity to provide an essential service in Jesus' burial;

For the worship that fills our hearts just now, as we meditate on the love of Jesus in his sacrificial death on the cross for our sins;

IN JESUS' NAME, AMEN

111. Luke 24:1 - 12
The Empty Tomb

Luke 24:1 - 12
On the first day of the week, very early in the morning, the women took the spices they had prepared and went to the tomb. ² They found the stone rolled away from the tomb, ³ but when they entered, they did not find the body of the Lord Jesus.

⁴ While they were wondering about this, suddenly two men in clothes that gleamed like lightning stood beside them. ⁵ In their fright the women bowed down with their faces to the ground, but the men said to them, "Why do you look for the living among the dead? ⁶ He is not here; he has risen! Remember how he told you, while he was still with you in Galilee:⁷ 'The Son of Man must be delivered into the hands of sinful men, be crucified and on the third day be raised again." ⁸ Then they remembered his words.

⁹ When they came back from the tomb, they told all these things to the Eleven and to all the others. ¹⁰ It was Mary Magdalene, Joanna, Mary the mother of James, and the others with them who told this to the apostles. ¹¹ But they did not believe the women because their words seemed to them like nonsense.

¹² Peter, however, got up and ran to the tomb. Bending over, he saw the strips of linen lying by themselves, and he went away, wondering to himself what had happened.

When Joseph and Nicodemus placed the body of Jesus in the rock-tomb belonging to Joseph, Luke noted that *'the women saw the tomb and how his body was laid in it'* (23:55). They were observing carefully so that they would know its location and remember how the body had been arranged within it.

It was now Sunday morning, and the women went to the tomb carrying the spices they had prepared to complete the embalming of Jesus' body. They expected that it would be in the tomb where they had left it on Friday evening.

They found the stone rolled away from the tomb, but when they entered, they did not find the body of the Lord Jesus. (vv. 2-3)

This is the Resurrection Chapter, the record of an event that turned the world upside down. If this was all we knew about Jesus' resurrection, it would not be proof that he had risen. But the testimony of the empty tomb is backed up by the resurrection appearances of Jesus, from this point forward. 'He is Risen' is the essential creed of all believers.

The women entered the tomb but when they entered they did not find the body of Jesus. They were wondering about this when, suddenly *'two men in clothes that gleamed like lightning stood beside them.'* The women were frightened and in the presence of these angel-like messengers, they bowed low to the ground. Some words spoken by the men gave them a better understanding of what had changed about the tomb and the body of Jesus.

"Why do you look for the living among the dead? He is not here; he has risen! Remember how he told you, while he was still with you in Galilee: 'The Son of Man must be delivered into the hands of sinful men, be crucified and on the third day be raised again" (vv. 5-7). Here is a 'golden' sentence*: 'Then they remembered his words.'(v. 8)* How precious those words were at that moment! Perhaps, like the disciples, they had missed those words when Jesus had spoken them at the first. But now – they were the most thrilling words in the world!

When they came back from the tomb, they told all these things to the Eleven and to all the others. It was Mary Magdalene, Joanna, Mary the mother of James, and the others with them who told this to the apostles. (v. 9-10) The women returned to Jerusalem to where the Eleven and other friends of Jesus were gathered. Luke gives the names of the women: *'It was Mary Magdalene, Joanna, Mary the mother of James, and the others with them.'* They told the apostles about their experience at the Tomb.

The first witnesses of the resurrection were women – the women who had stood by Jesus when the men fled out of fear. But they were met with unbelief! *They did not believe the women, because their words seemed to them like nonsense. (v. 11)*

It was Sunday morning, the third day since Jesus died and was buried, but not one of the apostles was thinking about the possibility of resurrection! However, something stirred within Peter and he ran to the tomb: *Bending over, he saw the strips of linen lying by themselves, and he went away, wondering to himself what had happened.*

THANK YOU, HEAVENLY FATHER:

For the resurrection message 'He is not here, he has risen!' We believe in a Saviour who lives (1 Corinthians 15);
For the gospel of Jesus Christ, it is the power of God for the salvation of everyone who believes: first for the Jew, then for the Gentile;
IN JESUS' NAME, AMEN

112. Luke 24:13 - 35
On the Road to Emmaus

Luke 24:13 - 35
Now that same day two of them were going to a village called Emmaus, about seven miles from Jerusalem. [14] They were talking with each other about everything that had happened. [15] As they talked and discussed these things with each other, Jesus himself came up and walked along with them; [16] but they were kept from recognising him.

[17] He asked them, "What are you discussing together as you walk along?"

They stood still, their faces downcast. [18] One of them, named Cleopas, asked him, "Are you only a visitor to Jerusalem and do not know the things that have happened there in these days?"

[19] "What things?" he asked.

"About Jesus of Nazareth," they replied. "He was a prophet, powerful in word and deed before God and all the people. [20] The chief priests and our rulers handed him over to be sentenced to death, and they crucified him; [21] but we had hoped that he was the one who was going to redeem Israel. And what is more, it is the third day since all this took place. [22] In addition, some of our women amazed us. They went to the tomb early this morning [23] but didn't find his body. They came and told us that they had seen a vision of angels, who said he was alive. [24] Then some of our companions went to the tomb and found it just as the women had said, but him they did not see."

[25] He said to them, "How foolish you are, and how slow of heart to believe all that the prophets have spoken! [26] Did not the Christ have to suffer these things and then enter his glory?" [27] And beginning with Moses and all the Prophets, he explained to them what was said in all the Scriptures concerning himself.

[28] As they approached the village to which they were going, Jesus acted as if he were going further. [29] But they urged him strongly, "Stay with us, for it is nearly evening; the day is almost over." So he went in to stay with them.

[30] When he was at the table with them, he took bread, gave thanks, broke it and began to give it to them. [31] Then their eyes were opened

and they recognised him, and he disappeared from their sight. ³² They asked each other, "Were not our hearts burning within us while he talked with us on the road and opened the Scriptures to us?"

³³ They got up and returned at once to Jerusalem. There they found the Eleven and those with them, assembled together ³⁴ and saying, "It is true! The Lord has risen and has appeared to Simon." ³⁵ Then the two told what had happened on the way, and how Jesus was recognised by them when he broke the bread.

This is a lengthy section but we need to think about as a whole. This post-resurrection evidence about the two believers meeting Jesus on the Road to Emmaus is unique to Luke's gospel. Were these two men who were among the disciples we had not met before, or were they husband and wife? Several touches in the narrative might lead us to think they were a married couple. We cannot be dogmatic about this.

These two had decided to leave Jerusalem and the other disciples and go home. Jesus was dead, and they had few other options. We can easily imagine their conversation as Luke records it in vv. 13-14. The most beautiful touch is in vv. 15-16:

'As they talked and discussed these things with each other, Jesus himself came up and walked along with them; but they were kept from recognising him.'

They did not know the 'stranger' because they were divinely kept from recognising him. As before his resurrection, so after it Jesus had an aptitude for entering into other people's conversation: *"What are you discussing together as you walk along?"* (v. 17a) Jesus could see that these two were carrying a burden of anxiety – it was written in their faces (v. 17b). The one who was called Cleopas (a masculine name) spoke first. (v. 18) *"Are you only a visitor to Jerusalem and do not know the things that have happened there in these days?"*

Jesus had only to say two words and the whole story came tumbling out.

'What things? he asked. Cleopas kept talking for the next six verses! (vv. 19-24).

The two poured out their grief about the death of Jesus; they pinned the blame for Jesus' death where they believed it belonged; they spoke about their cherished hopes about him; they spoke about the significant passing of time since his death; they told him of the women who had been to the tomb and found it empty; they told him of the message the angels had given the women; they said that some of their colleagues had gone to the tomb and found it empty, but they didn't find Jesus.

At last, Cleopas is perhaps out of breath, but Jesus interjects. We can try to imagine the tone of his voice.

He said to them, *"How foolish you are, and how slow of heart to believe all that the prophets have spoken!* [26] *Did not the Christ have to suffer these things and then enter his glory?"* [27] *And beginning with Moses and all the Prophets, he explained to them what was said in all the Scriptures concerning himself.*

If they had believed the Scriptures they would not have been sad (v. 17) or confused (vv. 19-24). There were two emphases in what Jesus said:-

'Christ had to suffer' and *'then enter his glory'*

Time and miles pass quickly when there is a good conversation in progress: by this time they had arrived at Emmaus. *As they approached the village to which they were going, Jesus acted as if he were going further. But they urged him strongly, "Stay with us, for it is nearly evening; the day is almost over." So he went in to stay with them. (vv. 28-29)*

Soon a meal was spread, and, in the custom of a devout Jew, Jesus gave thanks for the food, broke it into portions and gave it to them. In that moment the truth dawned on them. *Then their eyes were opened and they recognised him, and he disappeared from their sight.* [32] *They asked each other, "Were not our hearts burning within us while he talked with us on the road and opened the Scriptures to us?"*

The adrenaline rushed in their veins. We can't keep this to ourselves. We must tell the others back in Jerusalem. Late though it was, they got up and returned to Jerusalem (v. 33).

There they found the Eleven and those with them, assembled together ^{34} *and saying, "It is true! The Lord has risen and has appeared to Simon."* ^{35} *Then the two told what had happened on the way, and how Jesus was recognised by them when he broke the bread.*

By leaving Jerusalem when they did, they had missed at least one other appearance of Jesus to the other disciples. They were in no way disappointed and were pleased to add their story to the testimony of the others that Jesus was alive. It was true, the Lord had risen indeed!

THANK YOU, HEAVENLY FATHER:

For the growing body of evidence that Luke is compiling that Jesus is alive and has appeared to the disciples;
For the fact that Jesus Christ is the same, yesterday, today and forever;
For the joy of knowing Jesus, indwelling our hearts by the Holy Spirit; and committed to be with us always;

IN JESUS' NAME, AMEN

113. Luke 24:36 - 43
Jesus Appears to the Disciples

Luke 24:36 - 43
While they were still talking about this, Jesus himself stood among them.
[37] They were startled and frightened, thinking they saw a ghost. [38] He said to them, "Why are you troubled, and why do doubts rise in your minds? [39] Look at my hands and my feet. It is I myself! Touch me and see; a ghost does not have flesh and bones, as you see I have." [40] When he had said this, he showed them his hands and feet. [41] And while they still did not believe it because of joy and amazement, he asked them, "Do you have anything here to eat?" [42] They gave him a piece of broiled fish, [43] and he took it and ate it in their presence.

Jesus' body was the same body that was laid in the tomb, but in some respects it was different. One of the contrasts was that it was not confined to space and time as before the resurrection. He could now appear and disappear at will, but he possessed flesh and bones.

While they were still talking about this, Jesus himself stood among them and said to them, "Peace be with you."

Just as Jesus supernaturally disappeared from the home in Emmaus (v. 31) so he appeared among the disciples gathered in the Upper Room (v. 36). There was the sound of his voice when he greeted them *'Peace be with you.'* However they were not too sure of what was happening. Some thought they had seen a ghost (v. 37). So Jesus enabled them to adjust to his presence with them (vv. 38-40).

"Why are you troubled, and why do doubts rise in your minds? [39] Look at my hands and my feet. It is I myself! Touch me and see; a ghost does not have flesh and bones, as you see I have." When he had said this, he showed them his hands and feet.

The Risen Christ was the same person as Jesus of Nazareth.

Luke writes carefully, anxious to prove to his readers that Jesus' body was real. Why show them his hands and his feet? These carried the scars from his crucifixion, even if the wounds had started to heal. Luke doesn't record whether any of the disciples physically touched Jesus.

While they still did not believe it because of joy and amazement, he asked them, "Do you have anything here to eat?" [42] They gave him a piece of broiled fish, [43] and he took it and ate it in their presence.

If it were needed Jesus gave them a further proof of his resurrection (vv. 41-42). He asked them for food. They gave him a piece of fish, which he ate before them. We don't blame the disciples for their natural hesitancy to believe their eyes and ears. To some degree, we understand it. Jesus understood their hesitancy and helped them overcome it. Visions don't sit down and break bread with people (v. 30), and ghosts don't have appetites (v. 41).

Luke 24:44 – 49
He said to them, "This is what I told you while I was still with you: Everything must be fulfilled that is written about me in the Law of Moses, the Prophets and the Psalms."
[45] Then he opened their minds so they could understand the Scriptures.
[46] He told them, "This is what is written: The Christ will suffer and rise from the dead on the third day, [47] and repentance and forgiveness of sins will be preached in his name to all nations, beginning at Jerusalem.
[48] You are witnesses of these things. [49] I am going to send you what my Father has promised; but stay in the city until you have been clothed with power from on high."

In v. 44 Jesus is recalling the years he had spent with the disciples before his death. He recalled telling them '*Everything must be fulfilled that is written about me in the Law of Moses, the Prophets and the Psalms."*

Then he opened their minds so they could understand the Scriptures.

What a wonderful experience this must have been (v. 45). To this day we must look for Jesus Christ in all the Scriptures when we are reading our Bibles.

He told them, "This is what is written: The Christ will suffer and rise from the dead on the third day, and repentance and forgiveness of sins will be preached in his name to all nations, beginning at Jerusalem (v. 46-47).

The work of world evangelisation must be undertaken by the apostles and all believers until Christ shall come again in his glory. Jesus made this a personal challenge for each of those present (vv. 48-49).

You are witnesses of these things. I am going to send you what my Father has promised; but stay in the city until you have been clothed with power from on high."

Jesus promised that they would be divinely empowered for this mission.

THANK YOU, HEAVENLY FATHER;

For the over-arching message of the Old and New Testaments: they testify about Jesus (John 5:39);
For the special ministry of the Holy Spirit, who takes the things of Christ and makes them known to us (John 16:13-15);
For the refreshing experience it is to meet Jesus as we read the Scriptures;

IN JESUS' NAME, AMEN

114. Luke 24:50-53 & Acts 1:1-11
The Ascension of Jesus

Luke 24:50 - 53
When he had led them out to the vicinity of Bethany, he lifted up his hands and blessed them.
⁵¹ While he was blessing them, he left them and was taken up into heaven.
⁵² Then they worshipped him and returned to Jerusalem with great joy.
⁵³ And they stayed continually at the temple, praising God.

For completeness Luke included mention of the Ascension of Jesus, an event that the prophetic Scriptures had looked forward to for centuries. The most vivid of such Scriptures is Psalm 24 which is a Psalm by King David. The third section of that Psalm (vv. 7-10) anticipates the arrival of Jesus the King in heaven. The ancient gates are exhorted to be lifted up so that the King of Glory may enter in. What a scene! What worship!

The location of the Ascension was near Bethany. There was no long farewell speech, in fact it seemed very ordinary, just like old times before Jesus was arrested and crucified. Jesus led, and his disciples followed.

He had led them out to the vicinity of Bethany,
He lifted up his hands and blessed them. While he was blessing them, he left them and was taken up into heaven (vv. 50-51).

It was not a farewell speech, it was better than that by far. It was a farewell blessing from the hands of the Risen, now Ascending Lord.

Then they worshipped him and returned to Jerusalem with great joy. And they stayed continually at the temple, praising God (vv. 52-53).

The early believers did not give worship to Satan or to any man, but only to God. The disciples worshipped Jesus in glad adoration because they believed that he was God, and beside him there was no Saviour.

For the sake of completeness, and in order to introduce Luke's second book, we conclude this section with a brief look at the Acts of the Apostles.

Acts 1:1 - 11
In my former book, Theophilus, I wrote about all that Jesus began to do and to teach ² until the day he was taken up to heaven, after giving instructions through the Holy Spirit to the apostles he had chosen. ³ After his suffering, he showed himself to these men and gave many convincing proofs that he was alive. He appeared to them over a period of forty days and spoke about the kingdom of God.

⁴ On one occasion, while he was eating with them, he gave them this command: "Do not leave Jerusalem, but wait for the gift my Father promised, which you have heard me speak about. ⁵ For John baptised with water, but in a few days you will be baptised with the Holy Spirit."

⁶ So when they met together, they asked him, "Lord, are you at this time going to restore the kingdom to Israel?"

⁷ He said to them: "It is not for you to know the times or dates the Father has set by his own authority. ⁸ But you will receive power when the Holy Spirit comes on you; and you will be my witnesses in Jerusalem, and in all Judea and Samaria, and to the ends of the earth."

⁹ After he said this, he was taken up before their very eyes, and a cloud hid him from their sight. ¹⁰ They were looking intently up into the sky as he was going, when suddenly two men dressed in white stood beside them. ¹¹ "Men of Galilee," they said, "why do you stand here looking into the sky? This same Jesus, who has been taken from you into heaven, will come back in the same way you have seen him go into heaven."

Observant readers will recognise these paragraphs in Acts 1:1-11 as the connection between Luke's first and second books.

"Do not leave Jerusalem, but wait for the gift my Father promised, which you have heard me speak about. ⁵ For John baptised with water, but in a few days you will be baptised with the Holy Spirit" (vv. 4-5).

The Gift of the Holy Spirit would be poured out on the infant Christian Church to equip it for the task of world evangelisation (v. 8).

"But you will receive power when the Holy Spirit comes on you; and you will be my witnesses in Jerusalem, and in all Judea and Samaria, and to the ends of the earth."

In the meantime Jesus had to return to His Father. Here Luke gives a slightly expanded report of the Ascension of Jesus (vv 9-11).

After he said this, he was taken up before their very eyes, and a cloud hid him from their sight. They were looking intently up into the sky as he was going, when suddenly two men dressed in white stood beside them.
   "Men of Galilee," they said, "why do you stand here looking into the sky? This same Jesus, who has been taken from you into heaven, will come back in the same way you have seen him go into heaven."

The group of believers returned to Jerusalem in obedience to the command of Jesus that they wait there for the advent of the Holy Spirit.

THANK YOU, HEAVENLY FATHER:

For the promise given by the two men who appeared at Jesus' Ascension: *This same Jesus, who has been taken from you into heaven, will come back in the same way you have seen him go into heaven."*
For those believers whom God has called away from this life before Jesus comes again: we thank You for their testimonies to Jesus their Lord and Saviour;

For the gift of the Holy Spirit who was poured out on all your people at Pentecost; for his many ministries and gifts to the church; and for his indispensible ministry in enlightening those who in sin and need to turn to Jesus for salvation;

IN JESUS' NAME, AMEN

Soli Deo Gloria